Overcoming Deficits of Aging

A BEHAVIORAL APPROACH

APPLIED CLINICAL PSYCHOLOGY

Series Editors: Alan S. Bellack, *Medical College of Pennsylvania at EPPI,
Philadelphia, Pennsylvania,* and Michel Hersen, *University of Pittsburgh, Pittsburgh,
Pennsylvania*

A Continuation Order Plan is available for this series. A continuation order will bring delivery of
each new volume immediately upon publication. Volumes are billed only upon actual shipment.
For further information please contact the publisher.

Overcoming Deficits of Aging

A BEHAVIORAL APPROACH

ROGER L. PATTERSON
Director, Gerontology Program
Florida Mental Health Institute
University of South Florida
Tampa, Florida

with

LARRY W. DUPREE, DAVID A. EBERLY,

GARY M. JACKSON, and MICHAEL J. O'SULLIVAN
Gerontology Program, Florida Mental Health Institute
University of South Florida, Tampa, Florida

LOUIS A. PENNER
Department of Psychology, University of South Florida
Tampa, Florida

and

CARLA DEE KELLY
Institute for Health Maintenance, Tampa, Florida

PLENUM PRESS • NEW YORK AND LONDON

Library of Congress Cataloging in Publication Data

Patterson, Roger L.
  Overcoming deficits of aging.

  (Applied clinical psychology)
  Bibliography: p.
  Includes index.
    1. Aged—Mental health services. 2. Behavior therapy. I. Title. II. Series [DNLM: 1.
Behavior therapy—In old age. W1 150 P3180]
RC451.4.A5P35 1982   618.97'689142   82-18076
ISBN 0-306-40947-X

© 1982 Plenum Press, New York
A Division of Plenum Publishing Corporation
233 Spring Street, New York, N.Y. 10013

Printed in the United States of America

Foreword

That older patients can be successfully *treated* has only recently been recognized by professionals and by older persons themselves. That older persons can also be *taught* new skills or retaught previously existing skills constitutes even newer knowledge. By focusing on the *reversibility of behavioral deficits* in the elderly the authors, under the leadership of Dr. Roger Patterson, have made both a scientific and a humanitarian contribution to the well-being of older persons. In this volume they have presented a theoretical basis and a practical how-to method of overcoming behavioral deficits. They have demonstrated that their modular technique of fostering improved functioning in such areas as activities of daily living and social skills not only has been successful but also has allowed individuals to return to less restrictive environments or to completely independent living.

The approach is an interdisciplinary one, appropriately since older people often experience difficulties in multiple areas of functioning. The authors have tried to integrate social, medical, and behavioral approaches, with an emphasis on behavioral methodologies. Although this book deals primarily with behavioral approaches to treatment of the elderly in a single setting, the volume clearly constitutes a challenge to other scientists and clinicians to apply the techniques described here in other settings.

A medical colleague of mine, a geriatrician, recently expressed the opinion that he had never encountered an older patient for whom he could not do something to improve health. What Patterson and his colleagues are saying in this book is something very similar, along behavioral lines. They are saying that behavioral deficits in aging are subject to modification, with surprising and gratifying results. Both of these views are new and refreshing. As a gerontologist interested in improving both physical and mental well-being, I heartily concur.

Now such views and the attendant requisite skills must be widely disseminated among professionals working with the aging.

ERIC PFEIFFER, M.D.

Suncoast Gerontology Center
University of South Florida
Tampa, Florida

Preface

This book is a report of an unusual experience. In November 1975 Roger Patterson was given responsibility for developing a treatment program for elderly people using behavioral methods assembled in a modular fashion. The general idea for such an approach had been proposed by Henry Bates (1975), who developed the idea from an extensive review of the literature. Dr. Patterson directed this effort from its beginning as a basic concept throughout its development and implementation, and continues to direct the operation. This program was to be directed to returning chronic hospitalized patients to community living and was to be developed into a full-fledged treatment program and evaluated for effectiveness of the treatment. Furthermore, it was to serve as a model for dissemination throughout the state of Florida. No part of the program was in existence: staff, clients, program, and treatment evaluation all had to be assembled and developed. The opportunity for evaluation of the treatment was unusual in that it was possible to look at three aspects: (1) treatment effects produced by each treatment module, (2) overall behavioral changes produced in the clients during treatment, and (3) what happened to the clients after discharge. Many studies look at one or two of these aspects, but few deal with all three. In order to complete this effort, the work of many individuals was required.

Michael O'Sullivan joined the effort very early and handled most of the day-to-day administration of the treatment units in addition to helping develop several modules. For example, the existence of Self-esteem training is largely due to his efforts. Louis Penner joined the effort in its second year as an evaluation consultant and remained affiliated formally or informally through the completion of this book. Carla Dee Kelly was recruited as a clinical psychologist to lead the staff in the development of individual psychological treatment plans and did much work to improve the functioning of the treatment team.

David Eberly had the responsibility of creating a data system, managing ongoing evaluation efforts, and designing and managing training programs in the dissemination efforts. After much of the modular program was developed, Gary Jackson introduced a new system of developing and implementing individual behavioral treatments, provided the staff with excellent training in behavioral methodology, and did much to improve the management of both the residential and day treatment components of the program. Larry Dupree joined the program to improve our integration with the community and was later put in charge of the day treatment project for the purpose of developing it into a true community project.

One may see that these individuals who worked to put an idea into practice each made a unique and valuable contribution. It is for this reason that each of them is an author of this total book and also has additional credits on certain chapters. Individuals with special responsibilities in a certain area took major responsibility for preparing the corresponding chapters, but no segment of the program or book chapter stands alone. Each of the authors is in some way responsible for completion of the whole.

In addition to the authors, many other individuals contributed greatly to the development and daily functioning of the program. Manuel Garcia Alvarez was the physician with the program who not only provided excellent medical care to the residential clients but was supportive of staff efforts to develop the behavioral program. Richard Gordon was Director of the Florida Mental Health Institute during the implementation phase of this program and offered encouragement and administrative support. Gail Smith, Tamara Harrell, Constance Miller, JoAnn Vogel, Dana Kessler, and Peggy Goodale had major supervisory and creative roles in many aspects of the program. Jack Anderson organized the data, conducted analyses, and prepared the illustrations for this book. Joan Piroch wrote or edited most of the training manuals for the modules, and these were used in preparing the module descriptions in Chapter 4. Ms. Piroch also edited much of this book.

The final production of this book was made possible by the secretarial efforts of Betty Alfonso, Lillian Barry, and Audrey Weislo. Ultimately, the whole work was possible only because of the efforts of very high-quality care staff, to whom gratitude is expressed.

Contents

1

The Setting and the Clients

MICHAEL J. O'SULLIVAN
AND ROGER L. PATTERSON

This book tells about the Gerontology Program of the Florida Mental Health Institute (FMHI), hereinafter referred to simply as *the program*, or *our program*. Founded by the state legislature with state funds in 1971, the FMHI is the primary change agent for shifting public policy away from custodial institutional care toward active treatment and rehabilitation. As conceived and implemented, FMHI has a tripartite mission: to provide service by conducting demonstration projects of new treatment and restorative and rehabilitation approaches; to conduct evaluative research in order to establish the effectiveness of new modalities; and to train public and private service providers in those methods and techniques that have been proven to be effective in addressing the problem of the state's mental health clients. The institute was built on land provided by the University of South Florida and became operational in July 1975.

From the outset, it was deemed important that FMHI should devote a part of its resources to work with the mental health needs of the elderly because of the relatively large proportion of these people in the population of Florida. The Florida Statistical Abstract (Bureau of Economic and Business Research, 1980) assesses the percentage of elderly in this state as 17.6%, and several counties in Florida have elderly populations in excess of 30%.

Although of special concern in Florida, the situation of elderly people in this state may provide a preview of what may be expected by other states in years to come. Florida is coping currently with a proportion of elderly people that other states will begin to encounter because of the accelerating nationwide increase in this population. The Bureau of the Census projects that by the year 2000 the elderly will represent 12.7% of the total population of the country (U.S. Bureau of the Census, 1979).

The Gerontology Program, which is the subject of this book, began in 1975. There was a statewide concern over a number of the elderly with problems of considerable magnitude, namely, those in state hospitals and those considered at risk of institutionalization. This concern was largely prompted by information that many of the elderly in the state hospitals could be placed in less restrictive settings. A survey by the American Psychiatric Association (1963) concluded that many elderly residents of such facilities could be restored to community care. A research study conducted by the state mental health agency (Ray, 1971) concluded that placement of some hospitalized elderly mental patients in community settings was economically sound, administratively feasible, and humanely warranted, with the proviso that such persons could be adequately screened and evaluated. These findings in Florida are similar to the conclusions reached in many other states and by national bodies which have studied the issue of deinstitutionalization (Becker & Schulberg, 1976). Based on such information, an objective of the Florida Division of Mental Health in the fiscal year 1975–76 was to reduce the census of geriatric patients in state hospitals and to increase the community care caseload. Primary methods of meeting this objective were to identify and place in the community those persons who did not require psychiatric hospitalization and to prevent such persons from entering the state hospitals.

The Gerontology Program was developed in response to this objective, and both the nature of the program and the particular population served were determined by it. The population in the state hospitals could be impacted in two ways: (1) by selecting individuals in the institutions and those in local hospitals who could benefit and providing them with intervention which would prepare them to return to the community, and (2) by providing similar services to persons residing in the community but considered at risk of institutionalization, in order to prevent their institutionalization. The two major units of the program were a residential unit, which served those already hospitalized or scheduled to be hospitalized; and a day treatment unit, which provided service to those still living in the community but considered by knowledgeable others to be at significant risk of being institutionalized. The residential unit contained space for 32 residents, and the day treatment served an equal number of daily attendees. The two units were separately located in opposite ends of a large building.

The nature of the major objective dictated that the program be restorative in nature. Furthermore, the demand of the situation was such that *rapid* restoration, within a period of a few months, was required. The hospitals needed to reduce populations rapidly because of limited resources. Also, there were legal requirements to remove those not receiving active psychiatric treatment. An additional requirement of the program was that the population to be treated must be aged 55 years or older, because this age had previously been defined as "elderly" by the state mental health agency and the legislature.

According to an accepted model of rehabilitation program development and evaluation (Reagles, 1980), large groups of clients must be subdivided into smaller groups, each group having its own objective(s). For example, a group of physically handicapped young people may be divided into those who can be helped to obtain competitive employment, others whose handicap is such that they may learn only to function in a sheltered environment, and still others for whom employment is not feasible. The characteristics of the clients admitted to particular programs must relate to the program. Such a systematic relationship between clients and programs not only facilitates treatment but also makes program evaluation simpler and more meaningful. Unfortunately, neither treatment programs nor objectives are usually well specified for any group considered mentally ill; and "psychogeriatrics" in particular are too frequently thrown together as if they were a homogeneous group merely because of their age.

The mental health population age 55 or older, even just the segment in institutions or at risk of institutionalization, is actually extremely heterogeneous. For example, there could be an age range of as much as 40 years within a group of elderly clients. Also, since the only characteristic all clients have in common is a minimum age, one would expect that the clients will vary considerably in their biographical/demographic characteristics and in the magnitude and type of dysfunction. Therefore, it was necessary to develop criteria which identified a subgroup of the elderly population who would benefit most from a program designed to produce rapid restoration and noninstitutional placement.

It is obvious that there are some elderly mental health clients for whom short-term, intensive, restorative treatment of a behavioral nature aimed at community placement is not likely to be successful, will not be beneficial, and may even be harmful. There are some people who need a type of institutional care for reasons of physical health and will likely need this type of care for a long period of time. There are also those who require institutional care for reasons of being dangerous to themselves or others. The criteria for the program were developed to permit the selection of those who did not require institutional care for any of several such reasons.

Persons selected for the program met the following criteria:

- At least minimally ambulatory by some means
- Continent, except for occasional accidents
- Not in need of acute medical service or skilled nursing care
- Not considered to be a danger to themselves or others
- Capable of being in an open setting without one-to-one supervision

Persons who cannot meet these criteria will probably require some sort of institutional care (including general hospitals, psychiatric hospitals, and nursing homes) for some time and are not suitable candidates for rapid restoration to community living. Persons who do meet these criteria but who are in need of institutional-type mental health services probably have a number of difficulties in community living which should be amenable to treatment by restorative behavioral approaches.

The program's efforts began with the general concept originated by Bates (1975) that several modules or treatment components were to be developed specifically for the treatment of elderly mental health clients which could be replicated both across individuals and across other treatment programs in the state. These modules were to incorporate modern behavioral technology and evidence of the efficacy was to be well established. Furthermore, the efficacy of the entire program as a treatment entity was to be established.

The period of January 1976 to August 1977 was devoted to developing and initiating a program which met the requirements for a behaviorally based modular system and to designing and eliminating errors from the data collection and analysis system to permit evaluation. An extremely important issue also resolved during this early period was the acquisition of human and other resources necessary to conduct superior treatment, evaluation, and training. Although some data from the developmental stage of the program are reported in Chapters 9 and 10, the majority of this book describes the program as it existed after August 1977. That is, the program description in this book covers the three-year period following the development and standardization of appropriate treatments, data systems, and evaluation methodologies. It was during this period that treatment and follow-up data were gathered and training and dissemination initiated.

On the basis of what we learned during this time, we have added new treatment components and modified others. Also, as new needs and priorities were established by the state, the program was changed in response to these. Therefore, the program as it exists today differs somewhat from what you will read about. Such change does not indicate a lack of clarity about the program and its goals but rather is a necessary characteristic of any healthy, viable organization. We chose to describe the program as it was because the newer aspects of the program have not yet been fully evaluated. What this book describes is the program as the clinical staff hoped it would be and the extent to which these aspirations were realized.

2

Problems Relating to Aging

Rationale for a Behavioral Approach

Larry W. Dupree,
Michael J. O'Sullivan,
and Roger L. Patterson

Old people are subject to the same problems as younger people. Therefore, when we speak of the problems of the elderly, we are usually referring to common human problems found in greater abundance among older people. A large number of problems of the elderly may be said to be related to major losses which tend to occur more frequently in later life. Those losses include loss of family and social contacts, reduction in work, economic loss, physiological and health impairment, decreased social and cultural status, and lowered self-evaluation. Usually the losses are gradual but also incremental. Thus, the transition from middle to older age may be experienced as a stressful, difficult, and sometimes prolonged period of readjustment, necessitating fairly substantial (and frequent) changes in the individual's life and behavior. This transition period can elicit diverse behavior, with some individuals being unable to adapt to the changes taking place, changes occurring in many areas and often overlapping in time.

THE AGED AS A HIGH-RISK GROUP

Because of the rapid accumulation of changes and the consequent accumulation of stress, the aged are a high-risk group in the area of mental health (Ingersoll & Silverman, 1978). An estimated 15–25% of the elderly have significant mental health problems (U.S. President's Commission on Mental Health, 1978). Kramer and associates summarized seven studies of prevalence rates for mental illness among noninstitutionalized older age groups and estimated that 10–20% were in need of mental health services (Kramer, Taube, & Redick, 1973; Redick, Kramer, & Taube, 1973). Furthermore, older adults account for approximately 25% of the reported suicides each year (Butler, 1975; Butler & Lewis, 1977). It appears to be difficult to obtain highly reliable estimates of prevalence rates for mental illness among the elderly because, as the President's Commission on Mental Health (1978) indicates, a growing trend in recent years has been to transfer older patients out of costly state hospitals into other less expensive boarding situations. This often results in two things: (1) inadequate medical, nursing, social, and mental health care and (2) an exclusion of these residents from prevalence studies of mental disorders among the elderly. Therefore, the rate of mental illness among the elderly may be vastly underestimated. Prevalence data more often are based upon mental hospital and community mental health center data. Yet, the National Center for Health Statistics (1977) reports that 58% of all nursing home residents are considered confused some or most of the time. Thus, a significant population for whom mental health services might be appropriate may not be incorporated within prevalence estimates upon which current need and future services are determined. Libow (1977) points out the applicability of diverse services to confused individuals by noting that among adults who suffer from senile dementia as many as one-third may be reflecting *pseudosenility* or a reversible brain syndrome as a result in errors in medication, malnutrition, metabolic imbalance, and other causes that have the potential for being reversed.

Underutilization of Mental Health Services by the Elderly

Even though the aged do appear to be a high-risk group in the area of mental health, this population receives a disproportionately small share of mental health services (Butler & Lewis, 1973). For example, the President's Commission on Mental Health (1978) reports that only 4% of the clients seen at public outpatient mental health clinics are elderly, whereas others have reported that 2% of those seen by independent practitioners are elderly (Butler & Lewis, 1977). Not only are the elderly receiving less care than younger individuals, but their rate of care per 100,000 elderly population is dropping (U.S. President's Commission on Mental Health, 1978). The paucity of such services results both from the reluctance of professionals to deal with this group and from the hesitance of older people to seek psychological help (Ingersoll & Silverman, 1978).

CULTURAL "AGEISM"

Several explanations have been given for the underutilization of services by the elderly. Most of them are in some way related to "ageism." Ageism is age discrimination or the prejudice by one age group toward other age groups (Butler, 1969). Ageism reflects "a personal revulsion to and distaste for growing old, disease, disability; and fear of powerlessness, 'uselessness,' and death" (Butler, 1969, p. 243). Cultural attitudes reinforce these feelings and compound the stress associated with growing older. Yet aging is what our national population is doing. In 1900 there were three million older Americans (age 65 and above) representing 4% of the total population, whereas in 1977 the aged represented 11% (approximately 23 million) of the nation's census (U.S. Bureau of the Census, 1978). Between 1900 and 1977 the total United States population increased by approximately 288% while the category of older Americans grew by approximately 683%. More recently, between 1970 and 1977, the older age group increased by approximately 18%, whereas those under age 65 increased by about 5%. During this period the total population increased by approximately 6%. Thus, both the number and proportion of the elderly have increased and these trends are likely to continue. The total number of older Americans is expected to increase from approximately 23 million in 1977 to 32 million in the year 2000. Even though our national population is aging, aging has been transformed from a natural process into a social problem in which the older individual bears the negative consequences. The extent to which ageism is an obstacle to the apt treatment of elderly individuals is of particular interest in the present context.

PROFESSIONAL AGEISM

In the mental health field ageism has become professionalized. Butler and Lewis (1977) refer to "professional ageism," which in turn refers to the negative attitudes of mental health professionals toward the elderly (Gaitz, 1974; Kastenbaum, 1978; Waters, Fink, & White, 1976). Professional ageism includes a belief that aging means inevitable decline, pessimism about the likelihood and speed of change, and the belief that it is futile to invest effort in a person with limited life

expectancy. Of course, such beliefs may not be verbalized, but resultant behavior manifested by professionals correlates highly with such
views. For example, estimates are that

> from 10 to 30 percent of all treatable mental disorders in older people are
> misdiagnosed as untreatable, frequently because the physician assumes
> that mental impairment is to be expected with advancing age and there-
> fore makes no effort to rule out reversible disorders. (Butler, 1980, p. 9)

Also, as Palmore (1973) points out, the views associated with professional ageism (particularly those noting that mental illness in old age
is inevitable, untreatable, disabling, and irreversible) become a self-
fulfilling prophecy, leading to a lack of prevention and treatment
which in turn tends to confirm the original belief. Caplovitz and
Rodin (cited in Rodin & Langer, 1980) noted, that furthermore, professionals often use age as a cue for interpreting behavior and that the
labels assigned by professionals affect the behavior of the elderly. In
this study, a group of psychologists and psychiatrists were presented
with identical descriptions of behavior, with six cases being presented
as persons young in age and six as persons in their sixties or seven-
ties. Age influenced both diagnosis and recommendations for treatment, with the elderly more often diagnosed as having an underlying
organic condition. Treatment recommendations for this group were
more often drug-related and demanded institutionalization. The
younger population received recommendations involving less use of
drug therapy and more community-based treatment.

GENERATIONAL DIFFERENCES IN PROBLEM DEFINITION

Another view of underuse of mental health services by the aged
is that the elderly are at present reluctant to define their problems in
psychological terms (Lawton, 1979). However, an increasing trend
toward defining one's mental health problems as such and an increased use of treatment centers has been noted by Kulka and Tamir
(1978). They replicated the study of Gurin, Veroff, and Field (1960) on
how Americans view their mental health and found that 13% of those
65 and over had actually sought professional help for personal problems. This was a significant increase of 7% over the previous findings. Even more significant, perhaps, was Kulka and Tamir's finding
that of the elderly who defined a personal problem in mental health
terms 67% had sought professional help. Also suggested was a slight
increase in help-seeking attitudes and behavior with age cohorts over
time. Thus, it is possible that today's adults between the ages of 20
and 49 (of whom about 44% defined problems in mental health

terms) will be seeking assistance for mental health problems during the later years of their lives, and at a much greater rate than does the current population 65 and above (Kulka & Tamir, 1978). Moreover, this trend should be potentiated due to the current emphasis placed on nonmedical intervention relative to personal problems.

CONCEPTUALIZING PROBLEMS OF THE ELDERLY

It is useful to examine briefly three models used in conceptualizing the problems of the elderly: (1) the social model, (2) the behavioral model, and (3) the medical model. It is the opinion of the authors that these are different but valid and indispensable conceptualizations for dealing with the matter at hand.

THE SOCIAL MODEL

This model attributes the differences between the elderly and younger adults in part to different roles prescribed for these groups by our society. In different societies roles for the elderly may be more or less satisfying. In China, for example, old people are traditionally viewed as being very wise because they have lived very long and are accorded an honored placed in the household and the community. Among the Eskimos, however, old people were formerly sometimes abandoned to die because they were considered useless. Although the United States is a multicultured nation, we generally fall somewhere between the old traditions of the Eskimos and the Chinese in our treatment of our elders.

Although gross generalizations about the treatment of its older population by any pluralistic nation such as ours are inevitably somewhat unfair, it seems to be true that we often expect less responsibility and decreased functional ability on the part of our society's older members. L. M. Miller (1979) proposed three categories of behavior for which we accept lesser levels of functioning from the elderly. These are (1) self-care behavior, or habits related to daily functions such as eating, sleeping, toileting, grooming, and health; (2) task behavior, defined as the management of tasks assigned by membership in specific social groups, including housekeeping and employment responsibilities; and (3) relationship behavior, meaning all kinds of social relationships with other people. According to this view, there is a continuum of behavior within each category. Each continuum runs from those actions which society considers acceptable as part of the normal social role of an old person to those which are considered unacceptable. For example, acceptable relationship behavior demonstrating decreased responsibility is that of elderly parents accepting some control of their affairs by their children. An example of unacceptable relationship behavior would be extreme argumentativeness. Within the category of task behavior, withdrawal from more difficult housekeeping duties is an acceptable form of decreased responsibility and functional status, but unsanitary homemaking is not acceptable. Various changes in self-care behavior are acceptable, including moderate changes in grooming and toileting habits, but incontinence is not.

The Medical Model

The traditional medical model considers deviations from normal functioning as due to illnesses or diseases. These diseases are seen as ultimately caused by improper internal or physiological functioning. External disease-producing factors such as stress, smoking, or improper diet are considered of importance only because they produce improper physiological functioning. Therefore, when confronted with changes in behavior of the elderly, adherents of the medical model seek to find alterations in physiology which produce the changes. For example, changes in the structure and the functioning of the brain are frequently blamed for altered behavior in the elderly.

The Behavioral Model

The behavioral model seeks to identify, define, and measure behavior with great specificity and to relate the occurrence and nonoccurrence of this behavior to observable *environmental events*. Dependent upon the history and heredity of the individual, different environmental events may prompt, strengthen or weaken, maintain or fail to maintain, behavior of concern. Therefore, when confronted with the problem behavior, the behaviorist seeks to determine events occurring immediately before and after the behavior and to alter these events in order to change the behavior.

The Behavioral Model in Intervention with the Elderly

A current view of the behavioral model is more appropriately presented as reflecting a general orientation to problem resolution (Goldfried & Davison, 1976; Hersen, 1981; L. M. Miller, 1976) than as simply a compilation of techniques. Thus, the behavioral model represents an empirical approach. Behavior is assessed as lawful and is believed to be a function of specifiable antecedent, (intra)personal, and consequent conditions. Within this framework, treatment strategies are empirically rather than theoretically based, stressing objective, observable assessment, systematic evaluations of outcome, and the use of empirically validated procedures. Thus, the behavior therapist in his or her approach to clinical problems operationally defines the problem behaviors, attempts to measure them reliably, designs interventions specific to the targeted behaviors, and attempts to document objectively any resultant changes in behavior. Such an approach, being problem-oriented rather than age-specific, appears to be applicable to many of the well-documented problems noted in later life (Patterson & Jackson, 1980b). Those behaviors which have been targets of successful modification attempts include daily living skills (behavior necessary for the successful maintenance of one's life on a daily basis), social and leisure activities, social skills (behavior necessary for the development and maintenance of one's social support network), and intellectual performance. In light of this approach it would appear that behavioral techniques have sufficient utility for geriatric populations. Several authors have encouraged the use of behavior therapy relative to problems associated with late life (M. M. Baltes & Barton, 1977; Cautela & Mansfield, 1977; Hoyer, 1973; Hoyer, Mishara, & Reidel, 1975; Lankford & Herman, 1978; Lindsley, 1964; Patterson & Jackson, 1980a,b).

COMPLEMENTARY IMPORTANCE OF THE THREE MODELS

It is very unfortunate that these three models have sometimes been viewed as being in conflict; as if *either* social, medical, or behavioral variables were the true causes of functional changes in older people. It is obvious that changes in all three classes of variables occur throughout the life span. One changes roles from an infant, a preschooler, a schoolchild, an adolescent, a mother, a worker, to a retired or a nonretired elder. These roles (as shared expectancies) have profound effects upon behavior. In addition, there are vast changes in physiological functioning occurring during the life span due to both normal development and various disease processes. Similarly, learning experiences which serve to produce and modify behavior continue throughout life. It is worth stressing that the modification of behavior throughout life because of individual experience is a continuous and natural process which occurs to everyone. New learning, as well as the modification of old learning, is stopped only by death.

Because all three classes of variables change simultaneously throughout life, all three may be considered as causes of changes due to the aging process. This statement may seem in conflict with the topic of this book, a behavioral treatment program for the elderly. Any conflict is only apparent and not real. It is true that the authors *chose* to develop a treatment program that concentrates on behavioral interventions, but this choice was not intended to imply that variables which are properly the subject matter of medical and sociological science are not of importance.

Gerontology has been heavily dominated by input from sociology, medicine, and developmental psychology. However, with regard to effective therapeutic intervention, Kastenbaum (1968) noted that psychologists had contributed very little to the welfare of the aged beyong "counting their wrinkles." Patterson and Jackson (1980a) reviewed the literature regarding behavior modification and the elderly and found a paucity of *well-developed* interventions, although almost all the behavioral research supports the plasticity of the behavior of the elderly. The field of actively applied, programmatic approaches to the use of behavioral procedures relative to the enhanced welfare of the aged would seem to be an almost open one, particularly concerning the elderly residing in the community.

In order to understand this lack of application of behavioral approaches, it is useful to examine the difference between historical causation of behavior and interventions to change existing behavior. It is unfortunately true that medical model approaches have sometimes been misused to lead to a dead end when applied to the functioning of the elderly. Adherents of the medical model have sometimes seemed to take the approach that because nothing could be done to cure the basic physiological changes of aging, nothing useful could be done to alleviate most age-related problem behavior until such time as appropriate cures were developed. This situation was particularly true with regard to functional changes assumed to be caused by alterations in the brain. Clearly, this is a misuse of the medical model, but it is a misuse which the authors have found to be dismayingly prevalent. A more proper use of the medical model would be to continue to encourage medical research regarding the physiological changes related to aging, while *also* recognizing and actively encouraging research and application of social and behavioral methods.

Students of the social model have studied various social situations and have determined that some may be valued as better than others with regard to promoting the well-being of the elderly. Some have even advocated the development of specific types of residential arrangements for this purpose. As valid as such interventions may be, they require large-scale, expensive developments which can be applicable to only a very few persons in the near future. Furthermore, rearranging communities is not likely to remediate totally the problems of any individual. It is probable that even if every elderly person in the United States were transported to some type of ideal community, there would still be great need for individual intervention to improve many types of problem situations. In addition, it can be debated that this type of approach does not really remedy problems, but instead may actually *discourage* remediation by providing compensations for problems rather than seeking to overcome them.

Some advantages of including behavioral approaches to interventions with problems of the elderly will now be discussed. It is important to note that what is advocated is that appropriate behavioral interventions be used concurrently with the best medical and social interventions available. The addition of behavioral interventions and concepts is of great importance because too many efforts in the past have included only medical and social approaches. The first advantage to be considered will be that of overcoming an unfortunate discriminatory attitude toward the elderly which has existed in this country.

SPECIFIC BENEFITS OF THE BEHAVIORAL MODEL TO THE ELDERLY

Ageism is pervasive, and any model of intervention which intentionally or otherwise places primary or sole focus on the age of a person is susceptible to its intrusion. The tendency is to accept behavioral change as a one-to-one correlate of physical change; yet such an age/behavior correlation is quite arbitrary (M. M. Baltes & Barton, 1977). Such purported correlations, when maintained either by a culture or treatment model (either explicitly or implicitly) affect the expectations of the targeted age group as well as those attending to them. Thus, an important value of the behavioral approach is as a means of avoiding the negative impact of cultural expectations and allowing the treatment specialist to focus on the task at hand: the resolution of problem behavior regardless of the age of the client. The behavioral model minimizes the encroachment of ageism on treatment programs.

Within the behavioral model, an older person's physical changes and existing illnesses (if any) are not considered as the sole cause of behavior; also to be taken into account are the changes in the environment. This directs the behavior therapist to consider factors other than age and physiological changes as the bases of behavior and limits the probability of the intrusion of ageism with its negative attitudes (particularly relative to the reversibility of behavior). Support for the reversibility of (functional) age decrements, as well as the reversibility of apparent cognitive impairment, has been reported in reviews of the literature by Baltes and Barton (1977) and Patterson and Jackson (1980a,b).

The literature dealing with the direct modification of problem behavior associated with later life supports the viewpoint that behavior is a result of the interaction of organismic variables with environmental variables and that the interaction of changes in the internal and external variables produces behavioral changes (M. M. Baltes & P. B. Baltes, 1977; M. M. Baltes & Barton, 1977; P. B. Baltes & Willis, 1977; Hoyer et al., 1975; Patterson & Jackson, 1980a,b; Rebok & Hoyer, 1977). Prior to this behavioral view, physiological changes were given undue emphasis as the bases for changes in behavior. More will be said regarding the interaction of variables later in the chapter.

In directing treatment specialists to consider factors other than age, the behavioral model permits, if it does not prompt, an optimistic attitude regarding the mental health problems of older people. Rebok and Hoyer (1977) state that, notwithstanding such labels as senility and organic brain syndrome, the behavior therapist proceeds to ascertain the extent to which a particular behavior can be remedied. Problems are defined in terms of occurring behavior, and are treated on the assumption that they can be remedied.

The heterogeneity/variability of the aged is not lost in the behavioral approach to problem behavior. The design of an appropriate treatment plan within the operant model usually requires that the treatment specialist establish appropriate antecedent conditions and reinforcers for behavior change. The individualized plans are monitored for efficacy on an ongoing basis. As a group, the elderly may be more heterogeneous in their behavior, as well as in the bases for the behavior, than any other group; and this variability can be taken into account by the treatment specialist through individualized treatment plans (Hoyer, 1974; Rebok & Hoyer, 1977). Such an approach promotes successful intervention with older individuals either for prevention, maintenance, or rehabilitation (Hoyer, 1973, 1974).

Cautela and Mansfield (1977) have also noted the specific value of the behavioral model to the problem behavior of the elderly: (1) time is not unnecessarily spent on determining the "true" impact of all past life experience, (2) present behavior is the target for change (rather than seeking some unconscious motivator of behavior), (3) older individuals profit more from active therapists and treatment involving problem-oriented behavior rehearsal (as opposed to the more passive insight therapy), and (4) no attempts are made to apply negative diagnostic labels. Labels are rarely removed, and usually once designated no attempt is made to change the behavior. However, "even when organic dysfunction is noted it can be of practical value to assume that many behaviors can be modified somewhat by applying specific behavior therapy procedures regardless of past history or organic involvement" (Cautela & Mansfield, 1977, p. 23). Also, the notion of behavioral inflexibility often attributed to the elderly becomes an empirical question rather than a "fact" based upon sociocultural attributions relative to old age. Such an empirical approach has resulted in doubts as to the general validity of a biological decrement model and given a better accounting of problem behavior in old age in terms of the interaction of organismic (e.g., biological) and environmental determinants (Baltes & Baltes, 1977; Baltes & Barton, 1977; Baltes & Willis, 1977). Baltes and Burton (1977) report findings challenging many of the neurophysiological explanations for "older behavior" in the area of intellectual/cognitive behavior and also report on studies demonstrating that various patterns of behavior thought to be irreversible and a result of some disease process can be positively altered by means of contingency management. Such change was the result of the rearrangement of events antecedent to and consequent to the occurrence of behaviors. Other behaviors thought to be age-related were also positively altered by operant procedures. These included reversal of social isolation, increasing interest in one's environment, reversal of poor hygiene and grooming habits, modification of self-injurious behavior, and increased social and verbal behavior (Baltes & Barton, 1977).

Another value of the behavioral approach is that self-management or control can be augmented. The initial therapist can be faded, further enhancing independence. Individuals of all ages can be taught behavior analysis (identification of antecedents and consequences to behavior) and how to implement change and maintenance procedures. Also, teaching elderly individuals to shape and control actively those parts of their environment contributing to functional as well as dysfunctional behavior increases their belief in personal efficacy. Thus, the elderly can be taught to attribute through behavior analysis the basis of problem behavior to the appropriate sources: organismic, environmental, or both. By more accurately attributing responsibility for behavioral events, rather than invoking some global concept referred to as the *aging process*, dysfunctional behavior is seen as less inevitable and remediation or prevention more likely. Rodin and Langer (1980) point out that overattribution to aging rather than to remedial sources, in conjunction with a negative labeling process apparent in our culture relative to the elderly, generates decreased self-esteem and diminishes performance. Over time, and with disuse, the abilities themselves may also decline (Langer, Rodin, Beck, Weinman, & Spitzer, 1979; Rodin & Langer, 1980). To reverse these effects, older people might be encouraged to attribute responsibility for behavior to the more appropriate source rather than attributing consequences in a manner consistent with cultural stereotypes. By doing so, many supposed irreversible and age-determined behaviors can be remedied.

The behavioral model is also useful in the treatment of older individuals in terms of cost effectiveness, the replicability and/or consistency of treatment, the value of negative results as well as positive, the structure afforded staff in attending to individuals in treatment, and suitable community placement based upon individual circumstances. Often the resources for treatment are scarce, and behavioral treatment programs in diverse settings have successfully used paraprofessional staff (Rebok & Hoyer, 1977), as well as employing the rearrangement of existing resources rather than adding new ones (Patterson & Jackson, 1980a,b). In many treatment programs there is a lack of consistency of treatment application or a lack of quality control (Hersen, 1981). Within the behavioral model, fairly detailed treatment manuals can be made available so as to minimize the personalization of a treatment approach by the various therapists in the setting. Such standardization procedures also help prompt the treatment specialists to maintain their active participation and modeling rather than allowing treatment to drift toward approaches reflecting more cognitive and passive attitudes. Thus, the value of behavior therapy to any treatment program is a sense of quality control including treatment stability over time and replicability both within and without the program.

Replicability of treatment results is also a goal of the behavioral model. Obviously replicability of positive results is valuable, but so too is replicability of negative results (Rebok & Hoyer, 1977): "Negative results are important because they often suggest procedures that are ineffective or harmful" (p. 32). Another value of operant-based intervention is that it requires observation on the part of those who are involved in the treatment plan. The attention of the staff and others is intentionally directed toward the individuals' behavior. By using structured intervention approaches (e.g., a token economy system) and basic learning principles, treatment specialists can be "forced" to attend to desired (targeted) behaviors and then function as both providers of tokens and social reinforcers. Richards and

Thorpe (1978) also report studies in which behavioral techniques were successfully applied to the behavior and attitudes of treatment staff caring for elderly in institutional settings.

Lastly, the precision or clarity of most information produced in treatment programs emphasizing the behavioral model also is valuable relative to client placement. For example, if an individual does not know *what* medications to take *when*, and even with continued training and assessment never significantly improves over baseline, then placement for such an individual should incorporate the behavioral data relative to medication. The community placement setting should provide enough structure and/or assistance to ensure that all who require medication are prompted to take it properly.

This chapter has thus far emphasized the benefits and appropriateness of the use of the behavioral model in the treatment of elderly clients. To follow is a presentation of how these potential benefits assisted in the formulation and direction of the clinical intervention approaches of the Gerontology Program at the Florida Mental Health Institute.

BEHAVIORAL INTERVENTION WITH THE ELDERLY AT FMHI

An underlying premise of the Gerontology Program is that older adults who are suffering from behavioral deficits and/or personal and social losses can learn or relearn skills to overcome these deficiencies. Three major problems often associated with later life are attended to: (1) skill deficits, when older individuals have discontinued taking care of themselves; (2) psychosocial losses, when there is a loss of the significant interactions with others which serve to maintain mental health in general; and (3) the occurrence of inappropriate or excessive behavior which is sometimes a result of the other two factors. Even though the approach is problem-oriented (rather than age-oriented), an emphasis is placed on acquisition of skills that lead to increased self-enhancement, self-control, and self-management. Thus, in contrast to a debilitation or decline model of aging, attempts are made to foster self-improvement and self-maintenance.

A number of reviews dealing with the direct modification of problem behavior in the elderly support the viewpoint that such behavior is the result of interaction of organismic (people) variables with environmental variables (Patterson & Jackson, 1980a). Many instances of behavioral deficits are determined to be promoted by the environment and/or the lack of encouragement (prompts and reinforcers) from the environment for the desired, more functional behavior. This research-founded conclusion is the basis of the Gerontology Program's approach in treating older individuals. Thus, in agreement with Goldfried and Davison (1976), whether a client engages in certain behavior is believed to depend not only on the availability of the behavior within the individual's response repertoire, but also upon the degree to which certain environmental determinants elicit and/or reinforce the designated behavior. The application of the antecedent–behavior–consequence (ABC) analysis of behavior paradigm has proved to be very useful with the elderly. Baltes and Barton (1977) and Patterson and Jackson (1980b) cite numerous studies detailing the impact of poor environmental living conditions in age-performance decrements, particularly as the environment interacts with changing biological processes. Such findings seem to suggest that not only should the traditional (ABC) analysis of behavior be used with the elderly, but that such an analysis should heavily incorporate as interaction variables those deficits associated with aging (Patterson & Jackson, 1980b). Deficits associated with aging (such as those of vision, hearing, or memory) interact with environmental antecedent and consequent events so as potentially to decrease the effectiveness of those events on the acquisition and maintenance of desired behavior and/or on the reduction of dysfunctional behavior.

The Gerontology Program staff have noted a major difference in the application of behavioral procedures with different age populations (e.g., children versus elderly). With young populations, behavioral intervention is more often used to establish new behavior; whereas with the elderly behavioral procedures are more often used to reestablish responses to an appropriate strength and/or frequency. Thus, the elderly are more likely to have the target behavior within their response repertoire, and very often minimal prompting initiates quick, if not almost spontaneous, recovery of such behavior (Patterson & Jackson, 1980b). However, the maintenance of such behavior must be carefully considered. The behavioral approach relative to the elderly certainly removes the mystery from how to go about eliciting appropriate behaviors, how to maintain them, and how to eliminate dysfunctional behaviors. Nothing works as simply as stated, but the process is understandable (to both client and treatment specialist) and replicable.

Lastly, it would appear that the major factors in aging-related behavior are disuse, sparsity, and expectancies (Baltes & Barton, 1977). When performance deterioration through disuse (in combination with a sparsity of environmental reinforcers and cues) interacts with the negative cognitions (expectancies/prophecies) held by older people, response decrements are further augmented. The behavioral model is appropriate to the alteration of any of these factors; disuse, sparsity, expectancies. Because of this, the Gerontology Program incorporated the behavioral model in its treatment program in the belief that behavior therapy, when viewed as an integrated approach to problem behavior, would provide the most effective and workable framework both for the elderly and for the treatment staff.

3

Behavioral Principles and Techniques

Gary M. Jackson
and Roger L. Patterson

The Gerontology Program at the Florida Mental Health Institute was primarily based on the principles and techniques of behavior modification. Such principles and techniques stress the importance of one's immediate environment in determining the occurrence and maintenance of one's behavior. In fact, the actual aging process may be viewed as an interaction between a biologically maturing individual and his or her immediate environment (Hoyer, 1973).

Generally speaking, socially acceptable and independence-related behavior is maintained throughout the aging process only if the environment interacts with the individual by providing ongoing support for this behavior. Many clients who are deficient in several areas of skills in old age may have had rich behavioral repertoires in the past. However, their more recent immediate environment prior to admission into our program may not have provided the support that would have encouraged and maintained these skills.

From a behavioral point of view, the immediate environment provides support by interacting with the individual in two ways. First of all, the environment prompts or signals the occurrence of behavior. Secondly, the environment provides consequences to behavior that either increase or decrease the probability of future occurrence of the behavior. This chapter will describe how behavioral principles and techniques were used in the Gerontology Program to provide a behaviorally therapeutic environment. This type of environment interacts with the client to support the development and reestablishment of behavior necessary for as independent and socially meaningful a life as possible.

The ABC Model

The individual/environment interaction formed the basis for the behavioral interventions in the Gerontology Program and is explained by the ABC model. This particular model of behavior indicates that behavior does not occur as an independent entity, but rather is inexorably tied to the environmental events immediately preceding and following the occurrence of behavior. The three components of the model are: antecedents (A), behavior (B), and consequences (C). These components are defined in the following manner:

Antecedent: The observable environmental event(s) or situation(s) occurring immediately before the observed behavior.

Behavior: The observable response of the client.

Consequence: The observable environmental event(s) or situation(s) occurring immediately after the observed behavior.

As we mentioned previously, the aging process may be viewed as an interaction between a biologically maturing individual and the immediate environment (Hoyer, 1973). This interaction would appear to be supportive of specific skills as long as the appropriate discriminative stimuli (antecedents) and reinforcers (consequences) remain in effect and barring debilitating physical deficiencies that inhibit performance of these behaviors.

For example, if one is to maintain a skill such as proper hair care throughout the aging process, then the appropriate antecedent events or situations must be present to signal the occurrence of brushing, combing, and shampooing. Many of the clients in the Gerontology Program may normally live a life of isolation with no significant other in their immediate environment to prompt such behavior. There may have been no one to say "Martha, let's go shopping," or "Martha, I like your hair when you fix it." Therefore, program staff members implemented such antecedent events to signal the reoccurrence of essential behavior.

Consequences of behavior are just as important as antecedents. Staff members were well trained and quite adept at providing immediate social and/or tangible reinforcers as consequences for appropriate behavior. It appeared that if adaptive behavior was to be reestablished and maintained, someone in the client's immediate environment had to provide reinforcing consequences such as "Martha, your hair looks so nice today." If environmental support is not present through appropriate prompts and reinforcers, appropriate behavior may not be developed or maintained.

Although the ABC approach is now almost commonplace and is used extensively by behavioral clinicians for children and younger adults, a technological lag has occurred between accepted practice with these populations and applications with the elderly (Patterson & Jackson, 1980a). Recognizing this oversight, the Gerontology Program successfully pursued the development of behaviorally based interventions that were consistent with the ABC model. Such an approach resulted in supportive, behaviorally therapeutic environments in the Gerontology Projects that supported the reestablishment of necessary adaptive behavior.

TYPES OF ENVIRONMENTS FOR BEHAVIORALLY DYSFUNCTIONAL ELDERLY

If behavior is truly a function of the immediate environment, the characteristics of that environment are very important in promoting and maintaining desirable behavior. Environments can be classified according to specific characteristics. Patterson and Jackson (1980a) classified environments for the elderly into these categories:

1. *Custodial Care Environment:* A protective, medically oriented environment in which nursing care is provided for the prevention and treatment of physical deficiencies but which offers no systematic behavioral approach to establish or reestablish appropriate behavior.

2. *Prosthetic Environment:* A physically supportive environment that makes physical disabilities less debilitating by the provision of prosthetic devices to assist in the maintenance of appropriate behavior. Such behavior cannot occur without the aid of a prosthetic device (e.g., artificial limbs, walker, cane, wheelchair ramps, hearing aid, or grab-bars).

3. *Training Environment:* An environment in which behaviors are established or reestablished by the systematic application of learning principles, with particular attention given to antecedents and/or consequences of behavior. Behaviors are maintained in that environment by the design of supportive antecedents (i.e., prompts and discriminative stimuli) and reinforcers specific to that environment.

4. *Therapeutic Environment:* An environment in which behaviors are established or reestablished by the systematic application of learning principles, with particular attention given to the antecedents and/or consequences of behavior, and with emphasis placed on generalization and maintenance of behavior. Behaviors are not only maintained in the immediate training environment but are also generalized to the "usual" environment, where they are maintained by naturally occurring antecedents and consequences.

Environments for the elderly do not always fit clearly within a single category. For example, a nursing home may contain elements of both custodial and prosthetic environments. A particular medical/ behavioral treatment program may contain elements of both prosthetic and training environments. Therefore, the categories describe environments on the basis of the approach or approaches taken directly to assist the elderly or to support the reemergence and maintenance of appropriate, adaptive behavior.

It is important to emphasize the difference between a training and therapeutic environment. A *training environment* exists for the purpose of developing and reestablishing appropriate behavior which is maintained and generalized within that specific programmatic environment. Many behavioral treatment programs fall within this category since maintenance often appears to be an elusive entity. A *therapeutic environment* is a training environment which not only results in the maintenance and generalization of behavior within the programmatic setting but also results in generalization and maintenance of appropriate behavior to the postdischarge setting. This latter component is, of course, essential if the client is to be placed and successfully remain in the community. The Gerontology Program sought to provide a therapeutic environment. Behavior was changed through the proper manipulation of environmental antecedents and consequences and attempts to generalize and maintain behavior were routinely made. Data provided in Chapters 9 and 10 of this book show evidence that at least some success at generalization and maintenance was obtained.

There were essentially three behaviorally based treatment systems that maintained the therapeutic nature of the Gerontology Program. The first system, the *modular treatment program*, was used to facilitate the reestablishment of certain self-help and social skills with large numbers of clients. In brief, modules are preplanned procedures for teaching specific categories of skills to many clients (Chapter 4 describes modular treatment in detail). The second system was *single case behavioral treatment (SCBT)*, which was designed to focus on idiosyncratic behaviors serving as barriers to community placement and not addressed by modular treatment (Chapter 5 describes SCBT in detail). The third system may best be described as the *behavioral program milieu*. The use of the term *milieu* is intended to imply that the use of behavioral technology on the part of the staff was much broader than the application of techniques specifically planned and recorded as part of SCBT or modular treatment.

In terms of time and effort spent by both the clients and most of the staff, the conduct of the modules with their accompanying assessments and recording was by far the major treatment effort. The modules were planned on the basis of the needs of many clients and occurred on a scheduled daily basis. Most clients and staff spent most of the normal work week involved in modules and other scheduled activities, similar to the program in a school. However, there were almost always a few clients (usually about 10–15%) who required highly individualized attention. This might be because they displayed types of behavior not addressed by the modules, or because they were not responding adequately to modular treatment, or both. It was for these clients that SCBT plans had to be developed on an as-needed basis. Such SCBT treatments could be critical to meeting a particular client's needs. For these clients, just providing skills train-ing in the usual fashion in the modules would accomplish little of significance.

In addition to modules and SCBT, there was a third way in which the behavioral approach affected treatment. All staff–client in-teractions, as well as many staff–staff interactions, were influenced by the behavioral system and training. For example, the use of social reinforcement for any of a great variety of daily incidental desirable behaviors was strongly encouraged and occurred very frequently. Visitors to the units often remarked about this type of approach and how pleasant it made the general interaction.

It is important to note that a *token* reinforcement system was an integral component of all three treatment systems. The token system was not separate, but rather was considered to be embodied in the total unit environment. The use of tokens provided a convenient and effective method of providing positive reinforcement almost anywhere and at any time on the units. An elaboration of the use of this system is presented later in this chapter.

The three behavioral approaches inherent to the Gerontology Program were based on identical behavioral principles and tech-niques. The remainder of this chapter will consist of a description of the major principles and techniques used. Although it is well beyond the scope of this book to provide a detailed explanation of all princi-ples and techniques involved, major principal elements will be dis-cussed.

BEHAVIORAL PRINCIPLES AND TECHNIQUES

A variety of behavioral principles and techniques were used in the Gerontology Program. All staff members received detailed inser-vice training in the rationale and application of such procedures. All behavioral principles and techniques used in the Gerontology Program were subsumed within the following operational categories and are presented in this chapter in that order: increasing the occurrence of existing adaptive behaviors; establishing the occurrence of adaptive behaviors; decreasing the occurrence of maladaptive behaviors; and maintaining and generalizing established adaptive behaviors in the program and postdischarge setting.

INCREASING THE OCCURRENCE OF EXISTING ADAPTIVE BEHAVIORS

Clients admitted to the Gerontology Program typically exhibited some degree of adaptive behavior. A major problem was that the adaptive behaviors, although obviously present in the client's behavioral repertoire, occurred only at very low frequencies. The frequency of occurrence of adaptive behaviors was often so low that, for all practical purposes, they were functionally nonexistent. The procedures used to increase the occurrence of already existing behaviors were different from procedures to establish new adaptive behaviors. To increase the occurrence of behavior, these principles and techniques were used: (1) prompting and (2) positive reinforcement, including (a) identification of positive reinforcers, (b) verbal contracting, (c) social reinforcement, (d) token system, and (e) various schedules of reinforcement.

Prompting

Prompting is the use of verbal, gestural, or physical assists presented to the client for the purpose of initiating or completing a response appropriately. Clients did not always initiate a response, or if they did initiate a response, it was not always completed appropriately. The correct use of prompting by staff members assured that the response, when initiated, was completed appropriately. The prompting used in the Gerontology Program was divided into the following four types of prompts:

Verbal Prompt. A verbal prompt consists of asking the client to initiate a response or the provision of instructions to guide the appropriate completion of a response.

Modeling/Gestural Prompt. A modeling prompt consists of demonstrating the appropriate response for the client to imitate. A gestural prompt consists of using gestures to initiate or guide the appropriate completion of a response.

Occasional Physical Assistance. Occasional physical assistance consists of occasionally touching the client in such a manner as to guide him to a degree in completing a response appropriately.

Complete Physical Assistance. Complete physical assistance consists of continually touching the client in such a manner as to guide him physically in completing a response appropriately.

The levels of prompts were hierarchically arranged from minimal staff assistance (verbal prompts) to complete staff assistance (complete physical assistance). *It was essential in working with a client that the least amount of assistance resulting in the appropriate completion of the response be provided.* For example, in the ADL I module, we often found that we had to start with occasional physical assistance to ensure that the client completed fingernail care appropriately. The key to successful prompting, however, was the ability then to use only gestural prompts and finally only verbal prompts to get the client to complete the behavior appropriately. Once the client was completing fingernail care appropriately with only a verbal prompt to initiate the behavior, the verbal prompt was faded. The client then initiated fingernail care.

When approaching a client for the purpose of prompting him to complete a specific response, the staff member first tried a verbal prompt since it was the least amount of assistance that one could provide. If the client was provided with a verbal prompt and did not initiate or complete the behavior appropriately, the next level of prompt was used. This approach allowed a client to be as independent of staff assistance as possible. This is an essential point which cannot be overemphasized.

Positive Reinforcement

1. *Process:* The term *positive reinforcement* describes a process whereby the probability of occurrence of a response is increased as a result of a stimulus immediately following the emission of that response.

2. *Operation:* The presentation of verbal feedback, praise, a tangible object, or access to an activity immediately follows the occurrence of a response for the purpose of increasing the probability of occurrence of that response.

Positive reinforcement was used operationally in the Gerontology Program on an ongoing basis. Staff members were trained and were quite adept at selecting appropriate behaviors to be reinforced and at presenting positive reinforcers immediately following the occurrence of specified behaviors. Positive reinforcement was essential in facilitating adaptive behavior in modular treatment, SCBT, and the behavioral program milieu.

The use of staff-directed prompts was tied directly to the use of positive reinforcement. For example, if a client was in the process of reestablishing telephone skills, the trainer typically prompted the appropriate completion of a specific target behavior and immediately reinforced the client on completion of the target behavior. The prompt assured that the appropriate behavior would be initiated and completed correctly while the immediate presentation of a positive reinforcer at the completion of the behavior increased the probability of occurrence or strengthened the behavior.

Staff members were also quite adept at "catching a client being appropriate." In other words, staff members were quick to reinforce clients immediately when they initiated appropriate behavior without staff-directed prompts. It was extremely important to reinforce clients for exhibiting appropriate, adaptive behavior on their own. The reinforcement of self-initiated adaptive behavior not only strengthens the occurrence of that particular behavior but also facilitates the independence of the client.

Identification of Positive Reinforcers. In any behaviorally based treatment program, the identification of positive reinforcers is a necessary first step in the process of establishing appropriate changes in behavior. It is important to remember that reinforcers are highly individualized. The old saying, "different strokes for different folks," is very real when it comes to the identification of reinforcers. In other words, what may be reinforcing to one client may not be reinforcing to other clients.

How does one identify positive reinforcers? Perhaps the easiest and most effective method is the appropriate use of the *Premack Principle.* This principle states that if two behaviors are observed to occur at different rates in the natural environment, the opportunity to engage in the more frequently occurring behavior can be used as a positive reinforcer to increase the rate of the less frequently occurring behavior (Favell, 1977).

The Premack Principle was widely used in the Gerontology Program and was especially useful when it was difficult to identify reinforcers. To identify specific reinforcers, a client was observed in the unrestricted unit environment and a determination of the frequency of certain activities was made. For example, if during leisure time the client usually played cards, the staff knew that card playing could be used as a reinforcer for lower frequency behaviors.

If bed-making occurred at a low frequency of occurrence in relation to card-playing, the opportunity to play cards was made contingent on the client's making his bed. If a client initiated walks at a high frequency but did not attend the assigned modules on a regular basis (low frequency behavior), walks were made contingent on attendance at modules.

The major advantage of the Premack Principle was that, almost without exception, reinforcers could be identified. The use of the principle taught the staff not to rely solely on traditional reinforcers. By simply observing clients and the frequency of their behaviors, reinforcers were readily identified. This approach is far superior to the trial-and-error method of identifying reinforcers.

Verbal Contracting. Verbal contracting consists of specifying verbally to a person a planned contingency of reinforcement in which the occurrence of a specific behavior will be immediately followed by an identified reinforcer.

Verbal contracting consists of two parts: (1) specification of the desired target behavior and (2) specification of the reinforcer that will follow the occurrence of the target behavior. One of the most effective ways to use verbal contracting is to combine it with the Premack Principle. The use of the Premack Principle allows one to readily identify positive reinforcers, and verbal contracting provides a format for expressing a contingency between a target behavior and the identified reinforcer.

Staff members in the program soon learned that clients typically pariticipate in some activities at high frequencies. Popular, high-frequency activities were watching television, listening to music, going for a walk, and playing table games. Following the Premack Principle, these activities were identified as positive reinforcers. Staff members would establish a reinforcement contingency whereby the opportunity to participate in a reinforcing activity was used to increase the occurrence of low-frequency behaviors (e.g., making one's bed, participating in modules, or dressing appropriately). These contingencies were stated in a verbal contracting format.

Staff members learned that there was a correct and an incorrect way to use verbal contracting. An incorrect way would be to phrase a contingency in the following manner: "Joe, if you don't make your bed, you can't listen to the radio." A correct way of expressing the contingency was to phrase the same example in the following manner: "Joe, when you make your bed, you can listen to the radio." Obviously, the first example was more likely to be perceived as a threat with all of the disadvantages that a threat has to offer. The latter example was expressed as a privilege rather than a threat and was more likely to result in the occurrence of the behavior.

A combination of the Premack Principle and verbal contracting was easily used operationally. The combination assured that reinforcers could be readily identified and reinforcement contingencies established and expressed in an appropriate manner to the client.

Social Reinforcement. Social reinforcement is an increase in the probability of occurrence of a response as a result of presenting verbal feedback and/or verbal praise immediately following the occurrence of that response.

Social reinforcers were widely used in the program. There were a variety of reasons why social reinforcers were so widely used. First of all, social reinforcers could be delivered immediately following the occurrence of appropriate behavior. It was often difficult to reinforce a client with a token immediately following the occurrence of a specific response since the trainer might not have been within arm's reach of the client and stopping immediately to give tokens could disrupt modular training. However, the process of reinforcement was started as soon as the staff member acknowledged the appropriate completion of a behavior by verbal approval. Social reinforcers were always available and easily delivered.

Second, much empirical evidence exists to indicate that social reinforcers are very powerful positive reinforcers. It appears that most people enjoy or even seek out acknowledgment or praise for completion of specific behaviors or tasks. Clients in the program appeared to enjoy the positive attention that the staff provided as reinforcers. *Staff members realized the strength of social reinforcers and provided social interactions for clients contingent only on appropriate behavior.*

Third, social reinforcers were easily paired with the presentation of other reinforcers such as tokens. By doing so, staff members were sometimes able to withdraw eventually the use of tangible reinforcers and maintain appropriate behavior with social reinforcers alone.

Social reinforcers must also be presented to the client in a correct manner if they are to be maximally effective. For example, our staff members were very careful not to belittle the clients when interacting socially with them. It is important to remember that elderly clients are adults and expect to be treated as such. Social reinforcement must be accomplished with proper regard for their age. A handshake, for example, may be more effective than a pat on the back. All social reinforcers should be delivered in a sincere and nonpatronizing manner.

1. *Token.* A token is a previously neutral object with no reinforcing value which becomes a secondary, generalized reinforcer when that object is exchanged for other reinforcers.

2. *Token economy* is a system whereby a person is reinforced with tokens contingent on prespecified, appropriate behaviors with the

tokens gaining reinforcer value by being exchangeable for other reinforcers.

Although token economies were not new, very few token economy programs had been used exclusively with the elderly. Since the inception of the token economy as a treatment modality in the latter 1960s, the vast majority of applicants have involved such populations as psychiatric inpatients not categorized by age, the developmentally disabled, juvenile delinquents, and children in the classroom setting (Patterson & Jackson, 1980a).

The token economies in the program were viewed as adjunctive systems for delivering positive reinforcers. Staff were trained always to provide feedback as to why a token was being given along with praise for exhibiting the appropriate token-earning behavior. The combination of token reinforcement and social reinforcement was assumed to be more powerful than tokens delivered without social reinforcement. It was also assumed that the constant pairing of social reinforcement with the delivery of tokens served to increase the value of social reinforcement for those clients who did not initially respond well to social stimuli.

Social reinforcement and informational feedback are frequently encountered in the noninstitutionalized environment. Although token reinforcement would cease upon discharge from the program, it was hoped that social reinforcers would continue to be present in the postdischarge setting and would therefore maintain the skills reestablished in the Gerontology Program.

As positive reinforcers, tokens were used in all behavioral treatment components of the program. For example, tokens were used to reinforce attendance to and participation in the assigned modules. Tokens were also used in SCBT to reinforce nonmodular related adaptive behaviors which occurred during the conduct of modules as well as at other times. (See Patterson, 1976, for a detailed explanation of individualized treatment with a token economy.) Lastly, tokens were used as a part of the overall behavioral program to encourage and support the initiation of independence-related adaptive behaviors whenever they occurred. In addition, the token economies provided structure for staff members in that the system served as prompts to staff to reinforce clients for appropriate behavior on a consistent and ongoing basis.

The token stores were managed on a daily basis with scheduled access times. Staff members kept daily records of the number of tokens earned in addition to the number of tokens exchanged. An interesting finding in the program was that clients often appeared to complete specified behaviors for the token itself and not for the exchange value. This was assumed since many clients often accumulated large numbers of tokens without exchanging them for objects in the token store.

A token economy can be a very convenient and effective means of providing positive reinforcers for appropriate behavior. First of all, tokens can be delivered immediately upon the occurrence of targeted behaviors. In cases in which they cannot be delivered immediately (e.g., when the client is not immediately accessible but is in the immediate vicinity), the delivery of tokens is easily preceded by a social reinforcer. This bridges the gap between the occurrence of the behavior and the delivery of tokens. In addition, social reinforcement and token reinforcement are paired. Secondly, tokens are generalized reinforcers, that is, a single token may be exchanged for a variety of other reinforcers. This adds to the strength of the token as a reinforcer and prevents the process of satiation that can occur when a client receives too much of a single reinforcer.

Lastly, tokens are easily delivered. Staff members would obviously have had great difficulty in carrying around on their person such tangible reinforcers as coffee, cigarettes, soft drinks, clothing items, or toiletries. It would have been virtually impossible to carry around certain intangible reinforcers such as Guy Lombardo or Lawrence Welk music. However, after reinforcement with a generalized reinforcer such as a token, the client could exchange the token for any of the mentioned tangible or intangible items or activities. Tokens were, of course, easily carried and delivered by staff members. Such ease of use ensured that clients received the continuous reinforcement that was required in the reestablishment of adaptive behavior.

Schedules of Reinforcement. A schedule of reinforcement specifies the contingency established between the repeated occurrence of a response and the delivery of a reinforcer on either a sequential or temporal basis.

Of all the schedules of reinforcement, five schedules are more commonly used. These schedules are labeled continuous reinforcement (CRF), fixed ratio (FR), fixed interval (FI), variable ratio (VR), and variable interval (VI), and may be defined in the following manner:

1. *Continuous reinforcement (CRF)* is a schedule of reinforcement in which a response is reinforced on each occasion that it occurs.
2. *Fixed ratio (FR)* is an intermittent schedule of reinforcement in which a response is reinforced only after a specified number of such responses have occurred.
3. *Fixed interval (FI)* is an intermittent schedule of reinforcement

in which the first response after a fixed interval of time is
reinforced.

4. *Variable ratio (VR)* is an intermittent schedule of reinforcement
in which a varying number of responses occurs before the last
response in that sequence is reinforced with the varying number of responses expressed as the average number of responses.

5. *Variable interval (VI)* is an intermittent schedule of reinforcement in which the first response after a variable amount of
time is reinforced with the varying time periods expressed as
an average time interval.

Although continuous reinforcement is essential in teaching a new
skill or in initially strengthening the reestablishment of behaviors
lying dormant within a person's behavioral repertoire, it is well established that if continuous reinforcement is interrupted, extinction of
the previously reinforced behavior occurs quite rapidly. Staff members in the Gerontology Program used continuous reinforcement only
to initially strengthen an appropriate behavior or for skill acquisition.
After the behavior was occurring at an appropriate frequency, intermittent reinforcement was used to maintain the occurrence of the
behavior. The intermittent schedules of reinforcement increased considerably the resistance of the new behaviors to extinction.

Of the four major types of intermittent schedules of reinforcement (FR, FI, VR, and VI), the FI schedule was the most useful. An
approximation to an FI schedule was used in the Conversation Training module. Basically, clients were reinforced on an interval schedule
for engaging in conversation with other clients (see Chapter 4 for a
complete description). Because the approach used resulted in practical
application problems, the approximated FI schedule was later converted to a VI schedule. The VI schedule of reinforcement is known
to generate high, stable rates of behavior since the person never really
knows when reinforcement is to occur. Since it is highly unpredict-
able as to when the opportunity to be reinforced is present, the
person typically exhibits the target behavior on an ongoing basis to
secure the reinforcer when the opportunity is present. This is in fact
what happened in Conversation Training. The VI schedule resulted in
a high rate of conversation among all clients in the module.

ESTABLISHING THE OCCURRENCE OF ADAPTIVE BEHAVIORS

Frequently it was evident that many elderly clients either did not
initiate specific target behaviors or did not on their own complete a
target behavior correctly. If the correct form of the behavior did not

occur at all, then, of course, the frequency of occurrence could not be increased. This indicated that specific behaviors, or at least the correct forms of the specific behaviors, were not presently in the client's behavioral repertoires.

Therefore, behavioral techniques designed to develop new behaviors were used. The major techniques widely used to establish new behaviors within the Gerontology Program were prompting (previously described), modeling, behavioral rehearsal, shaping, and backward chaining

Modeling

1. *Process:* The term *modeling* refers to a process whereby an observer learns new behavior by observing and imitating the behavior of a model.

2. *Operation:* Modeling as an operation consists of demonstrating a behavior to a person who is then reinforced for imitating the behavior.

Modeling was perhaps the most widely used teaching technique of the Gerontology Program. Much empirical evidence indicates the effectiveness of modeling as a procedure for establishing new behavior. Not only is the specific modeled behavior adopted by the client, but similar, even innovative, responses are developed. Contrary to popular belief, novel behaviors can emerge through the modeling process.

When exposed to several models, observers rarely pattern their behavior after a single model. Instead, observers typically combine aspects of various models into new amalgams that differ from the original source (Bandura, Ross, & Ross, 1963). Modeling specific behaviors then appears to initiate the acquisition of other appropriate responses in a similar situation (response generalization).

Staff members in the Gerontology Program used some form of modeling in virtually every module that was offered. Examples included modeling components of proper nail care in ADL I, correct use of the telephone and making change in ADL II, how to prepare a budget in ADL III, the appropriate expression of pleasure and displeasure in Communication Training, and modeling appropriate and positive statements about self and peers in Self-esteem Training. The reader will recognize the importance of modeling in these modules as well as other modules when reading Chapter 4, which describes the modules.

Modeling could be observed as an ongoing process both in the modules and in the overall behavioral program milieu. Clients observed other clients performing certain skills and being reinforced. Hypothetically, clients could learn vicariously by modeling reinforced behaviors of other clients. An example of vicarious learning through observation could be observed in Communication Training. The staff member modeled appropriate communication behaviors for a single client. However, other clients in the group also observed this process. It is quite possible that other clients in the group benefited from observing this process as it was repeated for each client in the group.

Staff members also served as models of appropriate and adaptive behavior on a daily, shift-by-shift basis. Staff members were well aware that clients were likely to adopt components of their behavior through the modeling process. Therefore, they maintained appropriate behavior in the presence of clientele.

Modeling was also occasionally used in SCBT plans. If a client had difficulty in mastering a specific skill within a module, the client received specialized SCBT on a one-to-one basis to learn the skill. For example, if a client failed to acquire proper fingernail care in a training group, the case manager would work with him on an intensive one-to-one basis and use modeling, along with other behavioral techniques, to assist the client in acquiring the specific skill.

In order for modeling to work effectively as a teaching technique, staff members learned that they must first gain the attention of the client. Modeling is an observational technique and the client must be actively attending to the model if the behavior of the model is to be adopted. If a client was not actively observing, a special effort was made first to achieve the undivided visual and auditory attention of the client.

Behavior Rehearsal

Behavior rehearsal is a training technique in which a client demonstrates behavior in simulated practice sessions in order to learn how to perform the behavior in real-life situations.

Behavior rehearsal is very convenient for teaching many skills because the use of simulated situations to practice behaviors allows for training to occur at the time and place of the trainer's choosing rather than having to do all training only where and when the target behavior would normally occur. These advantages also allowed many types of training to occur in groups which might otherwise have to be done on a strictly individual basis. All training techniques were applied with the rehearsed behavior that would be applied with more naturally occurring behavior.

Behavior rehearsal was used extensively in the program in specific modules or pilot modules as well as in SCBT. In modules, behavior rehearsal was closely associated with the use of modeling. For example, in the Communication Training module, the client was first asked to demonstrate his response in a simulated situation. If the demonstrated behavior in the simulated situation needed improvement, the staff member then modeled an appropriate response for the client. The client was then given another opportunity to demonstrate appropriate responses in the same simulated situation with the added opportunity of adopting the behavior of the model.

In the preceding example, behavior rehearsal was used for two purposes. First of all, asking the clients to demonstrate how they would respond in a simulated situation provided the staff member with an assessment of the clients' usual way of responding. Much can be learned from careful observation of an initial behavior rehearsal. Inappropriate ways of responding can quickly be targeted as areas needing improvement. In addition, appropriate ways of responding can be reinforced and therefore strengthened.

Second, the client again had the opportunity to demonstrate how he would respond in the same simulated situation. However, the client had the benefit of having observed appropriately modeled responses provided by a staff member immediately following the initial behavior rehearsal. This, of course, increased the probability that more appropriate responses and concomitant positive reinforcement would occur as a result of the modeling process.

The focused attention of the client is essential with both modeling and behavior rehearsal. When the client completed the first behavior rehearsal, the staff member would immediately provide feedback to the client regarding the adequacy of the performance. The verbal feedback occurred in the following two-part sequence:

- The client was informed of the appropriate components of the rehearsal behavior, and
- The client was informed of the components of the behavior that would be better changed.

Following the verbal feedback after the initial behavior rehearsal, the staff member instructed the client to attend to specific behaviors that he (the staff member) would model for the client. The staff member then modeled an appropriate rehearsal of behavior in the same simulated situation. The client was then given the opportunity to repeat the behavior rehearsal. In most cases, the clients in the program adopted the appropriate, focused behaviors modeled by the staff member and were reinforced for doing so.

Shaping (Method of Successive Approximations)

Shaping is a technique used to develop a new target behavior not presently in the client's behavioral repertoire by reinforcing successive approximations of that target behavior. The first behavior reinforced may only slightly resemble the target behavior; however, each succeeding reinforced approximation more closely resembles the target behavior until finally the target behavior occurs and is reinforced.

In addition to modeling, shaping was widely used in all components of the program to produce previously nonexistent behaviors. That is, some approximation to a desired behavior might occur spontaneously; or prompts and/or modeling might set the occasion for such an approximation to occur. Shaping served the purpose of improving upon such approximations until the appropriate behavior was completed.

Although shaping was used in all modules in some form, a simple example will illustrate the use of this very effective technique. If a client in ADL I had trouble with a certain skill such as filing the fingernails appropriately, staff members would initially reinforce any attempt at filing the nails. That is, the reinforcement would occur even if the attempt at filing the nails was a hit-and-miss process. However, in future training sessions, reinforcers were withheld until the fingernail filing attempts were closer approximations to appropriate filing. Eventually, by requiring closer approximations before reinforcers were presented, clients successfully mastered the fine motor behaviors required in proper fingernail care.

Shaping was also used in SCBT. For example, if a client had trouble learning how to write a check in ADL III, one-to-one training occurred in which the trainer would initially reinforce any approximation to the final target behavior and require closer approximations in successive trials at filling out a check appropriately.

Shaping was an ongoing component of the overall behavioral program. The staff were well aware that often clients could not be expected initially to exhibit target behaviors appropriately or correctly. Therefore, approximations of the target behavior would be reinforced. If the goal for a specific female client was to dance with a male client partner, the first approximation could be to dance with a female staff member. In other words, this was the first approximation to be reinforced. Then, of course, closer approximations to the target behavior were reinforced, such as dancing with a male staff member and then dancing with a male client.

When using shaping, it is essential to reinforce only the closer approximations to a target behavior. In the Gerontology Program, staff members were careful not to reinforce initial approximations after closer approximations were obtained. The only exception to this occurred when a client could not acquire the approximation that was presently being taught. In this case, it appeared that the more recent approximation was too big a jump for the client to make. The procedure was therefore to back up a little and accept an approximation between the last successfully completed approximation and the approximation which the client was then having difficulty mastering. After the interim approximation was successfully acquired, the staff member taught or required the completion of the approximation which had created some difficulty.

The important point is that shaping is a fluid, dynamic process. It is often difficult to determine just what approximation will be reinforced prior to implementation of the procedure. The appropriate shaping technique involves reinforcing the client's self-initiated approximations rather than reinforcing a client for conforming to predetermined steps. When using shaping, one must be flexible enough to allow for a "molding" of behavior just as a potter does in molding a vase from an initial amorphous piece of moving clay.

Backward Chaining

Backward chaining is a technique used to teach a complex task by dividing the task into separate, sequential steps (behaviors); the chain is then taught sequentially beginning with the last step first and progressing backward until the entire chain is acquired.

Backward chaining is an extremely useful technique in teaching relatively complex tasks (tasks that can be divided into separate and distinct behaviors) to persons with limited learning and memory abilities. Very often, backward chaining has been successfully used to achieve results in the acquisition of certain skills when other techniques have failed.

An example of backward chaining in the Gerontology Program was in memory development, an activity the development of which was begun during the evaluation period reported here but which continues in a developmental stage (Dee, 1980). Clients were taught to orient themselves to their immediate environment for the purpose of seeking out specific locations without staff assistance. Orienting themselves to the new project environment was often very confusing to recently admitted clients. Although there were very few turns in the approximately 50-yard trip from the Gerontology Residential Treatment Unit to the cafeteria, some clients had difficulty in traversing this distance unassisted.

Basically, the backward chaining technique consisted of first dividing the trip from the unit to the cafeteria into steps. Then, true to backward chaining procedure, the last step was taught first. In other words, the staff member accompanied the client most of the way to the cafeteria, stopped short of the cafeteria door by several feet, and prompted the client to walk to the cafeteria. The first step taught was therefore the last component in the chain.

When the client could complete the first step, the second step was taught. This step consisted of again accompanying the client most of the way to the cafeteria, but this time the staff member stopped further away from the cafeteria door. The prompt, "Walk to the cafeteria," was again given and the client walked the remainder of the way to the cafeteria. This process was repeated on each excursion to the cafeteria, with the staff member reducing the distance for which he accompanied the client. Eventually, the client could leave the unit and traverse the distance to the cafeteria without any staff-directed location prompts.

There are several key components to using the backward chaining technique successfully. First of all, the reinforcer must always be presented to the client at the successful completion of the chain. For example, if one is teaching a client to locate the cafeteria, the client would be reinforced only when he opened the cafeteria door, regardless of where he started the unassisted portion of the trip. In any type of behavioral chain, any new step, or link, is a signal for the occurrence of the next step, with each completion of a step also serving as a reinforcer for the preceding step. The terminal reinforcer (the reinforcer following the last step in the chain) serves to strengthen and maintain the entire chain.

Second, if a client has difficulty in mastering a step in the chain, this could mean that the step is too much to ask of the client. Therefore, a new step is added falling between the last successful step completed and the step with which the client is presently having difficulty. Finally, additional prompting may be needed at crucial parts of the chain to obtain successful mastery of that step. For example, it was not unusual for some clients to require additional verbal prompts in learning spatial components of steps involving turns in the chain of going from the unit to the cafeteria.

Decreasing the Occurrence of Maladaptive Behaviors

A number of gerontology clients exhibited maladaptive or inappropriate behaviors. An inappropriate behavior was considered to be maladaptive if such behavior presented an obstacle to community placement. The goal in working with a client who exhibited maladaptive behavior was to decrease the occurrence of such behaviors.

Many behavioral techniques exist for decreasing the occurrence of inappropriate behavior. However, it is essential that such techniques not be used alone. If deceleration techniques are to work effectively and have long lasting effects, then positive reinforcement procedures must also be used concurrently to strengthen the occurrence of appropriate behavior. Positive reinforcement of appropriate behavior was used along with the following techniques to decrease inappropriate behavior: social disapproval, extinction, exclusion time-out, seclusion time-out, household orderliness training, and differential reinforcement of other behaviors (DRO)/differential reinforcement of incompatible behaviors (DRI).

Social Disapproval

Social disapproval is a corrective technique in which verbal feedback is given to a client indicating that a specific behavior is not acceptable.

Social disapproval is obviously very common and it was usually the first approach used to decrease behavior; however, staff members were well aware that speaking to clients immediately after a behavior, to indicate either approval *or* disapproval, could well function as an attention reinforcer and actually increase the undesirable behavior. Therefore, it was necessary to keep frequency data on the occurrence of the behavior to ensure that the procedure was working. It was frequently found that social disapproval was effective with the elderly clients; therefore, more complex procedures were often avoided.

Extinction

Extinction is a behavioral technique used to decrease the incidence of inappropriate behavior by removing the reinforcer(s) maintaining that behavior.

The usual form of extinction used in the Gerontology Program was the withdrawal of staff attention contingent on the occurrence of inappropriate behavior. Extinction was widely used as a behavioral deceleration technique in modular treatment, SCBT, and the overall behavioral program. This technique combined with the positive reinforcement of appropriate behavior was the most common combined approach taken by far. The proper use of extinction and positive reinforcement accomplished the dual result of increasing the frequency of appropriate behaviors and decreasing the frequency of inappropriate behaviors.

Extinction was often used in modular treatment to decrease the incidence of excessive and inappropriate talking in a group. Clients very often disrupted a group by talking. Such disruption is harmful for two reasons. First of all, it interferes with the learning process for other clients because their attention is distracted and focused on the disruptive client rather than on the trainer. Second, the disruptive client is not exhibiting appropriate social skills. That is, one must learn to speak at socially acceptable times.

The actual extinction procedure consisted of simply ignoring the client when inappropriate talking occurred. All staff members used extinction systematically and consistently for such behaviors. Occasionally, a client would not respond to extinction in the modular setting; therefore, other techniques (e.g., social disapproval, exclusion time-out) were used in these instances.

Extinction was also a technique commonly used in SCBT. For example, one particular client would visit the nurses' station at such a high frequency of occurrence that her participation in the program was limited. She would often go to the nurses' station rather than attend the assigned module or activity. Careful analysis of the situation revealed that staff members might have been inadvertently reinforcing such behavior by interacting with the client on her visits to the station. Although the content of such staff–client interactions might have consisted of no more than "Mary, please do not come to the nurses' station so often," it was apparently enough to maintain this high rate of behavior. In other words, Mary could be assured of receiving attention from staff by visiting the nurses' station. (This was obviously a case in which social disapproval had an effect opposite to that which was desired.)

The extinction procedure used was very simple. All staff members in the nurses' station ignored Mary completely when she walked up to them. They were careful to avoid eye contact, not to talk to her, and were even careful not to face in her direction. The staff provided interaction only when Mary was away from the nurses' station. After approximately a week, the number of Mary's visits to the nurses' station decreased dramatically.

As previously mentioned, extinction was also very useful in the overall program. It was virtually impossible to include all inappropriate behaviors that might occur in a single treatment plan. The modules could not address all areas, and certainly one-to-one SCBT programs could not be designed to cover all behaviors with all clients. Therefore, the staff generally placed all inappropriate behaviors on extinction and reinforced all appropriate behavior. The only exceptions to this occurred when extinction did not work with a particular client or when a behavior was too serious to ignore. This overall approach appeared to be powerful, for many inappropriate behaviors present shortly after admission no longer occurred after several weeks in the program.

Exclusion Time-out

Exclusion time-out is a technique in which a client is immediately removed from the vicinity of an activity contingent on the occurrence of specified inappropriate behavior. The client is allowed to return to the activity after a prespecified period of time (e.g., five minutes) in which the disruptive behavior does not occur.

As we mentioned previously, not all clients responded to staff-applied extinction in a group setting. When extinction did not result in a decrease in the disruptive behavior in that setting, exclusion time-out was often used. There are many reasons why staff-applied extinction may not work well in a group setting. Perhaps the major reason is that the disruptive behavior may be maintained by attention from other clients and not maintained simply by staff attention. Therefore, when only staff attention is removed from the total amount of combined staff and client attention, little if any effect is noticed. The rationale for using exclusion time-out by removing a client from a specific setting when disruptive behavior occurs is that such removal separates the disruptive client from any group-produced reinforcers that are maintaining the inappropriate behavior.

When exclusion time-out was used in a group setting, staff members implemented the procedure as the disruptive behavior occurred. The client would be assisted away from the group and taken to a neutral setting where additional attention was not available. This was accomplished with an absolute minimum of verbal interaction to assure that the process of removal from the group would not be reinforcing also. When the client had behaved appropriately for a period of time, he was asked to continue in the group.

When using exclusion time-out, it is essential to implement the procedure when the disruptive behavior is occurring or immediately after the occurrence. It is also essential that the procedure be implemented with a minimum of verbal interaction. Occasionally it is necessary to use *graduated guidance* in removing the client from the group and to direct him to a neutral area of the unit. Stated simply, graduated guidance is a prompting technique in which a specific behavior of a client is obtained by using the least amount of assistance necessary. In other words, the client is never provided with more assistance than that necessary to secure the removal and relocation of the client.

Seclusion Time-out

Seclusion time-out is a restrictive technique in which a client is immediately placed in an externally locked, seclusion time-out room contingent on severely aggressive and/or destructive behavior. The seclusion time-out room must be free from obstacles, well lighted, and well vented and must contain an observation window through which a client is visually checked every two to three minutes.

Seclusion time-out was used early in the program and with only three clients. These clients became seriously aggressive toward others on the unit and were placed in seclusion time-out for periods of from five minutes to one hour. Good results were not obtained with these clients. Apparently, the time-out room actually served as a reinforcer for one client who began to isolate herself there voluntarily with considerable frequency. Theoretically, the seclusion time-out procedure is effective because it temporarily removes the person from a reinforcing environment and in this sense functions as a punisher. One has to conclude that, in the cases of these clients, the time-out room was not significantly less reinforcing for these people, at least for the short durations they stayed there as permitted by then-existing policies.

Even during the time that exclusion time-out was used, it was regarded as only short-term emergency treatment for any client. The admission criteria for Gerontology excluded clients who were dangerous to themselves or others because of the nature of the program. Therefore, attempts were made to screen out dangerous clients prior to admission; if they did become dangerous after admission, they were transferred to a more secure facility as soon as this could be arranged.

It is important to note here that many program settings do not allow the use of seclusion time-out. One should always determine the acceptability of this technique in any program setting prior to use. Also, seclusion time-out is a very restrictive procedure. It should be used only with clients exhibiting aggressive behavior to a degree such that others in the environment require protection and should be used only after less restrictive deceleration techniques have failed to produce appropriate decreases in aggressive behavior.

Household Orderliness Training

Household orderliness training is an overcorrection technique in which a client who has disturbed the appearance of the environment not only restores the environment to its previous condition prior to the disruption, but also straightens an additional part of the environment.

Household orderliness training is only one of a number of overcorrection/restitution techniques developed by Dr. N. H. Azrin and his colleagues (Foxx & Azrin, 1972, 1973; Webster & Azrin, 1973). Household orderliness training was particularly useful in the Gerontology Program for those clients who exhibited behavior that was disruptive to the immediate environment. The technique appeared to be more effective than simply correcting the client by requiring him to restore the environment to its original condition. The added step of "doing more," or overcorrecting, seemed to be an essential component in decelerating this disruptive behavior. The reader is encouraged to review Azrin, Foxx, and Webster's work on overcorrection/restitution techniques for more information regarding a variety of such techniques.

DRO/DRI

Differential reinforcement of other behavior (DRO) is a technique used to decrease the occurrence of a specified inappropriate behavior by placing that behavior on extinction and reinforcing the client for exhibiting increasing lengths of time in which the inappropriate behavior does not occur. At the end of the time interval, the client is reinforced for having exhibited any behavior *other* than the specified inappropriate behavior. If the inappropriate behavior occurs during a time interval, that time interval is started over.

Differential reinforcement of incompatible behavior (DRI) is a technique used to decrease the occurrence of a specified inappropriate behavior by placing that behavior on extinction and reinforcing the client for exhibiting increasing lengths of time in which the inappropriate behavior does not occur. At the end of the time interval, the client is reinforced for having exhibited behavior that is *incompatible* with the occurrence of the specified inappropriate behavior. If the inappropriate behavior occurs during a time interval, that time interval is started over.

A careful reading of the definitions of DRO and DRI will indicate what appears to be only a slight difference between these two techniques. A DRO approach involves reinforcing behavior *other* than the specified inappropriate behavior undergoing extinction. In other words, as long as the client has not exhibited the inappropriate behavior for a specified time interval, he is reinforced. A DRI approach, however, emphasizes the reinforcement of behavior that is *incompatible* with the occurrence of the inappropriate behavior.

The DRO and DRI techniques have typically been used in retardation settings. For example, a DRI approach to self-injurious hair-pulling would be to prompt the client to exhibit some activity that is incompatible with hair-pulling such as brushing the hair and then reinforcing the client at the end of the specified time interval for exhibiting hair-brushing with no occurrence of hair-pulling.

In practice, it is often easier to begin with DRO and then change to DRI later. Since reinforcement in a DRI approach relies on both the absence of the inappropriate behavior and the occurrence of a specific incompatible behavior, the opportunity to reinforce a client may be hampered by difficulty in getting a client to exhibit the incompatible behavior even though the inappropriate behavior has not occurred. It appears that both schedules are useful in certain situations. A DRO is particularly useful if a client exhibits appropriate behavior on his own during the reinforced time interval. If the client tends to sit and not exhibit appropriate behavior during the time interval, it seems more advantageous to use DRI, which results in the strengthening of actual appropriate behavior during that time interval.

DRO and DRI were used as part of the SCBT approach in the Gerontology Program. A representative example is a woman client who remained in bed for most of the day, which of course interfered with her appropriate participation in the project—particularly the modular treatment component. The treatment team implemented a DRO plan which consisted of prompting the client out of bed and out of her room. The client was first reinforced with tokens for staying away from her room for 10-minute intervals. This interval of time was gradually lengthened until she was reinforced for 30-minute intervals.

The client was reinforced for any behavior other than being in her room. In fact, she usually sat in the day room area and did not do anything else. Therefore, the schedule was changed to a DRI with the intention of reinforcing her for staying out of her room by reinforcing participation in the modules. In other words, she was reinforced for exhibiting specific appropriate behavior that was incompatible with her being in her room and that would result in continued progress in the program.

MAINTENANCE AND GENERALIZATION OF TREATMENT EFFECTS

One of the most important components of any behavior modification or behavior therapy program is the maintenance and generalization of treatment effects. Generally speaking, it is not difficult to change behavior. However, the task of maintaining appropriate behavior and generalizing it to other environments may be difficult. The authors have the general impression that these tasks may be more easily accomplished for many of the behaviors that elderly subjects exhibited in the past. Our experience has been that such behaviors are relatively easy to generalize and maintain. Perhaps this was because these behaviors were previously widely generalized and therefore reinstating the behavior also reinstates its occurrence in many environments other than the training environment. Maintenance and generalization were considered to be of prime importance in the Gerontology Program.

Maintenance Procedures

Various types of procedures were used in the program to ensure maintenance of behavior following behavioral treatment. All staff members were trained in the rationale and application of such procedures and were quite adept at monitoring maintenance and making programmatic adjustments to facilitate this very important process. The common maintenance procedures used in the program consisted of the following:

- The amount of assistance provided to the client was decreased by using various levels of prompts.
- Prompting for desired behaviors was provided on a less frequent or less intense basis.
- Reinforcement of desired behaviors was provided on a less frequent basis.
- Target behaviors were reinforced in a variety of settings within the program.

The first procedure, maintenance through prompting, was probably the major technique used in the program to foster independence. Prompting, as presented earlier, consisted of various levels of assistance.

Prompting was widely used in the program for those clients requiring a one-to-one SCBT approach. For example, an occasional client would not benefit from the ADL I modular training in that he would require occasional or complete physical assistance in a one-to-one situation to complete bathing appropriately. In such cases, an SCBT approach was used which combined graduated guidance with reinforcement of appropriate behavior. In other words, complete physical assistance was required to teach the client how to complete all steps of the target behavior followed by occasional physical assistance, gestural prompts, and verbal prompts—in that order. Eventually, the client completed all bathing steps with only a verbal prompt to initiate bathing.

After behavior was maintained with a verbal prompt, more work on the part of the staff was necessary. If the client was left at the verbal prompt level, he would not initiate the behavior until that prompt was given. This is where the first maintenance procedure ended and the second maintenance procedure began.

Once the client was responding to a verbal prompt by completing the target behavior unassisted, the verbal prompt was faded. The staff did this in two ways. The first fading procedure consisted of giving a less complete verbal prompt on each occasion when a prompt was necessary. For example, on Monday, a staff member may have said, "Joe, it's 8:00 and time to take your bath." On Tuesday, the staff member may have said, "Joe, it's 8:00—bath time." On Wednesday, the verbal prompt may have been, "Joe, it's 8:00." Each time the prompt was decreased in content, the client learned to rely less on the prompt and more on himself.

The other fading procedure consisted of providing the prompt on an intermittent rather than continuous basis. Once the client began to initiate the target behavior on his own, a prompt was not necessary each time. As the client moved toward independence, only an occasional verbal reminder to initiate the target behavior was required.

The third maintenance procedure used in the program consisted of reinforcing desired behaviors on a less frequent basis. In the initial stages of working with a client, the client was reinforced for each appropriate occurrence of the behavior. This was a necessary first step. However, after the client demonstrated that he or she could exhibit the behavior, the presentation of reinforcers was changed from a continuous to an intermittent basis. In other words, the client was not reinforced for every completion of the target behavior. At approximately this point, reinforcers were presented after the completion of a random number of occurrences of the target behavior. If the behavior began to decrease in occurrence, we simply backed up a little and reinforced more often, making sure to decrease the frequency of presenting reinforcers again as soon as possible. It is important to note that the process of providing reinforcers less frequently was sometimes completed more systematically with the use of specific schedules of reinforcement.

An example of maintaining behavior with an intermittent schedule of reinforcement in our program was the Conversation Training module. Since this type of schedule did not easily allow the client to determine when a reinforcer would be presented, performance remained consistently high with no pauses. In some cases, such as our work with tardive dyskinesia, specific schedules were used in an SCBT approach to maintain the nonoccurrence of inappropriate behavior. Differential reinforcement of other behavior (DRO) was also used in an SCBT approach which made use of an advancing FI schedule of reinforcement to systematically reinforce longer periods of the nonoccurrence of inappropriate behavior by increasing the intervals of time between reinforcers.

The fourth maintenance procedure doubles as a generalization procedure. It is essential to reinforce new, adaptive behaviors in a variety of settings. Obviously, behaviors are not going to be maintained in varying stimulus conditions (environments) if the behaviors are not practiced and reinforced in the presence of these varying stimulus conditions. For example, if a client did not interact socially with other clients, an SCBT plan was developed to prompt and reinforce interactions with others. The second, and just as essential, component of this process was to prompt and reinforce social interaction in various situations within our program. *If behavior generalizes, it is more likely to be maintained.*

Generalization Procedures

Various types of procedures were used in the program to ensure generalization as well as maintenance of behavior. All staff members were trained in generalization procedures and were very sucessful in obtaining generalization of behavior throughout the program setting. In addition, according to Gerontology Program follow-up data (see evaluation chapters), behaviors have been generalized to and maintained in the placement settings following discharge.

There are two types of generalization, both typically used in the Gerontology Program. Stimulus generalization describes a process whereby a target behavior occurs in the presence of stimuli similar to the stimulus initially associated with the behavior. Response generalization describes a process whereby responses occur in the presence of a stimulus that are similar to the response initially associated with that stimulus. Both types of generalization are important, although stimulus generalization appears to be most frequently mentioned in the literature.

Within the Gerontology Program, generalization in SCBT was obtained by:

1. Reinforcement of the client for exhibiting the target behavior in a variety of settings (stimulus generalization)
2. Prompting and reinforcing of the target behavior to ensure that the behavior did not occur only in the presence of one staff member (stimulus generalization)
3. Reinforcement of the client for exhibiting appropriate behaviors similar to the initial target behavior (response generalization)
4. Inclusion of significant others in the SCBT process in the placement setting to reinforce appropriate behaviors in that setting away from the program (stimulus and response generalization)

The first generalization procedure was an extremely important programmatic operation if a client's newly established, appropriate behavior was to generalize and be maintained throughout the program setting. For example, the initial stages of SCBT took place in a controlled setting within the program. It was not unusual for appropriate behavior to be established in one setting in the program and not others until the client was liberally reinforced for exhibiting target behaviors in all environmental settings within the program.

The first procedure was closely tied to the second. Not only was it desirable for the established behavior to generalize to other settings within the program, but it was also important for the behavior to occur in the presence of many staff members. All staff members were made aware of treatment plans in detail so that all staff members could reinforce appropriate behavior. It was also not unusual to observe a client exhibiting target behaviors only in the presence of a particular case manager. In other words, the behavior had not yet generalized to other staff members. If this happened, the staff member requested that other staff members prompt and reinforce the target behavior. In some cases, the presence of the case manager was initially required, while a neutral staff member was paired with the reinforced occurrence of behavior. When this process was established, the case manager's presence was not necessary. The purpose of the first and second stimulus generalization procedures was to broaden or increase the stimulus conditions under which the target behavior would occur.

The third generalization procedure was designed to obtain re-

52

sponse generalization. Basically, the procedure consisted of reinforcing appropriate behaviors that were similar to the target behavior being taught. In other words, some flexibility not only was expected in the performance of target behaviors but was prompted and reinforced as well. For example, one female client in the program had difficulty interacting in a socially appropriate manner with her husband. During SCBT counseling sessions, she was taught socially appropriate behavior. The husband was then included in the plan by having him visit his wife in the program and interacting with her socially in a controlled session. The client exhibited socially appropriate behavior that had been prompted prior to the session as well as other appropriate behavior. Staff members were observant as usual and reinforced the target behaviors as well as these other appropriate responses. In this example, staff members actually assisted the client in establishing a repertoire of appropriate social interaction behaviors composed of specific as well as similar responses. Without such flexibility in the criteria establishing successful performance, behavioral training is almost certainly rigid and may result in the development of a limited behavioral repertoire.

The fourth generalization procedure was highly desirable but could occur in only a small minority of cases because of logistical problems and a lack of willing participants. This approach actually consisted of a combination of stimulus and response generalization by incorporating the placement setting as an extension of the program. This was accomplished by including family members or significant others in the treatment whenever this was possible by instructing them in prompting and reinforcement techniques as well as in appropriate social interaction behavior. In this way, stimulus generalization could occur since those behaviors established in various settings within the program could also be prompted and reinforced in yet another environment—the placement setting. Response generalization could occur with this method since significant others could reinforce not only specific target behaviors established in the program, but other similar appropriate behaviors as well.

4

The Modular Approach to Behavior Modification with the Elderly

ROGER L. PATTERSON
AND DAVID A. EBERLY

One definition of *module* is "any series of standardized units for use together" (Webster's Dictionary, 1979, p. 733). The Gerontology Program has developed treatment modules which conform to this definition. An interrelated set of behavioral skills is taught as a standard unit. This constitutes a module and is used with other standardized units to form an integrated program. Every module is self-contained, but each is complementary in content and method to the other modules so that the total of the components used together, within a compatible daily environment, provides a relatively comprehensive program designed to increase the independence of the elderly clients. As explained in the previous chapter, behavioral technology is used in the module for teaching and/or reteaching skills.

Each Gerontology Program module exists in the form of a manual which contains:

1. A general statement of what the module was designed to teach and to whom (admission criteria and training objectives for the module).
2. A brief explanation of relevant behavioral principles and procedures designed to supplement or refresh the users' formal training in behavior modification.
3. An assessment of the users' knowledge of relevant behavioral procedures in order to ensure that the user has sufficient knowledge of basic procedures that are needed to train clients in this module.

4. Client assessment forms and accompanying instructions for collection of assessment data. In most cases there are individual assessments to be used with each module, including assessments to be used before entry into a module and progress assessments to be used periodically to determine when a client has met criteria for having acquired module skills.
5. Descriptions of specific content to be taught including lists of materials, facilities, and teaching aids for each class.
6. Client objectives for each module describing specific target behaviors as operationally defined by the assessments. These objectives are not necessarily the same for all clients, but rather are specific to individuals based on functional level and deficiencies as measured by the assessment.
7. Forms and graphs (flow charts) to record data. These are used in the clients' records and medical charts.

In effect, the modules constitute a series of independently taught but related structured learning experiences for groups of elderly mental health clients, both those in day treatment and those in residential treatment.

The following pages of this chapter are designed to provide the reader with the rationale for the use of the modular approach to skills training with the elderly, as well as the rationale for the material in modules.

The Modular Behavioral Approach

There is broad justification for a modular behavioral approach to treatment. In the original proposal for a Gerontology Program at FMHI, Bates (1975) reviewed relevant gerontological literature and noted that highly structured learning situations with precise but limited objectives seemed most successful for promoting positive behavioral change in the older mental health population. Concrete support for this position was obtained in an experiment by Reichenfeld, Csapo, Carriere, and Gardner (1973). These researchers first tried to stimulate self-expression by the elderly in unstructured situations but found the result to be lack of participation accompanied by long periods of silence. In contrast, a structured classroom situation with emphasis on cognitive tasks resulted in much greater responsiveness.

A better developed and more highly structured model of group treatment using principles of behavior modification is the structured learning therapy (SLT) of Goldstein and his colleagues (Goldstein,

1973; Goldstein, Sprafkin, & Gershaw, 1976). Structured learning therapy was developed to provide social skills training to chronic psychiatric patients and applies the social learning theory of Bandura (1969), using modeling, feedback, behavior rehearsal, and reinforcement as behavior modification techniques. Research has demonstrated that SLT is very effective in teaching social skills to chronic psychiatric patients (Gutride, Goldstein, & Hunter, 1973, 1974). Since it was expected that many of the elderly clients in the Gerontology Program would be chronically mentally ill and institutionalized, the results obtained with SLT lent additional support to the idea that highly structured learning groups using behavioral principles might be a useful approach.

There are also other structured group techniques that do not deliberately use behavioral technology, and these are some of the most common institutionally based, nonmedical treatments for institutionalized elderly and the chronically mentally ill population. Two of these are reality orientation (RO; Taulbee & Wright, 1971) and remotivation therapy (American Psychiatric Association, 1968). Reality orientation attempts to make people more aware of important personal information as well as of their surroundings by providing a variety of reminders or prompts from the ward environment and from the staff. Classroom instruction is conducted several times weekly in RO.

Remotivation therapy consists of group sessions designed to encourage people to share various kinds of information and pleasant social experiences. The purpose of this therapy is to motivate people to interact socially and to establish a richer social environment than that which usually exists on a psychiatric ward.

On the basis of a review of the above treatment techniques, Bates (1975) concluded that

> structured group techniques are particularly serviceable and relevant to the elderly. These techniques make allowances for decreased motivation, sensory deprivation, memory loss, slowed information processing, rigidity, and fear of performance which have been reported in the psychogerontological literature. (p. 17)

Although similar in some respects to these other interventions, the modular approach used in the Gerontology Program is somewhat different from previous approaches. For a full understanding of the Gerontology Program modules, these similarities and differences must be discussed. The modules contain elements of (1) modern educational approaches as used in schools and colleges, (2) basic single case behavior modification and behavior therapy methodology, (3) token economies, and (4) structured learning groups. Each of these elements will be examined separately.

Modern Educational Approaches

The word *modules* has been used to designate components of educational curricula. The Gerontology Program modules are similar to structured educational modules in that both have (1) defined objectives, (2) defined teaching techniques and materials, and (3) specific assessment techniques. The existence of these three elements assures a high level of standardization which permits replicability. (This is very important if a real, integrated treatment *program* as opposed to a collection of treatment *techniques* is to be established.) Although the above similarities exist and the Gerontology Program does use psychoeducational approaches, a mental health treatment program for elderly persons is not the same as a school program. Differences in the two programs required differences in application and methods.

In the educational systems, conventional modules usually include sets of lesson plans to be taught in a designated sequence to groups of students within a specified time frame. For several reasons, the Gerontology Behavioral Modules were deliberately not structured as a series of lessons, each with its own plan and time schedule. People enter and leave mental health treatment on the basis of perceived need for treatment or service, not according to some established schedule such as the start of a semester or school year. In addition, this perceived need is frequently related to crisis situations. An individual may decide that Aunt Minnie needs mental treatment because her housekeeping, which used to be fastidious, has become so unsanitary and unsafe that it is a health hazard. This situation is quite different from one in which 6-year-olds enter a 12-year period of education because a law or their parents say they must do so.

Even if it were practical for people to enter treatment in groups at predesignated times, this would only control time of entry into the program. Maximal individualization was also required in the Gerontology Program because all persons do not enter the same modules or stay in particular modules for the same length of time. Our clients differ greatly in the types of training they need and also in their rate of progress. Entry into modules is based upon assessments designated to determine what specific types of training clients require. Completion of modules is by reassessment which demonstrates either that the client has mastered the particular training or that the client has reached maximum achievement level. Thus, Client A might be assessed as having low self-esteem and lack of personal grooming skills but also as having good knowledge of personal information and good interpersonal skills. Client B might show just the opposite strengths and weaknesses. Client C might have the same strengths and weaknesses as Client B but might progress more rapidly so that Personal Information Training, Communication Training, and Conversation Training could be completed in half the time required for Client B. In order to attain this level of individualization and to maximize learning, it is necessary to incorporate the methods of single case behavior modification into the modular training. This is the basic difference from modular educational practice.

SINGLE CASE BEHAVIOR MODIFICATION

As presented in the previous chapter, techniques employed in single case behavior modification are the basis of all behavioral change programs and also of both the modules and interventions for idiosyncratic problem behaviors not dealt with directly by modules. (Idiosyncratic behavioral excesses and deficits are frequently encountered with elderly individuals and will be discussed in the next chapter.)

Programmed instruction (Skinner, 1968) applies the basic concepts and techniques of behavior modification to skills training and education. The basic method used in programmed instruction is to teach a series of approximations which come successively closer to the desired response. This is usually accomplished by providing verbal instructions, prompting correct behavior, providing immediate reinforcement for correct responding, and gradually eliminating or fading the prompts or cues as learning occurs.

Programmed instruction in educational settings is usually accomplished by means of programmed textbooks or teaching machines. The use of such materials has been highly successful in providing instruction in rehabilitation settings (e.g., Cohen & Filipczak, 1971). This success is possible because proper assessment of deficits followed by the use of individually prescribed programmed texts permits each trainee to study only what he or she needs and to proceed at an individuated rate of learning. Furthermore, there is no required time of entry or completion of the program.

Unfortunately, the use of programmed texts or teaching machines was impractical in our program. Most of our clients would experience great difficulty in using these types of programmed teaching materials: many suffer visual impairments that make reading difficult, and many have poor reading ability. Additionally, most require close personal supervision to become involved consistently in any task, the antithesis of common programmed instruction.

It was the opinion of the staff that an approach other than conventional programmed instruction which still allowed the application of behavior modification principles was needed. The approach that was developed required that the module trainers themselves serve as the programmers rather than using programmed texts or teaching machines. This means that the trainers had to know how to present the material to be learned, how and when to prompt behavior, and how and when to reinforce responses. In summary, they must apply the basic techniques of behavior modification to individuals, within highly structured group training situations. The modular behavioral approach as developed in the Gerontology Program is actually the synthesis of educational approaches with behavioral methodology.

The Gerontology Program is similar to all other behavior modification approaches in that the basic methodology is the same. However, having the material to be trained available in a modular format does offer several advantages.

As the preceding chapter explained, in order to modify the behavior of any person, one must (1) specify the target behavior of concern, (2) record baseline measurements prior to any deliberate intervention, (3) identify and specify prompts to be used, (4) identify effective reinforcers, and (5) apply prompts and reinforcers appropriately so as to modify the target behaviors. Although effective, these procedures are very time-consuming and require a relatively high level of expertise. A well-trained person is needed to conduct these operations successfully with a variety of subjects, each with different target behaviors and requiring different specific techniques. The modules in the Gerontology Program involve the same basic steps to modify target behaviors, but the steps are simplified so that staff members with less training can apply the appropriate methodology to many people simultaneously.

An analogy with a computer analysis systems may be helpful in attempting to understand the usefulness of the modular system as a way of dealing with many behavioral problems. At present, there are several systems of predeveloped computer programs for data analysis. Thus, many analyses can be performed by persons with a minimum knowledge of computer programming. It is certainly more efficient to use these packages, or canned programs as they are frequently called, than to program every analysis completely from the beginning. The modular behavioral system works in an analogous way. Like the canned computer programs, there are prepared methods for dealing with frequently encountered behavioral deficits. Therefore, it is not necessary to devise new treatments for these common behaviors of clients. However, like the canned computer programs, the target behaviors must be common to many clients, must be a finite set, and must be specified and developed ahead of time of use.

In addition to simplifying application of technique, the use of the prepared modules overcomes another problem, that of relevance of the behaviors taught or the content of the behavioral program. Many of the early studies in behavior modification were not concerned with questions of relevance because they dealt with relatively isolated individual problem behaviors which were obvious. If someone is stealing, dressing in a bizarre manner, or banging his head against the furniture there is not much need to delve into issues of relevance in order to justify the modification of these behaviors. However, for elderly people who are having difficulties maintaining an adequate and satisfactory life in the community, the target behaviors are not so obvious, and *more* than expertise in behavioral technology is needed to deal with them. The derivation of relevant and common target behaviors for the modules of the Gerontology Program is explained below. The point here is that the modular program automatically assures relevant as well as consistent methodology for each content area. Thus, one who has received training in both basic behavioral methods and the specific modules is in a much better position to provide service to the target population than if he were trained *only* in behavioral methods.

TOKEN ECONOMIES

As explained in the preceding chapter, token systems are basically a technical improvement upon individual behavior modification approaches. Although it is clear that token economies are valuable adjuncts to behavioral treatment programs, it is a mistake to assume that a token economy *is* a treatment program. To have a treatment program, much more than a system of generalized reinforcers is needed. The Gerontology Program does utilize token reinforcement as a very important element, as well as many other types of reinforcement. However, the program also includes modular training with accompanying specification of content, teaching techniques, and assessments, as well as a variety of highly individualized techniques.

STRUCTURED GROUPS

Three existing structured group techniques influenced the development of the modular program concept: (1) reality orientation (Taulbee & Wright, 1971), (2) remotivation therapy (American Psychiatric Association, 1968), and (3) structured learning therapy (Goldstein *et al.*, 1976). Each of these techniques has contributed to the total Gerontology Program, but not in the original form.

Reality orientation (RO; Taulbee & Wright, 1971) is probably the best known method for providing nonmedical, ward or institution-wide treatment to the institutionalized elderly. Reality orientation was designed to prevent or alleviate disorientation and confusion in this population by providing a high frequency of suitable prompts 24 hours a day, 7 days a week. In addition to nonstructured prompting provided by anyone and occurring at any time and any place, RO includes structured classroom sessions in which visual and verbal prompts, questioning, and lecturing are used as training techniques. RO is similar to some aspects of the Gerontology Program in that RO was an early attempt at a structured ward-wide program for the psychogeriatric population and also in that one gerontology module, Personal Information Training, is similar in content to RO. However, RO differs from the Gerontology Program in that it does not use behavioral techniques or assessments and in that the content of RO is limited to personal orientation.

Remotivation (American Psychiatric Association, 1968) is a structured group therapy which Butler and Lewis (1973) recommended as possibly helpful for institutionalized elderly, including those in psychiatric facilities. In this therapy, attempts are made to encourage participants to establish pleasant social relations and to share several types of information with defined content in specially formed groups. This procedure, when accompanied by a program of activity therapies, is designed to motivate participants to seek improvement and eventually to leave the institution. Remotivation resembles the Gerontology Program modules in that structured groups are used and there is definite content. However, as with RO, motivation therapy does not use assessments and behavioral technology, and the content is limited. In most cases, remotivation is not integrated closely with the activity therapies so as to form a coherent, individual treatment plan. The lack of assessments precludes such an approach.

Structured learning therapy (SLT) (Goldstein *et al.*, 1976) is a highly structured social skills training procedure which uses behavioral methodology. More specifically, small groups of trainees who are deficient in social skills observe models performing an activity correctly; then the trainees rehearse the behaviors which were modeled and receive reinforcement (praise and in some cases other reinforcers) for behaviors which resemble those of the model. The behaviors are taught in situations which encourage transfer of training outside the structured group setting.

Our modules resemble SLT in that specific categories of target behaviors are taught using modern behavioral techniques, including systematic contingent reinforcement. Modeling is also used quite freely in all the modules. However, no Gerontology Program module is exactly like SLT, primarily because of content. There are several types of modules which cover a broad spectrum of behavior which is crucial to promote deinstitutionalization and/or the prevention of institutionalization, and training in areas other than in social skills is included.

To summarize then, the Gerontology Modular Behavioral Program consists of a set of standardized behavioral training modules designed to be used by staff at least minimally trained in behavioral technology, single case behavioral treatments developed as needed, and a behavioral ward milieu which complements and makes possible the use of these techniques. The techniques and methods used in the modules are derived from educational technology, basic behavior modification, token economies, and structured training techniques. The content of the modules and their relevance will be addressed next.

THE CONTENT OF THE MODULES

The content of the Gerontology modules was derived directly from the goal of preparing elderly people in institutions or at risk of institutionalization to live as independently as possible in the community. There is relevant information in the literature to indicate what type of content is desirable for this purpose.

DEINSTITUTIONALIZATION

One major source of information was the work of Paul and his colleagues in their extensive research on deinstitutionalization (Paul, 1969; Paul & Lentz, 1977). Based on a review of the literature concerning rehabilitation efforts for chronic mental patients, Paul (1969) was able to identify four categories of intervention which are necessary to maintain chronic mental patients in the community: (a) resocialization, including adequate self-care, interpersonal relations, and social skills; (b) instrumental role performance, including housekeeping, the instrumental activities of daily living, and vocational skills when appropriate; (c) the reduction of bizarre behavior which may be distressing to others; and (d) the provision of at least one supportive significant other in the community.

BEHAVIOR MODIFICATION LITERATURE

A second input has been the literature on behavioral modification with the elderly. Previous behavioral researchers have identified deficits in the areas of (1) skills in daily living, (2) improving social and leisure participation, (3) training in social skills, and (4) improving performance on intellectual tasks (for a recent review, see Patterson & Jackson, 1980a). The great majority of this work was concerned with chronically institutionalized groups. In brief, most of the studies reviewed did show that limited improvements in these deficits could be obtained by using behavioral approaches; although most interventions were isolated experiments or treatments which were not combined into a systematic and comprehensive treatment program.

ENVIRONMENTAL SUPPORTS

A third important source of information regarding the needs of the institutionalized or at-risk elderly comes from a rather large body of literature regarding environmental supports. As frequently used, the term *environmental supports* refers to goods and services which should be supplied to at-risk populations to ensure that the target groups can remain in a noninstitutional environment. At least one group of researchers, Jenkins and his colleagues (Jenkins, 1977; Pascal & Jenkins, 1961) have used the term much more broadly to refer to a group of necessary elements required in the lives of everyone, not just special risk groups, in order to avoid institutionalization. According to this view, institutionalization in some form is much more likely for *anyone* with too few environmental supports.

On the basis of the work of Jenkins and his associates as well as other researchers, environmental supports can be usefully divided into physical supports, social supports, and psychological supports. Physical supports are those factors necessary to maintain life and health, such as medical care, adequate housing, diet, and personal hygiene. *Social supports* are interactions and relationships with other people which serve to maintain normal social behavior. *Psychological supports* refer to interactions of persons with themselves and with their environment, which serve to provide satisfaction and comfort with life. Psychological supports also help to maintain normal behavior, but they are not necessary to life and physical health and may not necessarily include social interactions. Solitary leisure activities, a positive evaluation of self and life, and freedom from fear and anxiety may be considered psychological supports. Each of these support systems will now be discussed in turn.

Physical Supports

These include appropriate and properly maintained living quarters, medical care, a proper diet, satisfactory clothing, and personal hygiene. An adequate income is usually necessary to obtain these and other related items, but an adequate income does not ensure that they will be obtained. Obviously, a person must have such physical supports in order to live independently. What is not so obvious to many people is that having the proper behavioral repertoire necessary to obtain and maintain these supports according to one's means is a critical factor for ensuring support, even at higher levels of income.

Social Supports

The importance of social supports for successful aging has been stressed by a number of gerontologists. Birren, Butler, Greenhouse, Sokoloff, and Yarrow (1963) concluded that

> as environment showed qualities of deprivation or displacement of the person (in loss of intimate persons, loss of income, in cultural displacement), the attitudes and behavior of the aged showed more deteriorative qualities. . . . Psychological reactions to the loss of friends and other environmental supports may amplify, if not initiate changes in the older nervous system and thereby the rest of the organism. (p. 314)

In a later article, Butler and Lewis (1977) suggested that problems associated with an inadequate social support system will be especially severe for those who experience losses in social support late in life.

Bourestom, Wolfe, and Davis (1961) conducted an empirical investigation of the factors related to successful community adjustment for elderly former mental patients. These authors reported that the presence of significant others in these people's environments was strongly associated with good postinstitutional adjustment.

Atchley (1977) goes even further than the previous authors in his judgment of the importance of social support systems for the elderly. According to Atchley, the breakdown in an older person's social support system is the primary cause of institutionalization of the elderly. On the basis of these and similar statements, it would seem reasonable to propose that an older person who is deprived with regard to a social support system runs a high risk of institutionalization.

Psychological Supports

These supports are perhaps the least obvious of all and are much more difficult to define, although they may be very important. One type of such support which was identified early in the development of the program was that many of our clients could perhaps benefit from having a better opinion of themselves or improved self-esteem. These observations were supported by the fact that decreased self esteem has been mentioned frequently In the gerontological literature as a problem for many elderly (Barrett, 1972; Clark & Anderson, 1972; Gurin *et al.*, 1960; Schwartz, 1975). Jenkins and his associates (Rehabilitation Research Foundation, 1977) included an item in their scale for measuring environmental supports called *fear*, which purports to measure to what extent the person feels that he can meet and successfully cope with the demands of everyday life. Freedom from such fear may be a significant source of support for an elderly person. A closely related, but different, source of support might be freedom from anxiety. Anxiety has also been frequently mentioned as an important problem for many elderly (Butler & Lewis, 1973; Kalish, 1977; Patterson, O'Sullivan, & Spielberger, 1980), and reduction of anxiety by learning to relax may be conceived as improving psychological supports.

Although the reader might well accept the argument that a variety of environmental supports are at least useful in maintaining elderly psychogeriatric clients in the community, the relationship between environmental supports and the Modular Behavioral Treatment Program may not be obvious. After all, most of the concern of those involved with improving support systems is with supplying support services, not in training clients.

Supplying goods, services, and materials is certainly necessary but is not always sufficient to meet the needs of many people. Some of the needed supports cannot be supplied by any public or private agency. How does an agency supply supportive interpersonal relationships? Or how does an agency improve self-esteem, especially when dependence on the agency may appear to denigrate one's own image? Another problem is that many of those in the psychogeriatric group do not make use of even those services which are relatively easily supplied such as day-care and leisure activities. Many of the elderly population are not sufficiently well informed about the existence or nature of these services; others are lacking in the social and daily living skills required for successful participation; and still others have not developed habits and attitudes which would cause them to seek and accept these supports. It was the experience of the authors that it was difficult to get many of our clients to participate in most activities and to accept many kinds of services even when they were actively offered as part of treatment. Outside of treatment, it is very difficult for such people to obtain and maintain a good support system in the typical community where some degree of an active, assertive approach is usually necessary to improve one's lot in life.

IMPLICATIONS FROM THESE SOURCES OF LITERATURE FOR A BEHAVIORAL PROGRAM FOR THE ELDERLY

From the above discussion it becomes apparent that our clientele could probably benefit from learning skills to help them become more accepted in the community, more accepting of themselves, and accepting of the community. The modules were designed to reduce areas of deficit in order that the elderly clients might be better prepared to care for themselves personally as well as to seek, obtain, and accept a better system of environmental supports. Accordingly, modules were developed within the areas of Activities of Daily Living, Social Skills, and Psychological Supports. In addition, a variety of less formally developed group activities were incorporated to supplement the modules and the individually developed behavioral interventions. A description of the modules and structured activities follows immediately. Evaluation information pertaining to the modules appears in Chapter 9.

THE MODULES[1]

All modular activities were conducted in groups insofar as this was possible for reasons of economy and efficiency. A major improvement of the modules over most previous behavioral systems is that many of these systems did not construct training activities in such a way that they could be provided to groups in a standardized way. However, as will be further discussed, portions of Personal Information Training and some ADL I activities (bathing, dressing, and some other grooming activities) required some individual training.

A staff member at any level could be a trainer for any module. In

---

[1]Only brief, general descriptions of the modules and their assessments are presented here. Interested readers may write the senior author for more details.

practice, leadership was determined partly by personal preference or personal expertise. One or more observers, in addition to the major trainer, was also needed and almost always present. These observers recorded performance during the module on a standard form (the daily observation sheet or DOS, discussed in Chapter 6) and dispensed tokens on the basis of established criteria for the particular client in the particular module. In general, tokens were awarded for attendance and for participation as defined by the nature of the module, but token payments for any clients were solely at the discretion of the treatment team.

Modular training activities were conducted in different parts of the unit which were most appropriate to the content. Most of these areas were also used for general living and leisure time purposes. Each unit contained a home-style kitchen and a home-style laundry which were used for some types of ADL training. There were also three large social areas adjoined by a total of four alcoves. The major social area directly in front of the nursing station was devoted to conversation, reading, listening to music (it had an AM–FM stereo record player), table games, and billiards. One large social area was used for dances and movies. The television set was placed in an alcove which was designated for television watching and usable for this only as part of a current events activity, for after-hours leisure time, or as a reinforcer. Another alcove contained simple, inexpensive craft activities which were used for leisure purposes. There was only one formal group room on each unit which had to be carefully scheduled for modules which required a more formal classroom type setting, including Communication Training, ADL III, and Self-esteem Training. The various modules will now be described.

Personal Information Training

Many people in psychogeriatric treatment programs are unable to remember important personal information such as their name, the date, or names of other people they know well. These people are labeled as disoriented or confused, and psychiatrists and others sometimes interpret this behavior as evidence of organic brain syndrome. Some types of therapy, most notably reality orientation (Taulbee & Wright, 1971), have claimed some success in alleviating the confused and disoriented behavior. When the FMHI Gerontology Program was first developed, it was noted that some of the elderly clients were disoriented and unable to recall personal information. Therefore, a training module was developed to deal directly with these problems.

Assessment

The first step in developing the Personal Information Training (PIT) module was to identify those who appeared confused, disoriented, and unable to recall personal information and to target these behavioral deficits for correction. Assessments for these deficits are relatively common and have long been included in mental status examinations (e.g. Pfeiffer, 1975). These examinations differ in specific content and are commonly used for establishing medical diagnoses rather than for pinpointing specific deficits for the purpose of applying behavioral intervention.

The PIT assessment consisted of 10 specific questions. These questions were selected because the information they required was considered useful for community survival. Persons who could not answer the questions would be likely to encounter difficulties in daily life. Questions which are sometimes used for diagnostic purposes, such as counting backwards threes, were not included because this information is not of immediate use. Other questions, for example, "Who is your doctor?" were included because of their practical importance. The 10 questions on the assessment were:

1. What is your name?
2. What is your address?
3. What is your phone number?
4. Who is the important person in your life (spouse, relative, guardian, representative, etc.)?
5. Who is your doctor?
6. What is the name of this place?
7. What month is it?
8. What year is it?
9. Is it morning or afternoon?
10. Who is the president of the United States? (The practical importance of knowing the name of the president may be questioned, but many mental health workers do attach importance to this item.)

The assessment was administered by asking the 10 questions on each of 3 consecutive days. This replication was important because clients sometimes varied from day to day in their ability to answer questions. A client was considered deficient in personal information if he failed to answer any of the questions on all three occasions, except for questions that the client could not be expected to know at the beginning of assessment (e.g., for residential clients, the name, address, and telephone number of the Gerontology Program).

Technique

Training techniques in PIT differed somewhat from the techniques used in other modules because of the individual nature of some of the information, the amount of individual verbal modeling and prompting, and the frequent use of primary reinforcers. All of the performance required in PIT was verbal; therefore, training depended upon the conveyance of spoken and written information. Tokens were routinely used in PIT as positive reinforcers, but because some clients experienced problems remembering what they were for, primary reinforcers in the form of candy and cigarettes as well as praise were sometimes paired with tokens, at least in the beginning of training.

Because of the nature of the information taught in PIT, training was divided into individual and group components. Items such as the name of the program, resident physician, day, month, and year, and name of the president were taught in a group situation. Items such as the client's name, important person, home address, and home phone number were taught individually so that clients were not confused by other people's personal information. The client's progress was assessed and recorded every day. Clients received both individual and group training on the same days.

Individual Training. Each client was given his own card containing personal information specific to that client to carry on his person. In the residential program, clients were questioned and trained on the information on this card four times a day, before meals and before medication. The person who awakened the client in the morning and helped him plan for the day made sure that the client had the card. In day treatment, there was time to question and train the client on this information only three times a day: in the morning when the client arrived at the Institute, before lunch, and before the client left the program for the day. The person who greeted the client upon arrival to the institute made sure that the client had the card. The card had spaces on it for staff to record the client's correct responses one time each day. An X was placed in the appropriate space if the information given was correct. This was done during the first training session of the day. A response was considered correct if the client was able to give the information without any prompting whatever.

Training the Client. After the card was given to the client and he had read every item, the trainer said, "Carry this card with you all day, and if you have it when I see you, I'll give you a token." The client decided where the card was to be carried. The trainer asked, "Where are you going to keep your card?" After the client chose a place, the trainer said, "I want you to keep your card in the same place all the time so you can remember where you've put it."

During the day, four times a day for residential clients, three times a day for day treatment clients, a staff member asked the client to see the card. The client was positively reinforced with a token, praise, a physical demonstration of approval, or a primary reinforcer each time he produced the card. Then, the staff member proceeded to question and train the client on the items written on the card.

The trainer reinforced the client following each correct response. If the client was unable to answer a question within 10 seconds, the trainer prompted the client by saying the answer and asked him to find the answer on the information card. The trainer praised the client for locating, pointing out, and reading aloud the correct response. For example:

> TRAINER: What's your name?
> CLIENT: I don't know.
> TRAINER: Joe. Say "My name is Joe Smith."

Later in training, the prompt could consist of just the sound *J*. The amount of prompting required gradually decreased as clients learned to make the correct responses.

The trainer repeated the above procedure for each item on the card. The trainer repeated any items the client missed and instructed the client to study the items missed.

Group Training. The advantages of training clients in small groups include: (a) staff efficiency, (b) peer group support (approval and encouragement from other clients in the group), and (c) modeling (clients could benefit from hearing other group members giving correct information and then watching them receive reinforcement).

The ideal group size for PIT was three to five clients but in any case no more than eight. With larger groups it was difficult to avoid confusion and keep clients involved.

The basic method of training in PIT was to ask clients for the correct information, to supply various types of visual and verbal prompts and modeling, if necessary, and then to reinforce correct responses. Visual prompts used in PIT included calendars, clocks, maps, and other written material that could be displayed in the classroom or carried by an individual client. We found that one useful technique was to use large (8½ by 11 inch) cue cards. Each cue card had only a single item of information printed in large letters. Cue cards were used *only* when needed and were not left on display when a client did not need a prompt.

Each group meeting began with the trainer stating his name and the purpose of the meeting, since some clients did not remember. After this reminder, the trainer asked clients to introduce themselves. This provided an opportunity for clients to receive group approval and also helped clients learn each others' names, which was important for their relearning of social skills.

Next, the trainer introduced a topic by asking the entire group a question, for example, "What month is it now?" Typically, some clients would answer correctly and others would not. The trainer immediately and individually reinforced those clients who responded correctly, and made notes of each client's correct responses on individual PIT records. Clients who did not respond correctly were then individually prompted until they gave the correct response, after which they were reinforced. Group members who knew the correct response were used as models for those who did not. This procedure was repeated until all topics had been covered.

ACTIVITIES OF DAILY LIVING

Activities of daily living (ADL) refers to a variety of instrumental behaviors which all people must learn to do on a regular basis in order to care for and provide for themselves. Included in ADL are personal hygiene, eating activities, care of personal living space, and obtaining community resources. Obviously, these activities must be performed adequately if one is to maintain oneself in a noninstitutional setting.

It is well known that many persons who are in mental institutions or who are at risk of institutionalization do not perform many of the above activities very well. As we noted above, Paul and his colleagues (Paul, 1969; Paul & Lentz, 1977) reported that a lack of skills in daily living is one of four major areas of deficiency contributing to institutionalization. Unfortunately, training in ADL skills is rarely provided to elderly people either in institutional settings or in the community. In fact, many agencies actually encourage dependency in the elderly, apparently because they do not believe that old people can or should do things for themselves.

The experience of the staff in the Gerontology Program has been that training in a considerable array of activities is needed by elderly persons considered in need of or at risk of institutional treatment. If one considers simply the number of activities necessary to prepare for work in the morning, the complexity of the problem of providing adequate training in ADL is apparent. One must perform various grooming activities, wear suitable clothing, prepare or arrange for breakfast, and obtain transportation to the place of employment. Many people must also take medications. These activities involve some skill in handling money, shopping, and budgeting time.

The array of activities involved in ADL may seem to be almost overwhelming, and previous attempts to correct deficiencies of elderly people in ADL by behavioral techniques have been very limited with regard to specific deficiencies addressed. There have been some studies concerned with severe deficiencies found in persons institutionalized for extended periods in nursing homes and state hospitals. Problems with self-feeding (M. M. Baltes & Zerbe, 1976a,b; Geiger & Johnson, 1974; Risley & Edwards, 1978) and with ambulation (DiScipio & Feldman, 1971; McClannahan & Risley, 1974) have been researched. These studies did find that prompting and reinforcement techniques could be used to improve behavior. Rusin (1978) studied somewhat more complex behaviors of elderly women patients in a state hospital. She found that both an incentive condition and a structured role-playing condition were effective in prompting room cleaning, hair washing and use of the telephone, but the improved behaviors were not maintained after the experimental conditions were terminated. Although results such as these are encouraging, the training and retraining of elderly persons to perform necessary daily living tasks have not been well researched.

Because of the importance of acquiring skills necessary for successful and independent community living, the FMHI Gerontology Program has placed considerable emphasis on ADL skills training. Because of the number of skills involved, the ADL training was divided into three separate modules called simply ADL I, II, and III. A listing of the skills taught in these three modules is presented in Table 1.

TABLE 1. Topics Covered in Each ADL Module

ADL I	ADL II	ADL III
Oral hygiene	Laundering	Budgeting time and money
Bathing	Mending clothing	
Hair care	Managing money	Meal planning and preparation
Shaving	Meal selection	
Dressing	Maintaining a room and bathroom	Housekeeping
Nail care		Obtaining community resources
Personal eating habits	Use of the telephone	

Some types of community placement, including many boarding homes, foster homes, and family settings, provide meals, laundry, major housekeeping, help with a financial budget, and assistance in obtaining community resources. However, residents are expected to care for their own personal hygiene (perhaps with prompting) and to be able to feed themselves appropriately and safely. ADL I provides training for these latter kinds of skills.

Other types of placement are available which provide less personal service. These include boarding homes which provide only room and board including major housekeeping, but which do not provide assistance with personal hygiene, money management, using a telephone, laundry of personal clothing, selecting proper foods, or keeping the residence room neat and tidy. Clients who live in these types of settings need to have all the skills provided in ADL I, plus additional skills taught in ADL II.

Not all of the clients in the Gerontology Program are placed in situations in which some assistance with ADL is available. Some clients are able to obtain independent living quarters, be it a house, apartment, mobile home, or other independent residence. Persons living independently need all the skills provided in ADL I and II, plus additional skills taught in ADL III, that is, budgeting time and money, meal planning and preparation, housekeeping, and obtaining community resources.

As with all of our modules, entry into and graduation from the three ADL modules was based on assessments. Thus, on admission to the program a client might be admitted immediately into any of the three ADL modules, or none at all, depending on which assessments he had passed or failed. However, the modules formed a sequence, and a person had to pass ADL I in order to enter ADL II, and had to pass ADL II to enter ADL III.

Not everyone completed the ADL sequence. On the basis of progress assessments, some people seemed to plateau at one level and were unable to progress further. This seeming inability to progress provided very important placement-related information. The assessments indicated what particular ADL skills the client had and had not learned and therefore what type of assistance the person would probably continue to need on a long-term basis. It was important, then, that these types of assistance be provided by the placement selected.

Assessments

The ADL I assessment consisted of asking people a series of 10 questions regarding hygiene and dressing and observing the person eating to determine whether he could use proper care and acceptable table manners. The replies to the questions about hygiene and dressing were verified by inspection. For example, if in reply to a question a client said that he had shaved that morning, his face was observed by the person administering the assessment to determine if in fact the client had shaved. All items missed consistently became target behaviors for training.

ADL II skills were assessed in a similar manner, that is, by asking clients a series of questions and verifying the answers (for the most part) by observing the client perform a skill. For example, a client might be asked to demonstrate that he could make change, choose an appropriate diet, or dial a specific telephone number.

The original ADL III assessment was rather lengthy, requiring an hour or more for administration. With this form, there were many items grouped into four categories, and the questions asked the clients were accompanied by requests for demonstrations. For example, clients were asked to balance a checkbook, name three types of social organizations, plan a well-balanced meal, and describe how to clean a refrigerator. Each item was scored 1 if the skill was verified and 0 if it was not, thus yielding a maximum score of 34 points. This was the ADL III assessment which was used in the evaluation data reported in Chapter 9. All data concerning ADL III reported elsewhere in this book were obtained using this form.

Because of the time required for this assessment, a shorter form of the ADL III assessment was developed, but as yet it has not been studied psychometrically. This assessment consisted of the same four categories of skill areas as in the original ADL III assessment, but with only four questions in each category. Also, each item had separate scoring criteria which were developed so that a variable number of points could be assigned for different items on the basis of the quality and quantity of the responses. For example, when asked to name the basic food groups, clients could get one point for any of the six responses: protein, starch, vegetables, fruit, fat, and milk products. All of the ADL assessments were accompanied by specific instructions for delivering the assessment.

Technique

As previously described, the basic teaching techniques in all of the FMHI Gerontology modules were the same, regardless of the particular skills being taught. However, the modules differed in the way the techniques were applied and also in how frequently a particular technique was used. For example, much more prompting, motor guidance, and modeling was appropriate for ADL I and II than for ADL III. Similarly, far more use of verbal instruction was appropriate for ADL III than for the other two ADL modules. Breaking manual tasks into chains of component behaviors was also particularly important for ADL I and II.

The basic teaching paradigm for the modules was the presentation of initial verbal instructions followed by demonstrations. In most cases, these instructions and demonstrations were followed rapidly by opportunities for some or all of the clients to practice the new skills. Practice was always followed by social reinforcement (praise) for responding correctly. Those clients who responded incorrectly were given additional instruction and demonstrations until some level of correct responding was achieved. This sometimes involved greatly simplifying the responses expected from a particular client.

The initial instructions had to be thorough and demonstrations complete, and clients were encouraged to ask questions. Eventually, all forms of prompting had to be eliminated in order for clients to demonstrate that they had acquired some skill. Thus, after the initial demonstrations, only the minimal prompts required to produce the response were used with each client. Early in training, more directive and more frequent prompting was usually needed, and fewer and less restrictive prompts were necessary as training progressed.

Appropriate and skillful use of prompts, chaining (including backward chaining), and shaping were particularly important for the motor tasks such as making a bed, cleaning teeth, or bathing. Therefore, these tasks were divided into discrete steps within the modules, and each step was instructed and demonstrated separately.

Although we were well aware that training on these similar tasks has been accomplished by similar techniques with children and the developmentally disabled (e.g., Watson, 1976) we soon found that there were obvious differences when these methods were applied to teaching these tasks to the elderly. For the most part, the older people were recalling previously learned behaviors in ADL I and II and becoming motivated to perform them again. This meant that whole chains of activities could reappear abruptly rather than having each component in a chain or each successive approximation in a shaping procedure occur in sequence as it was taught. Also, very rapid generalization could occur for the same reason; once behaviors were recalled, they could appear in many forms in many situations, presumably because these behaviors had been well generalized previously. Subjectively on the part of the staff, this process of recall and remotivation was one of the delightful experiences of working with the elderly, but it made the appropriate use of the fading of prompts as explained in Chapter 5 especially important.

ADL III differed from the other two ADL modules in that a considerable amount of new, predominantly verbal learning was required. Many clients were relatively new to their present community or for other reasons had never learned about many community resources. Also, much of the information about budgeting, meals, and housekeeping probably differed from that which they had previously learned. For these reasons, much detailed instruction followed by reinforced practice was required to teach ADL III.

Social Skills

Deficits in social skills among the elderly are identified in a number of ways in different contexts in the professional literature. At one level, deficits in frequency of simple conventional social interaction have often been identified as a problem with some people. At a more advanced level, more complex interpersonal behaviors involving the appropriate expression of affect usually subsumed in the categories of assertion or social skills training have also been recognized as a problem with the elderly (Baffa & Zarit, 1977; Corby, 1975). Accordingly, two basic social skills modules were developed to overcome deficits in these areas: a Conversation module designed to increase frequency of conversation and a Communication module, intended to improve basic skills in expressing affect.

Conversation Module

Relatively simple manipulations of the residential environment have been found to increase greatly the frequency of casual conversations. Peterson, Knapp, Rosen, and Pither (1977) and Sommer and Ross (1958) found that furniture arrangements commonly found in institutions, such as chairs in a line against a wall, were not conducive to conversation. These researchers were able to produce dramatic increases in conversations by placing chairs and tables in more intimate groupings. McClannahan and Risley (1973) opened a "store" in the lobby of a nursing home which had the effect of greatly increasing social interaction when the store was open. Serving refreshments in a recreational area of a nursing home was also found to increase social participation (Blackman, Howe, & Pinkston, 1976). Risley, Gottula, and Edwards (1978) improved conversation at meal-

times by serving food in large bowls rather than in individual serv-
ings on plates.

In addition to these manipulations, the use of structured prompts
and reinforcers was also found to increase frequency of speaking in
poor communicators. Word games accompanied by primary reinforcers (candy and cigarettes), tokens, and praise were found to increase
social responding in elderly state hospital residents (Mueller & Atlas,
1972). A similar population was studied by Hoyer, Kafer, Simpson,
and Hoyer (1974), who noted that pennies which could be exchanged
for candy or cigarettes served to increase verbal interaction in nursing
home residents who rarely demonstrated communicative skills.

The above studies provide ample indication that the low level of
social conversation which is often a problem in elderly mental health
clients can be altered. On the basis of findings that lack of social
participation is a major factor related to reinstitutionalization (Paul,
1969; Paul & Lentz, 1977) and also of the gerontological literature
which states that social isolation is a major problem for some elderly
(Pfeiffer, 1977), it was expected that a modular program dealing with
social skills had to include procedures to promote social interaction.

Assessment and Technique. Specific areas in the Gerontology Program environment were designed to facilitate conversation and other
casual social interactions. Approximately half of each day room (both
day treatment and residential) contained chairs placed around low
tables which held magazines. A radio–record player was also located
in this area, which provided soft background music. (There was *no*
television set in the conversation area. The television was located in a
separate alcove used specifically for television viewing.) The other
half of the day room was devoted to space for various games. Meals
(except for those prepared in class) were served in a cafeteria where
there were small tables and booths. It was expected that the furniture
arrangements would facilitate social interaction throughout the client's
stay.

Clients in this module were scheduled and prompted to sit in the
day room conversation area and converse during a specific time period. The target behavior for this module was simply conversation.
Assessments were of two types: within-session assessments, which
provided the trainers with information as to when to reinforce as well
as indicating whether clients were learning; and generalization assessments administered every four weeks, which were used as the major
indicant of client progress.

Within-session, daily assessments were conducted by means of
interval recording by several observers (two to four) seated in various

locations around the edges of the room so that each observer could record behavior of approximately five clients. The time for rating conversations was divided into six 5-minute intervals. During each 5-minute interval, observers recorded whether or not each client spoke during the first half of each 1-minute interval. The 5-minute intervals were separated by a brief period of time to allow for observers to provide reinforcement.

With regard to the four-week generalization measures, day treatment clients were observed each day during a free period which occurred after lunch, and interval recordings were made to measure their frequency of conversation. The same procedure was used for residential clients, except that the observations occurred in the evening after dinner.

The teaching technology for the Conversation module was extremely simple. At the beginning of the conversation period, clients were instructed to sit in the conversation area and talk to someone. They were told that they would be observed and given tokens periodically by the raters if they were observed talking sufficiently often. Observations and timing then commenced. At the end of each 5-minute period, each observer walked over to the clients who had been observed talking during at least three of the five possible intervals and delivered praise and a token.

Communication Module

The Communication module was designed to teach more effective communication in two very basic types of situations: (1) those requiring the expression of pleasure and (2) those requiring the expression of displeasure. In other words, the clients were taught to say effectively that they liked specific favors done by other people, that they were grateful for the favors, and then to deliver a personal message to the other person (e.g., "You're a nice person to do that for me.") In different situations, clients were taught to say that they did not like unfavorable actions by another and to ask them to stop the behavior or correct the problem. Behaviors required in these types of situations were selected because they are more basic to effective social interactions than mere casual conversation and because they are incompatible with apathy, passivity, or hostility. Persons who cannot express pleasure and displeasure effectively are not likely to be able to maintain good social relationships (social supports) or to deal effectively with businesses or agencies which provide physical supports. Situations requiring the expression of pleasure and displeasure used in the training were very simple and not specifically related to any situation of any particular individual, because the emphasis of the training was on the behavior itself and not on the situation.

Assessment. For purposes of defining target behaviors and simplifying assessment, the total performance of the expression of pleasure and displeasure was divided into several component behaviors for both assessment and training. Verbal behavior included content, loudness, and voice feeling quality. Nonverbal behaviors were facial expression (including eye contact), body position and movement, and hand gestures. The complete performance was also judged as to its adequacy.

An assessment instrument called the Communication Behavior Rating Scale (BRS) was developed especially for use in the Communication module. In part, this instrument was designed to allow for rapid and simple feedback to clients during training immediately after they had performed in role-playing situations. The BRS had as its purpose the measurement of the target behaviors taught in the group. Therefore, it contained an item for rating each of six target behaviors (the verbal and nonverbal behaviors listed above). In addition, there was an item for rating the overall performance in both the pleasure and displeasure situations. All items were rated on a 6-point Likert scale with the lowest score defined as being an inappropriate or totally inadequate performance and the highest score meaning that a completely and consistently appropriate, highly emphatic response had been given. The authors are aware of the existence of more objective and precise measures of social performance such as have been described by Bellack and Hersen (1979). However, these latter measures were not used because of the requirements of simplicity and rapid feedback in the treatment situation. Although simple, the BRS had to allow for highly reliable and valid ratings so that the results could be used for clinical purposes and program evaluation.

Teaching Technique. All formal training in the Communication module took place with groups of 8 to 15 clients. The trainees were seated in a close, intimate semicircle, with two empty chairs in the center, located so that all persons in the semicircle could observe, hear, and converse with persons in these center chairs. Observers (raters) were seated at a table separate from the group, but they also had a good view of the two chairs in the center. One wall of the room contained an expanded display of the rating chart. This "scoreboard" consisted of seven columns, each containing six open envelopes labeled with a number from 1 to 6. (A score of 1 indicated the lowest score and 6 indicated the highest score.) Each column was headed by a card with the name of one of the items on the rating scale (target behaviors as well as the overall rating). Signs on the wall listed instructions as to how token reinforcers would be earned in this group, that is, by role-playing and by providing feedback to other members of the group.

The four crucial elements of the Communication Training were (1) modeling, (2) role-playing (behavior rehearsal), (3) feedback, and (4) reinforcement.

Modeling consisted of a client watching a staff member or other client performing the desired role-play behavior. Modeling was an especially relevant and valuable technique for Communication Training because it is difficult for even a highly skilled person to give or receive verbal instructions for the complex behaviors involved in social exchanges; modeling also facilitates role-playing, which is strange and uncomfortable at first for some people. A group discussion of what the model did that made the performance socially acceptable always followed the modeling session.

Behavioral rehearsal or role-playing consisted of having the client act out a specific interpersonal situation involving the expression of pleasure or displeasure. The group leader would describe a particular situation and then ask the client to enact the situation using a staff member or another client as the target of the expression. The type of situation most frequently used for expressing pleasure was that in which a neighbor, friend, or relative had spontaneously done a favor or brought a gift to the client. The client was asked to express gratitude to the benefactor and to express liking for that person. The displeasure situation most frequently used was that in which a neighbor had persistently been responsible for something annoying happening to the client. The client was given the task of telling the neighbor to change his behavior. For training purposes, the client was asked to exaggerate his expression somewhat.

During the role-playing sequence, the client could be given additional instructions or prompts by the group leader standing close to and whispering to the client when this was necessary to produce the desired behavior.

Feedback by both formal and informal methods was used in communication training. After each behavioral rehearsal, the client was given informal peer group feedback from the other group members. This feedback was directed by the group leader in a specified way. First the leader asked, "What did (the client) do best?" Then the leader asked, "What else did (the client) do well?" Finally the leader asked, "Now, what does (the client) need to improve upon?" The group was instructed to respond by naming the behavioral components, which they had learned very easily after having been in a few group sessions.

The mechanism for formal feedback involved use of the large display on the wall of the classroom (the scoreboard described above). After the informal feedback, the observer read the recorded ratings of the BRS to the group. After each rating was read, the client who had just rehearsed a behavior would put the score marker into the envelope corresponding to the behavior being rated and the particular rating given. It was believed that this combination of formal and informal feedback accomplished more than simply informing the client of the quality of the performance. The use of the wall display required that the client "do something," that is, get out of the chair, walk to the wall, and place the card in the proper envelope, and it also allowed all the clients in the group to participate.

Reinforcement consisted of both social reinforcement and tokens. Social reinforcement involved the use of praise given by the group leader and by other members of the group when a client performed correctly. Such praise was a natural accompaniment of feedback because of the way that feedback sessions were structured by the leader. The group was always asked first what the role-player did well. Only after this positive feedback was the group asked in what way the performance might be improved.

The normal procedure for the conduct of the group was that a scene to be rehearsed was described to the clients to enact. This was followed by either modeling or role-playing. If the scene was new to the client, or if a client was expected to have considerable difficulty with the scene, the situation was modeled for the client prior to the initial enactment. If modeling was not necessary initially, then role-playing was begun immediately after the scene was described. Either way, the first rehearsal was followed by feedback. Feedback was followed by modeling, then additional role-playing, then strong positive feedback. Clients almost invariably improved on the second attempt thus warranting strong positive reinforcement. Clients in the group were rotated through the procedure so that each client practiced several times a week and played the role of talker and listener in addition to offering feedback to other clients.

Self-esteem Training

The Self-esteem Training module was designed to improve clients' psychological support systems. It was noted that some of the first clients in the FMHI Gerontology Program were making negative

statements about themselves. They seemed to concentrate on expressing dissatisfaction with themselves and their lives, and this was dis-
turbing since many of the staff members were aware of positive
attributes demonstrated by the geriatric clients which the clients
themselves seemed to ignore. While we were disturbed, we were not
surprised. Barrett (1972) described this problem when he wrote:

> Despite the fact that he may have many talents and remain capable in a
> variety of areas, losses are magnified to the point that they blind the
> geronto to his continued self-worth. (p. 26)

Clark and Anderson (1972) related this problem to a proposed set of
adaptive tasks that people face as they age. One of these tasks is a
reassessment of criteria for self-evaluation, and many elderly people
do not adapt to this reassessment.

There is evidence both that, on the average, self-esteem decreases
with age (Gurin et al., 1960) and that it increases with age (Kogan &
Wallach, 1961). Schwartz (1975) proposed that self-esteem is the
"linchpin of quality of life for the elderly." His proposition receives
support from Riley and Foner (1968), who suggested that the relationship between self-regard and a positive view of one's life persists
even in circumstances such as poor health, low socioeconomic status,
and role discontinuity, all of which are typically associated with low
levels of life satisfaction. Our observations were that many of our
clients did not have high opinions of themselves and could probably
benefit from learning to appreciate more thoroughly their good qualities and to concentrate less on their real or assumed inadequacies.

The concept and basic methodology of the Self-esteem Training
module were derived from a procedure described by Todd (1972). He
used basic operant techniques to encourage depressed clients and
others whose problems appeared to include feelings of inadequacy,
lack of self-confidence, or low self-esteem, to acknowledge positive
and desirable attributes about themselves, and to increase the number
and frequency of such acknowledgments. Todd requested that clients
compose lists of positive characteristics about themselves. He arranged for these lists to be read frequently and for reinforcement to
occur each time the items were read. Todd reported successful results
when this procedure was combined with other therapy procedures
when necessary. One of the present authors also has noted success
using these techniques in a behavioral day treatment program (Patterson, 1976). Although the incidences of success reported above were
based on uncontrolled case studies, it seemed to the authors that
there was a good possibility that the operant techniques could be
modified to fit the modular format to benefit clients in the Gerontology Program.

Assessment

Self-esteem problems were assessed by the use of three instruments: the Self-esteem Scale (Rosenberg, 1965), a Life Satisfaction Scale (Neugarten, Havighurst, & Tobin, 1961), and a positive/negative statement scale designed by the project staff. This latter scale asked clients to state "the things which make you feel best about yourself and your life right now" and also "the thing you feel worst about yourself and your life right now." The score was a simple algebraic sum of these statements. Clients who did not have personal information deficits (either because there were no deficits initially or because they had graduated from Personal Information Training) and who scored less than 11 on the Life Satisfaction Scale were eligible for admission to the self-esteem group.

Technique

Each Self-esteem Training session began with a review of group expectations. Clients were reminded that they would be reinforced with praise and tokens for positive statements. A leader serving in the role of facilitator and an observer who recorded positive statements attended each session. During the group session, clients often provided positive self-statements that were very general in nature and/or that applied to the past. In such instances, the leader attempted to persuade clients to make the statements more particular and relate them to the present. The focus was always on the present, and the purpose of this emphasis was to help clients achieve a current basis for self-esteem. The leader sought to increase the number of positive self-statements made by clients and to enable each client to relate these to specific current behavior. If a client, for example, said that he was intelligent and proud of it, he had made a positive self-statement; however, this statement was considered far too vague. The leader would explore this with the client and attempt to find examples of ways in which the client was currently behaving intelligently. This was done to increase the intensity of this positive quality. In situations such as this, leaders found it very beneficial to enlist the aid of other group members to discover current concrete examples of the reality of the attribute expressed.

On occasion, new members found it difficult to make positive self-statements. There was reasonable basis for this behavior. Some people were simply very modest. The module leaders believed that this was a learned behavior resulting from the clients' having been seldom reinforced for positive statements in the past. The experience and upbringing of many people were in direct conflict with the precepts of the module. As children, some may have been reprimanded or ignored when they made positive self-statements and told that such talk refuted modesty, humility, good manners, or good taste. Some people may even have been reinforced by contradiction or sympathy for making self-deprecating statements. Group leaders found that explaining and discussing this with the group helped to overcome such prior experiences. As new members became accustomed to the group, the leader explained that unfounded negative self-statements were not true, not in the province of humility or modesty, and in no manner virtuous. It was also explained that positive self-statements were boastful only when it was the intention of the speaker to boast. In almost every instance, this orientation plus the positive milieu of the group sessions helped clients to overcome their hesitancy to make or accept positive statements.

As the development of the Self-esteem module progressed, a number of techniques were developed to evoke the desired response from group members. These included:

- Asking clients what they liked to do. Good qualities were likely to surface in replies.
- Challenging a quality the leader knew a client had. This would invariably lead to a self-defense which was strewn with positive self-statements uttered with strong conviction.
- Getting group members to state the qualities they admired in one another and instructing each member to accept what had been said of him or her by the others.
- Asking an individual: "What is there about yourself that you would not want to change?"
- Asking a person to write a reference for himself or another member of the group.

A problem particularly related to elderly persons developed when the techniques used by Todd (1972) were applied. One of the techniques was to request that clients list past accomplishments and use these to determine basic abilities. However, many elderly persons no longer possess the same skills they had when they were younger, and this change in their lives may serve to *lower* self-esteem. Therefore, developers of the Self-esteem module attempted to establish a current and continuing basis for self-esteem in their clients. Clients were trained to focus on their talents and on areas in which they were still capable so that they could be made aware of their continued self-worth. Group expectations were set. Members were expected to speak positively of themselves and of others. They were also expected to reinforce one another for positive statements made.

Negative statements were not appropriate in the group, and if made they were ignored by all. This procedure represents extinction of negative self-statements and is considered to be extremely important. There is an unfortunate tendency on the part of many people, including professionals, to argue with other people about negative self-statements and thereby give reinforcing attention to this behavior. Thus, someone might say that they feel worthless and a kindly listener might comment, "Why, you are not, you are a wonderful person!" This can serve as a prompt to the complainer to prove the point by giving illustrations of just how worthless he is creating a situation wherein he receives the attention of the entire group for the negative statement. It is better to provide gentle prompts for even the most minor positive self-statements than to risk reinforcing negative self-statements.

STRUCTURED ACTIVITIES OTHER THAN MODULES

In our program there were many structured activities conducted routinely at various times and for varying periods which never achieved the status of modules for several reasons. First, it was never assumed that every activity would be developed as a module. Second, some activities were intended to become modules but were never actually developed into modular format, usually because of difficulties in standardizing procedures and/or developing assessments. Nevertheless, these nonmodular activities were conducted because of assumed (though not empirically demonstrated) value to some clients. In some cases, attempts continue to develop these activities into modular format.

Leisure Activities

One example of a structured, nonmodular activity is leisure activities. Essentially, this activity was designed to teach clients to occupy spare time in a psychologically supportive way, both in large and small groups, as well as when a client was alone. This was considered clinically useful, and all clients spent some time each week involved in leisure activities. In large- and small-group activities, clients were encouraged to play bridge or other card and table games, engage in group craft projects, and the like. So far as individual activities were concerned, clients were prompted to read, write letters, listen to music, take walks, and so forth. Appropriate materials were supplied when necessary, and all clients were prompted to participate in leisure activities and then were reinforced with tokens and praise for their participation.

Although a leisure skills module was never completely developed, the objective of the training procedures described above was to teach clients new leisure skills, both by themselves and in group situations. Plans to develop and standardize assessments further, to standardize training techniques, and to evaluate the effectiveness of these techniques are still in progress, but at this time, priority has been placed on the previously described modules.

A variety of other less regular and less well-structured activities which involved leisure time utilization but also included community resource utilization, social participation, and self-care were also incorporated into our program. Clients who were able to do so frequently attended dances and other activities at local community centers on Friday afternoons. Residential clients had organized weekly shopping trips to a large modern mall located near FMHI. Clients also went outside the Institute to barbers and beauty shops.

Current Events

Another structured, nonmodular activity which was rather popular was current events. All clients participated in this activity, but they were divided into two levels. The general procedure was that beginning or lower-level clients brought a brief newspaper article to the current events group. Each client in turn read or otherwise described the article to the other group members. At a higher level, the same procedure was followed; however, a great deal more discussion was expected within the group concerning the content of the article. At both levels, clients were encouraged to participate and reinforced for their participation.

Relaxation Training

Muscle relaxation training was another structured activity conducted on a group basis. This training was usually done on the residential unit in late evening. Clients were taught to tense and then relax different muscle groups. The objectives of this training were to teach clients to become more immediately relaxed and also to teach clients to apply relaxation techniques at times or in certain situations in which they might feel tense or anxious. Clients were referred to this activity because of specific problems which were presumed to be related to tension, including insomnia, tension headaches, or high blood pressure.

Exercise

In addition to muscle relaxation training, brief exercise groups were conducted each morning. The exercises were not strenuous but were designed to increase range of motion and to strengthen muscle groups. All clients participated to the extent that they were physically able.

Medication Training

All clients also received training in the use of their medication. They were taught the names of their medications, purpose for taking it (this was not always certain for day clients), dosage levels, and when appropriate, the best ways of obtaining the medications. Residential clients who mastered the relevant basic information were given opportunities to learn to request their medications and to take them from their trays on the medication chart under observation of a nurse.

Advanced Social Skills Training

Several nonmodular activities were more clinical in nature than the aforementioned activites. One of these was an advanced form of social skills training using techniques similar to those published by Liberman, King, DeRisi, and McCann (1975), which they referred to as "Personal Effectiveness Training." The objective of this group was to train clients to learn to behave differently in interpersonal situations which were specific to the individual's life. During this training, clients were taught to interact effectively with others and to verbalize their feelings. For example, one client's niece wanted her put in a nursing home, but the client did not believe it to be necessary. The client preferred instead to go to an adult congregate living facility. The staff agreed with the client's assessment of her need but thought it desirable that the client learn to express herself more effectively with regard to this matter. Although the client was very anxious and subdued when the training was begun, ultimately she was able to state her case to her niece very convincingly.

The need for this type of training in the program varied greatly from time to time. Although the staff felt that many clients could benefit from the training, most clients were not interested in participating in spite of a great deal of coaxing. Often they refused to acknowledge intepersonal problems and, even if they did acknowledge them, did not relate the problems to their current situation in life. Therefore, this training was offered from time to time when it seemed appropriate for an individual client's situation and the client was willing to participate. Because of the infrequency with which this training was offered, it was never formally developed into a modular format. Also, rendering highly idiosyncratic, relatively complex problem-solving procedures as these into a module with a single assessment would be extremely difficult.

Rational Emotive Therapy

Another reputedly therapeutic activity which was sometimes used in the program employed the methods of rational emotive therapy (RET; Ellis & Grieger, 1977). In brief, RET seeks to teach people to overcome adverse emotional reactions by changing their beliefs about troublesome situations. In other words, a cognitive approach is used to teach clients to look at difficult or problematic situations in perspective. For example, a client might say that he *should* have spent more time with his son when the child was growing up. Now the parent feels guilty and negligent. In RET, the staff would suggest to the client that it would have been nice if he had spent more time with his son, but the word *should* is deemphasized, and the client is encouraged not to feel guilty or negligent.

Although some staff members thought that many clients could benefit from such therapy, there were considerable difficulties in getting many of our clients to participate in this type of training on a regular, programmatic basis. To begin with, most clients had difficulty in acknowledging or understanding psychological causation, that is, that there were specific events in their lives which were upsetting to them. (This result has been reported previously in the gerontology literature by Lawton, 1979.) Many clients also had great difficulty in acknowledging and defining emotion, or realizing and admitting that emotion (simply phrased as "being upset") had a role in their current situation in life. Therefore, RET techniques received very limited use.

As we mentioned earlier, although the activities described here were never formalized as modules, nevertheless we believe that they were important additions to our program and probably served to teach clients some skills and activities which they otherwise would not have learned.

5

Single Case Behavioral Treatment

GARY M. JACKSON
AND ROGER L. PATTERSON

Two behavioral treatment methods were used in the Gerontology Program at the Florida Mental Health Institute (FMHI). The first approach, the modular treatment method, was described in detail in the previous chapter. The second behavioral treatment method, which we have chosen to call single case behavioral treatment (SCBT), was applicable to idiosyncratic behavior problems or skill deficits of a particular individual. Both approaches were individualized; however, the word *individualized* had a different meaning for the two approaches.

The modular treatment method was individualized in the sense that each client was assessed for skill deficits that corresponded to existing treatment modules in the Gerontology Program. The treatment team then assigned each client on an individualized basis to a series of modules designed to increase adaptive skills in those areas in which he or she was deficient. Modules were designed to provide psychoeducational intervention for common skill deficits of the elderly. All clients were routinely assigned to several modules.

There were almost always present in the program some clients who exhibited idiosyncratic skill deficits or problem behaviors for which no modular treatment was available or for whom the modular treatment required supplementing. Since modular treatment was based on common problems of the elderly, less common problem areas were not addressed by the modules. It was obviously impractical, if not impossible, to have modules to address all problem areas, but the modification of highly idiosyncratic behaviors was crucial to the treatment of some individuals. Therefore, this type of situation required an additional approach to augment modular treatment. The

SCBT method was used in the Gerontology Program to provide this essential component.

THE SCBT APPROACH

Single case behavior treatment (SCBT) is an individualized behavioral treatment approach which consists of defining and analyzing observable, problematic, or skill deficit behaviors in terms of their naturally occurring antecedents and consequences. This information is then used according to known behavioral principles to develop interventions for the purpose of increasing the occurrence of adaptive behaviors and decreasing the occurrence of maladaptive behaviors.

SCBT employs the principles and techniques of behavior modification and behavior therapy. There are often differences among behaviorists with regard to the reasons that particular procedures work and even disagreements as to just what technique to use for a particular behavior problem or skill deficiency. Fortunately, such disagreement appears to be functional in that many alternative procedures have evolved.

Even though differences of opinion do exist among behavioral clinicians in terms of behavioral concepts, there appears to be very little disagreement as to the basic treatment approach. In other words, different behavioral clinicians will proceed in a similarly systematic, step-by-step manner. Within the Gerontology Program the approach was also standardized. It is safe to say that such an approach consists of the following sequential steps:

1. Directly observe and define behavior
2. Obtain baseline measurements of the behavior
3. Develop treatment for the behavior
4. Implement, the behavioral treatment
5. Evaluate results of the behavioral treatment

DIRECT OBSERVATION AND DEFINITION OF BEHAVIOR

When a client presents a problem of behavioral excess or skill deficits, the first step is to observe the client directly. The specific behaviors to change or develop are then identified and defined in behavioral terms, that is, in an objective manner so that two or more people can agree as to the occurrence of the behavior.

For example, one of our clients exhibited excessive mouth movements. The behavior was not identified as "the client moves her mouth excessively." It was more important to describe the actual behavior. Therefore, the behavior was defined in the following manner: *Mouth movement* is defined as any occasion in which the lips pucker in a forward direction. The latter definition was much better since all staff members knew the exact behavior that was being treated.

Words such as *frustrated, depressed, sad, obsessive, compulsive,* or *manic* are not useful in a behavioral program. Such words have different meanings for different people and do not specify exactly what behaviors to record.

It was common procedure to conduct an interrater reliability check between two observers to see if the definition of behavior was acceptable. Such reliability checks were conducted by two observers who simultaneously observed and recorded the clients' defined behavior from the same location. Measures of interrater reliability are usually stated in percentage agreement with a percentage agreement above 80% for new definitions and 90% for established definitions being the minimum acceptable agreement (L. K. Miller, 1975).

Obtaining Baseline Measurements of the Behavior

A baseline is a measure of how often (frequency) or how long (duration) a defined behavior occurs in the natural setting prior to any attempt at treatment. For example, in our program we were interested in attendance to modules; therefore, we recorded just how often the client in question attended scheduled modules before procedures were implemented to improve module attendance. If the concern was that the client was spending an inordinate amount of time in bed and missing important components of the program, both frequency (how often the client went to bed) and duration (how long the client stayed in bed) data were recorded during a baseline measurement. Since the concern was usually frequency or duration of behavior, data were depicted on frequency and duration graphs.

The baseline functions as a standard, or control, to which changes in behavior as a result of treatment may be compared. Obviously, data must be recorded in an identical manner through all baseline and treatment components if accurate comparisons are to be made.

The recording of data was an essential component of the Gerontology Program in general and of the SCBT approach in particular. Graphs are very useful ways to record behavior. A graph is to the behavioral clinician as a microscope is to the biologist or a telescope to the astronomer. In other words, all three professions use a tool to magnify and make visible the subject of their respective disciplines.

The graph has often indicated subtle behavioral changes before the staff could directly observe differences on a day-to-day basis. The detection of even minute changes in behavior has been essential in the program.

The behavior analysis form (BAF) has been very useful in the accumulation of baseline and treatment data in the Gerontology Program. In brief, the BAF is a form which permits the recording of the occurrence of specific behavior along with associated antecedent and consequent events. Rather than simply counting or timing the occurrence of inappropriate behavior, an entry was made on the BAF which objectively described the behavior as well as the accompanying antecedents and consequences. The BAF could, therefore, be analyzed in terms of individual/environment interactions as well as providing frequency and/or duration data. This type of analysis was essential for adequate development of behavioral treatment. Later in this chapter a complete description of behavior analysis using the BAF is presented.

One might ask just how long (days, weeks, months) a baseline study had to be conducted prior to implementing the behavioral treatment. In the Gerontology Program baseline measures were conducted until the data were stable. A stable baseline does not mean that fluctuation was expected to cease. As long as one is recording human behavior, variability in data will be quite evident. However, one should at least be sure that the variability of the baseline measure falls within a stable range if this is possible.

There were important exceptions to the rule of continuing baseline measures until some semblance of stability was achieved. We were occasionally presented with a relatively serious behavior problem. For example, if a client began to exhibit certain aggressive behaviors, it was often not feasible to conduct an extended baseline assessment waiting for stability to occur. In these cases, interventions were best implemented early.

DEVELOPMENT OF TREATMENT

Staff members relied on several sources of information in the development of SCBT for a client. They consulted the literature on an ongoing basis to keep abreast of recent developments. They also knew, through familiarity with the literature, where to look for specific information on treatment approaches for a given problem. The staff were also very much aware of the necessity of adapting previously developed treatments to meet the idiosyncratic needs of the client.

One of the richest sources of information concerning treatment ideas was the observations of direct care staff. These people had typically observed clients for long periods of time and were usually very knowledgeable about possible reinforcers to use. A wise clinician sincerely welcomes input from a variety of sources.

The previously mentioned ABC model was extremely useful in the development of SCBT planning. Viewing the clients' behavior with this model allowed the behavioral clinician to determine what antecedents signaled the occurrence of the behavior and what reinforcing consequences maintained it. The treatment assumption was that behavior could be changed by altering the identified antecedents and consequences that accompanied the behavior.

For example, if certain antecedents were signaling the occurrence of maladaptive behavior, these antecedents could be prevented from occurring. This decreased the probability of occurrence of the maladaptive behavior. On the other hand, adding an antecedent stimulus in the form of a prompt to signal the occurrence of adaptive behavior that was already in the clients' behavioral repertoire was also a very useful procedure. This latter point is especially relevant to the elderly.

Most elderly individuals in our program had probably exhibited many adaptive behaviors from extensive behavioral repertoires in the past that were not exhibited upon or shortly after admission. A series of prompts, or even a single prompt, could be all that was needed to initiate a "spontaneous recovery" of such behavior (Patterson & Jackson, 1980a). Therefore, prompting was an essential component in the Gerontology Program. The clients were, of course, reinforced for exhibiting the prompted behavior to assure maintenance.

Consequences could also be altered. On many occasions staff members discovered that a particular inappropriate behavior appeared to be inadvertently reinforced by attention from others. For example, one client in the program made somatic complaints at a very high frequency which interfered with her involvement in the program. The complaints did not appear to have a physiological basis. The SCBT plan was designed to include extinction as a technique. The actual plan consisted of ignoring the client when she voiced physical complaints and reinforcing her for talking appropriately. Within two weeks, the frequency of such complaints was decreased to an appropriate level.

Many approaches to treatment involved changing both antecedents and consequences of behavior. The addition of antecedents or prompts to the environment was sometimes used to increase the frequency of desired behavior. Maladaptive behaviors were also sometimes controlled by eliminating naturally occurring cues. Similarly, reinforcers could be added or eliminated to alter the occurrence of behaviors. The control of both antecedents and consequences was a powerful technique when this could be arranged.

The treatment plan was always to be written in a clear manner with care taken not to dispense with important details. Copies of the SCBT plan were made available to all staff members. The treatment was examined in detail with ample opportunity for staff members to question the procedure and request clarification on any part of the plan they did not understand.

Fortunately, not all clients in the program required a specialized SCBT plan. No more than 10–15% of the clients enrolled in the program at any one time needed such a plan. Otherwise it would have been extremely difficult if not impossible for all staff members to know all SCBT plans in detail if one existed for each of the clients. Since only a relatively small proportion of clients required SCBT at any one given time, all staff members were informed of procedural details. An SCBT plan was prepared in the treatment team meeting and was typed for distribution immediately following the meeting. Direct care staff then read the plan and initialed it to signify that they had read and understood it.

IMPLEMENTATION OF TREATMENT

Treatment was implemented by first talking to the client and explaining the treatment in detail. We often found, always to our surprise, that a particular behavior problem ceased to occur as soon as the client had been told of the specific contingencies involved in the SCBT plan. SCBT was not approached as if the client's behavior was going to be changed without his or her knowledge or assistance.

When the treatment plan was implemented, great care was taken to see that it continued on a systematic and consistent basis. An excellent SCBT plan can fail as a direct result of inconsistent application. Techniques of behavior modification and behavior therapy are extremely sensitive to inadequate implementation. For these reasons, SCBT plans required constant monitoring by staff. To ensure consistency in the Gerontology Program, all staff members were trained not only to maintain consistency but also to detect inconsistency when it occurred. Experience soon taught them not to develop a behavioral treatment and expect other staff members to implement and continue it without proper training, communication, follow-up monitoring, and accountability.

The physician is a key staff member and deserves special mention. The behavioral clinician should make a special effort to gain the cooperation of the physician when SCBT is implemented. The way in which this was done in our program is described in the following chapter.

EVALUATION OF TREATMENT

The first thing to remember in evaluating a behavioral treatment is not to rely on subjective progress reports, whether official or unofficial, verbal or written. Such statements as "I think the client is doing much better now than when he was admitted" are virtually worthless from an evaluation point of view (and also cause considerable dispute). It is important to remember that such statements are usually the result of casual observation at best and not a product of careful, objective determinations of behavior change.

SCBT is an empirically based approach. Evaluation of treatment involved comparing the results of treatment to the initial baseline. The concern was not with general statements of progress, but with the measures of defined adaptive or maladaptive behaviors. If data were recorded as the number of defined behaviors in a given unit of time (frequency data) the concern was with the change in frequency of the defined behavior during treatment as compared to the initial baseline. With some behaviors, both frequency and duration data were recorded within a single SCBT plan. In that case, changes in both frequency and duration data were objectively evaluated.

Once the graphs were observed to determine whether the defined adaptive behavior had increased or the defined maladaptive behavior had decreased, a decision was made regarding the clinical significance of the data. This was often a difficult decision. For example, was a 20% reduction in "talking out in group" clinically significant? How about a 40% reduction? 60%? At this point, a distinction between statistical and clinical significance was made. Various methods exist for evaluating behavior changes in terms of statistical significance (Kazdin, 1976); however, it is quite possible that a behavior change can be statistically significant at an alpha level of .05 to .01 but not be clinically significant, and vice versa.

The way out of the significance dilemma was to be more concerned with clinical improvement. In the treatment setting, the major objective was to assist individuals in improving their behavior from a clinical point of view so that their chances of being placed or continuing to live in the community were improved. This is not to say that tests of statistical significance were not important, rather that they were used for different purposes. Measures of statistical significance were indispensible for many types of research and for program evaluation involving large numbers of subjects in the Gerontology Program (cf. Chapters 9 and 10).

Evaluation of the SCBT plan was conducted to establish the effectiveness of the behavioral treatment. If the treatment was found to be ineffective, it was necessary to return to Step 3—the development of treatment. The treatment team regrouped and redesigned a more effective SCBT plan. Occasionally, several SCBT plans were developed or modifications were made to an existing plan to achieve treatment success. Such modifications were based on objective, data-based evaluations of treatment. Much was learned from the analysis of an SCBT plan which was not effective. This type of approach has appeared to increase the probability of success of subsequent SCBT plans.

The evaluation of the initial SCBT plan may have, on the other hand, demonstrated the effectiveness of the behavioral treatment. In that case, generalization and maintenance procedures were implemented to secure a high probability of enduring treatment effects. Many behavioral programs initially work in that behavior is quickly changed for the better, but they fail as the newly established behaviors are quickly extinguished following cessation of treatment. Without adequate attempts at gaining generalization and maintenance of behavior, the probability that the newly established behaviors will extinguish appears to be quite high (see Chapter 3 for a more detailed discussion of generalization and maintenance).

The Behavior Analysis Form in SCBT

SCBT was an objective behavior treatment approach based on recorded observations of behavior, beginning with problem definition and targeting of behaviors. The behavior analysis form (BAF) was an integral component of the SCBT process because it provided an instrument and a method for the accurate recording of behavioral observations.

The BAF, shown in Figure 1, is a behavior recording instrument designed to separate the individual/environment interaction into its various components. The ABC model presented in Chapter 3 is the basis of the BAF. The three components of the ABC model (antecedents, behavior, and consequences) are represented as major recording categories on the BAF. To reiterate, an antecedent to a specific behavior often functions as the environmental signal for the occurrence of

BEHAVIOR ANALYSIS FORM (BAF)		
NAME:_____ CASE NO.:_____ TREATMENT UNIT:_____		
ANTECEDENT(S)	BEHAVIOR(S)	CONSEQUENCE(S)
DATE: TIME: LOCATION: PERSONS IN VICINITY: SPECIFICS OF INTERACTION: OTHER EVENTS:	OBSERVED BEHAVIOR: DURATION OF BEHAVIOR	INTERPERSONAL INTERACTION: OTHER ENVIRONMENTAL INTERACTIONS: RECORDER:
DATE: TIME: LOCATION: PERSONS IN VICINITY: SPECIFICS OF INTERACTION: OTHER EVENTS:	OBSERVED BEHAVIOR: DURATION OF BEHAVIOR	INTERPERSONAL INTERACTION: OTHER ENVIRONMENTAL INTERACTIONS: RECORDER:

FIGURE 1. The behavior analysis form.

behavior. Consequences of a specific behavior often function as reinforcers resulting in either the acceleration or maintenance of behavior. Because the individual/environment interaction occurs in the order of antecedents–behavior–consequences, these three components are presented on the BAF in the appropriate sequence.

The following is a description of items that were recorded on the BAF with the items presented according to the recording category.

Antecedent Category

Date. An essential piece of data was the day and month the behavior was recorded. An accurate time base was essential in the appropriate analysis of behavior.

Time. This was a highly significant antecedent in that many disruptive behaviors appeared to occur as a function of the time of day. Very often, patterns emerged in which specific behaviors occurred at specific times of the day or night. For example, certain inappropriate behaviors occurred in the evening when the client was not as actively involved in the program.

Location. It was very important to indicate exactly where the client was when the inappropriate behavior occurred. If the client was away from the program setting when the inappropriate behavior occurred, the exact location was recorded. It was interesting to note that many behaviors occurred only in specific locations (e.g., bedroom, dining room).

Persons in Vicinity. If persons other than the client were in the immediate vicinity when the inappropriate behavior occurred, their names were entered under this recording category. It was also not unusual to find that specific inappropriate behaviors occurred only in the presence of specific persons such as staff members or other clients.

Specifics of Interactions. In this category, staff members briefly described the actions observed to occur between the client being considered and the other person or persons nearby just prior to the occurrence of the behavior. This category was used to elaborate the "Persons in Vicinity" category and often referred back to it.

Other Events. This category was reserved for events occurring just prior to the behavior which did not involve the presence of other people but which might have precipitated the occurrence of the behavior. Some examples of noninterpersonal events that could precipitate the behavior included a fire alarm, a telephone call, or an accident (such as dropping a food tray).

Behavior Category

Observed Behavior. The actual observed act (behavior) of the client. The entry was written in objective, observable terms. For example, staff members did not state that a client was "frustrated" or "anxious" since these are not actual behaviors. Instead, one stated exactly what was observed (the client cried, walked away from the ADL I group, etc.). The entry did not include suggested reasons as to why the behavior occurred but was simply a description of the observed behavior.

Duration of Behavior. It was also important to record how long a particular behavior lasted. This entry consisted of recording the actual elapsed time from the beginning of a behavior to the time it ceased to occur. For example, if a client became disruptive at 2:05 P.M. and continued nonstop until 2:10 P.M., the staff member entered "5 minutes" in this section.

Consequence Category

Interpersonal Interaction. This category contained the specifics of any interaction following the recorded behavior involving the client in question and anyone else. For example, if the recorded behavior stated that John Doe threw a vase against the living area wall, the recorded entry was "John was ignored by this employee" or "John was asked to pick up the broken pieces and sweep the floor."

Other Environmental Consequences. This entry included any environmental event immediately following the recorded behavior that was not an interaction with anyone else. For example, if John Doe was disruptive and did not get dressed in time to attend a special field trip on a bus, the entry was "John was refused permission to go on the field trip by the Unit Manager."

Recorder. This entry was simply the signature or initials of the person completing the BAF.

The success of the BAF recording in the Gerontology Program was a result of several principles. First of all, it was essential that recordings on the BAF be made immediately upon occurrence of the behavior. Experience soon taught staff members that a delay between the occurrence of the inappropriate behavior and the actual recording of the antecedents, behavior, and consequences only highlighted the imperfections of memory. It appeared that the longer the delay in recording, the less likely it was that the recording would be an accurate representation of the behavior occurrence.

A second principle was to record faithfully. It is very easy to fall into the trap of observing an inappropriate behavior and not taking the time to record its occurrence on the BAF. The staff members in the Gerontology Program were presented with the rationale of the BAF as well as the mechanics of completing it. It appeared that staff members faithfully used the BAF to record behavior because they understood the importance of the form and how it related to overall behavior changes of the client.

Third, it was essential to record behavior observations on a first-hand basis. In other words, the person who observed the behavior was the person who recorded the information on the BAF. It is important to note that all staff members in the program were trained in the use of the BAF. Such training was completed so that all staff members could complete the BAF as firsthand observers. If the information was obtained secondhand from an observer with the second person recording it, information that could be essential was almost certainly lost because the process of completing the BAF guided the observer from point to point in the chain of events. The BAF items, therefore, guided one through a systematic recall of various aspects of the occurrence of the behavior. If a person other than the observer recorded the event, a somewhat vague recollection of the antecedents, behavior, and consequences was recorded through a secondhand interpretation of the event.

Lastly, it was essential that the BAF entries be made on an objective basis. The observer/recorder stated exactly what was seen and heard. The appropriate use of the form did not include subjective impressions as to why the behavior occurred because different staff members would inevitably have made different interpretations of the behavior. However, staff members tended to agree with a high degree of reliability on specific behavioral events (e.g., John threw a chair or Mary went to bed and missed the Communications Training module).

USES OF THE BEHAVIOR ANALYSIS FORM

The BAF and its use gained widespread acceptance among all staff members in the Gerontology Program, apparently as a direct result of its demonstrated utility in the process of increasing the occurrence of adaptive behavior and decreasing the occurrence of maladaptive behavior through

- The provision of a data base for emerging problem behaviors (baseline)
- The provision of an analytic tool to aid in the identification of environmental events that resulted in the acceleration or maintenance of inappropriate behavior (treatment)
- The provision of an ongoing data base for the purpose of making comparisons between baseline and treatment conditions in order that the effectiveness of treatment might be determined (evaluation)

The first point is essential to any behavioral treatment program because a data base constitutes the foundation of such a program. Within the Gerontology Program, the BAF was used to document the occurrence of inappropriate behavior with its accompanying environmental components (antecedents and consequences). Two types of data were obtained. By obtaining duration and frequency data directly from the BAF, one could plot such data over a specific time base of hours, days, or weeks. Such information was invaluable. When the staff recorded any instance of inappropriate behavior, emerging problem behaviors were quickly identified and documented. For example, one client in our program began to leave the modular activities and go to bed. This information was routinely recorded on the BAF. When the treatment team met to review the client, the BAFs were reviewed and the problem of leaving the group to go to bed was identified. If the BAF recording had not been used, the problem may still have been evident; however, the accumulation of BAF recordings allowed the treatment team to view objective data on the frequency and duration of such behavior for each day of the week immediately preceding the meeting of the treatment team. With such a data base already initiated, the treatment team used the first meeting to design an effective SCBT plan to change the behavior.

Secondly, the BAF functioned as an analytic tool to aid in the identification of environmental variables that signaled the occurrence of and reinforced the presence of inappropriate behaviors. Staff members on many occasions reviewed multiple BAF entries and identified environmental variables that contributed to the maintenance of problem behaviors. The following examples indicate the usefulness of the BAF in ferreting out contributing variables:

- One male client's disruptive behavior was found to occur only when he was prompted by staff members to attend group activities.
- A female client visited the nurses' station several times per hour, disrupting her participation in modules. The BAF indicated that her visits were always accompanied by the reinforcing consequence of verbal interaction with staff members.
- A female client would become disruptive and combative only if prompted to participate in program activities by a specific staff member.
- A female client would exhibit delusional speech only if a specific staff member was present.
- The frequency and duration of sitting on the floor increased for a female client when she was prompted by staff members to stand up.
- A male client would become verbally abusive only when a specific female client was near him or when he was in the dining room.

In all of the preceding examples, SCBT plans were developed and implemented. The plans were based on altering the antecedents and/ or consequences responsible for maintaining the appropriate behaviors. In conducting such a pretreatment analysis of behavior it was very important to realize that antecedents and consequences were not always easily identified. The antecedents and reinforcing consequences responsible for maintaining the behavior were often so subtle as to elude or almost elude detection. In addition, reinforcers maintaining the inappropriate behavior did not always follow each occurrence of the behavior. Careful scrutiny of the BAF entries occasionally indicated that a supposed reinforcer followed the behavior only on an intermittent basis.

The best approach used in reviewing BAF entries was to look closely for patterns, which often emerged when one scrutinized a large number of BAFs. The staff were trained to look for specific antecedents and consequences that regularly or at least periodically accompanied the recorded behavior. Through experience, staff members discovered that very little, if anything, could be determined from only one or a few BAF entries.

Finally, the BAF furnished an ongoing data base which provided the treatment team with objective data tracking the client's progress throughout the duration of the SCBT plan. For example, if the treatment team met on a particular client and defined and prioritized inappropriate behaviors with which to work, the continued use of the BAF provided data that was used to evaluate the SCBT plan on an ongoing basis. The BAF, therefore, functioned as an ongoing data base to aid in both the identification and the continuing documentation of problem behavior.

SCBT: Treatment or Research

The term *behavioral research* has many different meanings; however, our concept can be stated by paraphrasing Wolman's (1973) definition of research in the following manner:

- *Behavioral research.* A detailed and systematic attempt to discover or confirm through objective investigation the facts pertaining to changes in behavior and the relevant principles involved.

To differentiate between *behavioral research* and *behavioral treatment* we define the latter term thus:

- *Behavioral treatment.* The manipulation of existing or presentation of novel antecedents and/or consequences of behavior to increase the occurrence of adaptive behavior and decrease occurrence of maladaptive behavior.

Combining the two definitions in the following manner results in our definition of *behavioral treatment research:*

- *Behavioral treatment research.* The manipulation of existing or presentation of novel antecedents and/or consequences of behavior to increase the occurrence of adaptive behavior and decrease the occurrence of maladaptive behavior, with a detailed and systematic attempt to discover or confirm through objective investigation the facts pertaining to changes in behavior and the relevant principles involved.

To quote Azrin (1977):

> As a clinical researcher, I have had two guiding principles. The first was to adhere to the tenets of an objective scientific research methodology. The second principle was to develop an effective treatment. (p. 141)

He further noted that this particular orientation is shared in the relatively recent, emerging fields of behavior modification, behavior therapy, applied behavior analysis, and, his own term, "learning therapies."

SCBT emphasizes a behavioral treatment approach as well as a behavioral treatment research approach. This, perhaps, is where SCBT extends beyond other approaches. Professionals, adhering strictly to a behavioral treatment research approach are typically interested in developing new treatments or investigating the efficacy of accepted behavioral treatments with new problems or populations. A research approach in this situation is therefore warranted. However, it is frequently evident that in the treatment setting a relatively common behavior problem or deficit emerges which has been changed successfully many times by using a specific, well-tested behavioral intervention. In our experience, the latter situation does not warrant a full-fledged research approach, but rather, a systematic and functional treatment approach.

There were many examples of common behavior problems in the Gerontology Program which were successfully changed with relatively routine behavioral procedures. For example, if a pretreatment analysis of behavior was completed with the BAF and it was discovered that a client's excessive or inappropriate talking in group was inadvertently and consistently followed by staff attention, extinction was usually applied as a behavioral treatment. In other words, the staff were instructed not to interact with the client in any way if the problem behavior occurred. The result was usually an eventual decrease in the occurrence of the excessive inappropriate talking.

If an initial assessment of a client indicated that she could shampoo her hair appropriately but did not exhibit this behavior on an ongoing basis, a very simple procedure was implemented whereby the client was prompted at appropriate times to engage in the target behavior and was immediately reinforced for completion of the behavior. Prompts and reinforcers were then faded. Referring back to the definition of behavioral research, we concluded that "a detailed and systematic attempt to discover through investigation the facts pertaining to changes in behavior and the relevant principles involved" was not necessarily relevant for these and similar examples in the treatment setting.

The treatment setting occasionally presented a situation in which a client exhibited a problem behavior or deficit for which no established behavioral treatment had been developed. For example, a client in the Gerontology Program exhibited high frequency mouth movements associated with tardive dyskinesia. Because no effective behavioral treatments were available, the behavior was defined and analyzed and several behavioral treatments were developed using a behavioral treatment/research approach (Jackson & Schonfeld, 1980, in press). Because new techniques were being implemented, appropriate experimental design and control of extraneous variables were of major concern. The SCBT approach was useful as a research investigation and in this case fit the definition of behavior treatment research.

The notion that the proponents of the SCBT approach separate efforts into either a behavioral treatment or a behavioral treatment research approach is, indeed, controversial. The traditional view of behavioral clinicians has been officially to approach behavioral treatment as research. This approach was obviously necessary in the early developing days of behavior modification.

Initially, principles governing behavior had to be discovered, evaluated, and adapted within a consistent methodology to effect appropriate behavior changes from a clinical point of view. This is not to say that experimental studies of the ground-breaking variety are no longer being conducted. On the contrary, new and exciting areas of investigation surface on a seemingly constant basis. However, since the inception of behavior modification, a technology of behavior change has developed which consists of the tools necessary for effective behavioral treatment.

It is true that behavioral technology is only in its infancy, but it has proved to be effective nevertheless. Technology, in this sense, is the application of the science of behavior and is the foundation of behavioral treatment. Why is it important to differentiate between behavioral treatment and behavioral treatment research in SCBT? The answer is deceptively simple; the two approaches have very different purposes.

According to Sidman (1960), experiments (research) are conducted for the following five reasons: (1) to evaluate hypotheses, (2) to indulge the investigator's curiosity about the nature of behavior, (3) to try out a new method or technique, (4) to establish the existence of a (behavioral) phenomenon, and (5) to explore the conditions under which a (behavioral) phenomenon occurs. The pursuit of any one or combination of the preceding endeavors qualifies as research within the general framework of SCBT. In fact, Sidman's reasons for conducting experiments serve as criteria by which we can define *behavioral treatment research*.

If the sole purpose of using behavioral principles and techniques is to provide behavioral intervention to increase the occurrence of adaptive behavior and decrease the occurrence of maladaptive behavior—and *not* to evaluate experimental hypotheses, indulge the investigator's curiosity, try a new method or technique, establish the existence of a behavioral phenomenon, or explore in detail the conditions under which a phenomenon occurs—then a *behavioral treatment* approach has been described. Within SCBT of the Gerontology Program the behavioral treatment approach was used more often than a behavioral treatment research approach. However, if the situation warranted a research approach, SCBT research was provided.

Experimental Design

Rigorous scientific methodology was required when behavioral treatment research was conducted in the Gerontology Program. Requirements of acceptable scientific practice were necessary to substantiate the effects of a new behavioral procedure or to demonstrate the existence of a behavioral phenomenon to the satisfaction of the scientific community. SCBT also required a standard methodology; however, the actual methodology was often an abbreviated version of a research protocol.

The heart of scientific methodology in behavioral treatment research is experimental design. Experimental design can be defined in the following manner:

- *Experimental design* is a systematic method of comparing the occurrence of behavior in a control condition with the occurrence of behavior in an experimental condition for the purpose of determining the presence or absence of causal relationships among independent and dependent variables.

An independent variable is the variable manipulated by the researcher or clinician. In SCBT studies, the independent variable is the behavioral procedure (manipulation of specified environmental events) that is applied in the experimental condition. A dependent variable is usually a measure of the frequency and/or duration of the appropriate or inappropriate behavior. A research study therefore consists of the manipulation of the independent variable(s) in terms of its absence or presence and the measurement of the subsequent effects of this manipulation on the dependent variable(s). If appropriate changes in behavior are clearly associated with the repeated application and removal of the behavioral procedure, either within or across subjects, it is fairly certain that such changes in behavior are a result of the behavioral procedure.

The SCBT approach as used in the Gerontology Program typically incorporated one or some variation of three major types of experimental designs (Hersen & Barlow, 1976, provide extensive discussion of these and other designs). The first type of design can be labeled as the *AB design* and is actually a case study design used for behavioral treatment. The second type of design is a true experimental design and can be labeled as the *ABAB design*. The third type of design, also a true experimental design, is the *multiple baseline design*. The ABAB, or any of its many variations, and the multiple baseline design are used for behavioral treatment research.

The AB Design

The AB design consists only of a single pretreatment baseline (A) and a contingency or treatment component (B). This case study design is often adequate in a behavioral treatment situation. Operationally, the first step after defining the behavior reliably is to conduct a baseline of the frequency and/or duration of the behavior until the behavior is stable. The behavioral procedure is then introduced. The baseline serves as the control condition to which one compares the results during the treatment condition.

Although the AB design is adequate for behavioral treatment, it is not adequate as a true experimental design for research purposes. Even if a dramatic change in behavior occurs during the treatment condition as compared to the baseline condition, it is not known whether the behavior change was actually a result of the treatment. It is quite possible that some other variable operating in the environment (e.g., visit by a relative, medication change) coincided in time with the implementation of the behavioral treatment and was responsible for the change in behavior. Since only one person is involved in the behavioral procedure and the AB sequence is not repeated, one cannot say with certainty that the procedure was the agent of the behavior change.

The AB sequence has been used for research purposes when modified. If the AB sequence is repeated, the design becomes an ABAB design. This design is acceptable since changes in behavior are repeatedly associated with the presence or absence of the behavioral procedure (Hersen & Barlow, 1976). The AB sequence can also be part of a multiple baseline approach (Hersen & Barlow, 1976) in which the AB sequence is repeated across subjects, behaviors, or settings. The multiple baseline design consists of the simultaneous occurrence of baselines with the procedure implemented at different points in time across subjects, behaviors, or settings (see the following discussion on multiple baseline design). The AB sequence could also be used for research purposes if a multiple schedule or multielement baseline component is added (Hersen & Barlow, 1976; Murphy, Doughty, & Nunes, 1979; Sidman, 1960; Sulzer-Azaroff & Mayer, 1977. The major point to be made is that the AB design without modification is suitable for behavioral treatment but does not substantiate the effects of a behavioral treatment to the degree necessary to meet the rigorous requirements of a research approach.

The ABAB Design

The ABAB design is actually two AB designs in sequence. The operation of repeating the AB sequence has many disadvantages. Perhaps the most important advantage of the ABAB design is its acceptance as a true experimental design. As mentioned previously, the AB design alone is a case study design. The single AB sequence is unacceptable from a research point of view since there is only one manipulation of the behavioral contingency. As previously mentioned, when comparing the A and B conditions, differences between them cannot be attributed solely to experimental manipulation of the behavioral procedure since another variable may have occurred by chance at the time the B component was implemented.

Early behavior modification research revealed an attempt to solve this problem by the addition of a "return to baseline" component (ABA design). The probability that variables other than the absence or presence of the behavioral contingency resulted in the observed changes in behavior is substantially decreased by completing the additional experimental manipulation of withdrawing treatment. If the experimenter achieved a stable baseline (A), introduced the treatment with a resultant change in behavior (B), and removed that procedure with another resultant change in behavior (A), then a strong case could be made for the presence of a direct causal relationship between the independent and dependent variables.

There is, however, a serious ethical problem with the ABA design. If a researcher is working with a problem behavior and shows that the treatment in the B condition decreased the occurrence of that behavior, it is not considered to be ethical to return to a baseline condition if the study ends at the end of the return to baseline condition. In other words, if the behavior during the return to baseline condition does return to the initial baseline level, the client is left with the same problem he or she had to begin with. The seriousness of this ethical problem is compounded by the fact that the experimenter has not only removed a treatment, but, rather, has removed a supposedly effective treatment. The researcher has removed a viable treatment only to add an experimental manipulation to substantiate the usefulness of his or her procedure.

The addition of a second B (ABAB) has two distinct advantages. The first and most important advantage is that the ABAB is an ethical design. The final condition is a treatment condition with the behavioral researchers assuming the ethical responsibility of also considering maintenance of behavior after the final B stage. The second advantage is that yet another experimental manipulation of the independent variable is added. This further substantiates the effectiveness of a behavioral procedure if the effects of the procedure result in changes in behavior that are associated with the experimental manipulations across all four conditions.

The Multiple Baseline Design

The multiple baseline design can be considered to be an AB design that is repeated across subjects, behaviors, or settings with the multiple baselines beginning at the same point in time and treatment being presented in sequence after a change in behavior is evident. The effects of treatment are substantiated by repeated presentations of that treatment.

Observation of a single AB sequence in the multiple baseline design does not convince one that the implementation of treatment was indeed the variable that resulted in the change of behavior. Just as in the single AB design, an environmental variable other than treatment may have coincided with treatment implementation with the resultant change in behavior being attributable to a nonexperimental variable. The strength of the multiple baseline design is derived from the replication properties of the repeated AB sequence.

One can make a strong case for the effectiveness of treatment if that treatment is presented at staggered times for different subjects, behaviors, or settings. It is highly unlikely from a probability point of view that environmental variables, other than the treatment variable, could coincide on a precise time base with the staggered presentation of treatment in the multiple baseline design. Therefore, when one evaluates behavior change with this design, the entire design must be taken into consideration. From a research point of view, if the effectiveness of the treatment is to be substantiated to the satisfaction of the scientific community, the change in behavior must be evident across the AB sequences. For example, if only one of the three AB sequences illustrated a substantial behavior change, then no case would be made for the effectiveness of treatment from a research viewpoint. In this particular case, treatment worked only in a single AB sequence. This, of course, is not acceptable since a single AB sequence contains all the disadvantages of the single, quasi-experimental AB design.

However, the multiple baseline design has been extremely useful in substantiating treatment effectiveness as behavioral treatment research. One major advantage stems directly from the design and is worthy of note here. If one uses the design appropriately, then one is working with three or more behaviors, subjects, or settings. Depending on the way the design is employed, this either results in improved treatment for a single subject, extends treatment to more than one individual when an across-subjects design is used, or increases the chances of stimulus generalization when used across settings.

Implications of Experimental Design

Although there is a conceptual difference between behavioral treatment and behavioral treatment research in SCBT, the two are by no means incompatible. On the contrary, the approach used in behavioral treatment is not operationally unlike the approach used in behavioral treatment research; it is simply an abbreviated version of the latter. This is an extremely important point.

What if the behavioral clinician has carefully conducted a baseline study and implements treatment only to find some surprising or serendipitous result? If the clinician has followed good treatment practice and has an AB sequence along with reliable operational definitions of behavior, has conducted reliability checks of behavioral definitions, and has controlled extraneous variables, he can extend the treatment design to a true experimental design by repeating the AB sequence. The clinician then has an ABAB design and has converted to a behavioral treatment research approach.

The reader probably noticed in the preceding paragraph that more is required in the conversion of behavioral treatment to behavioral treatment research than simply going from an AB to an ABAB design. In other words, good behavioral treatment practices share many methodological operations with the research approach. Good behavioral treatment means that we have operationally defined a behavior. Accurate data, whether for research or treatment, cannot be obtained unless the investigators observing and recording the behavior agree exactly on what they are recording.

Also, only one procedure should be implemented at any one given point in time regardless of the approach taken. If an appropriate change in behavior occurs when two or more procedures are implemented simultaneously, it is virtually impossible to determine which procedure resulted in the change. Furthermore, the simultaneous presentation of two or more procedures may complicate treatment by hopelessly confusing the client.

Accurate data are essential regardless of the approach taken. Unless data are recorded carefully with attention given to the precision of data collection, results can be meaningless. If an AB design is being used for treatment, it will serve no purpose to extend it to an ABAB design if collection of data has been inconsistent.

Consistency of application of a behavioral procedure is of extreme importance in treatment alone as well as in research. It is, in fact, surprising to find significant behavior change resulting from the inconsistent application of behavioral contingencies. In the unlikely event that appropriate behavior changes are occurring with the inconsistent application of contingencies, extending the AB sequence to an ABAB sequence adds little to the scientific merit of the approach.

In summary, SCBT represents a method of applying behavioral principles and techniques in a systematic and consistent manner to promote the occurrence of adaptive behavior and decrease the occurrence of maladaptive behavior. SCBT can be applied as treatment or as research depending on the nature and uniqueness of the problem and the scientific merit of the approach taken.

6

The Treatment Team

CARLA DEE KELLY
AND ROGER L. PATTERSON

HISTORY

The interdisciplinary treatment team has been defined by Horowitz (1970) as a small work group of helping or healing professionals from different disciplines. All treatment decisions in the Gerontology Program were products of deliberation by such teams. The subject of this chapter is a description of these teams and the nature of their functioning. First, some information regarding the historical development of these teams in mental hospitals will be helpful. The development of interdisciplinary mental health treatment teams is closely related to the introduction of more effective pharmacological and other treatments for mental illness. The development of the major tranquilizers, especially the phenothiazines, in the 1950s began what has been called the revolution in state hospitals (Bower, 1970). Prior to this time, inmates, as they were called, were expected to spend the rest of their lives in the hospital (Bower, 1970). As patients began demonstrating an ability to act responsibly when given increased freedom, attitudes toward them changed. Many were now seen as rehabilitable and only temporarily hospitalized, and more active efforts to return them to the community began to develop. In order to administer treatment preparatory to departure from the hospital, therapies other than psychoanalysis (then the standard treatment of choice) had to be legitimatized; otherwise, treatment would not be available to a large group of patients.

Albee (1959) discussed the trend of lower echelon staff agitating for increased recognition of their role in treating patients. Recognizing the important role of direct care staff in treatment of patients, he advocated the development of a new professional classification of mental health workers with a four-year college training program. The development of new treatment technologies such as token economies (Atthowe & Krasner, 1968; Ayllon & Azrin, 1968), attitude therapy (Taulbee & Wright, 1971), peer management techniques (Fairweather, Sanders, Maynard, & Cressler, 1969), and other total environmental approaches served to emphasize the usefulness of, and increase the need for, the broad representation of all types of staff in the planning and implementation of treatment.

These treatment developments resulted in the hiring of increasing numbers of social workers, psychologists, rehabilitation therapists, and other nonmedical personnel. The roles of these nonmedical groups also changed in the direction of greater participation in treatment. The physicians and nurses found themselves in the position of coordinating and directing the treatment efforts of a number of sub-professionals and professional level staff. Shortages of physicians and nurses, as well as the development of nonmedical treatment modalities, led to the desirability of selecting treatment team leaders from among other professional groups. This process has required a major adjustment by all staff to their new roles, especially physicians and nurses who have had to relinquish a great deal of authority.

Fry and Miller (1974) investigated the functional relationships among treatment team members. They emphasized the importance of role negotiations among team members and the necessity for the team to be given autonomy by the larger organization. They noted that any turnover of team members required a new set of role negotiations. Team effectiveness and authority patterns arise out of these negotiations and are a result of consensus among the members. Thus, interdisciplinary treatment teams are highly complex social organizations whose structure and function are dynamic and of wide-reaching importance to the individual team members, to the parent organization, and, most importantly, to the patients.

STRUCTURE

In the Gerontology Program, the treatment team members included the case manager (CM) of the client under consideration, the physician, the nursing supervisor, the clinical social worker, the clinical psychologist, the rehabilitation program supervisor, the unit manager, and the unit director, who usually functioned as the treatment team leader. The physician functioned as a consultant to the team on the day treatment unit because day clients were encouraged to have their own primary-care physicians from the community. (If FMHI had assumed medical responsibility for day treatment clients, it would have been contrary to efforts toward strengthening their community support system.)

The case managers were the direct care staff who were responsible for most of the treatment as well as the daily tasks associated with client care. They were generally people with two to four years of college who were provided with extensive on-the-job training, including a 30-hour course in behavioral principles and methods. Case managers had a case load of four to six clients. They oriented new clients; did most of the charting, including admission and discharge notes; ran the majority of the training groups; and performed all initial, monthly, and discharge assessments. The clients looked to them for guidance, to answer questions, and to resolve problems. They chauffeured clients to appointments outside of the Institute, took clients on field trips, and were the primary source of data regarding the specifics of clients' interactions with family and other significant members of the community. A very important function for the case manager was that of carrying out single case treatment plans developed by the treatment team. They had a significant responsibility for input to the treatment team plans because of their closer relationship with the clients. As was the case with all gerontology staff, the case managers provided training and were also responsible for collecting research data.

The physician was the medical expert of the team. He provided medical information and was, in the residential project, responsible for the physical well-being of the clients including the monitoring and adjusting of psychotropic medication as well as prescribing all other medicines and special diets. Although not medically responsible for day treatment clients, the physician examined them on admission and was called for emergency treatment. He also provided consultation to the treatment team regarding clients' physical status and the effects of prescribed medical treatments. (Day treatment clients authorized the release of information regarding their physical histories and treatments from community physicians.)

The nursing staff on the residential unit carried out the orders of the physician. They were alert to emerging physical problems and represented the physician at treatment team meetings. Nurses on day treatment frequently contacted the clients' physician in the community to obtain medical information and disseminate data about our treatment of the client. On both units, they taught clients about their medications and how to care for themselves if they had a chronic disease.

The clinical social worker and the social worker's assistant, the social service worker, were the experts on community resources and how to utilize them. For the residential clients, placement in the least restrictive community setting was a major goal, and placement for each client was considered from the time of admission. This placement effort occupied much of the time of the social worker. In order to do this successfully, it was frequently necessary to apply for financial aid or for clarification of the clients' financial status. The social worker also met with family members of the client, visited potential placement facilities, and wrote referrals to community mental health centers and to the state's aging services. The aging services placed clients in state-licensed boarding homes or foster homes and visited them monthly.

The social service worker was responsible primarily for the day treatment unit. The day treatment clients needed assistance in obtaining a variety of community supports, but their needs were different from those of the residential clients since placement was seldom an issue. The social service worker also performed other community liaison functions for day treatment, including case-finding and screening.

The clinical psychologist's role was nontraditional. In contrast to many other treatment programs in which psychologists' primary responsibilities are psychodiagnostics and conducting group and individual therapy, the psychologist in our program had as primary duties assisting and overseeing the development and implementation of a major proportion of the single case behavioral treatment (SCBT) plans, monitoring the overall treatment program for each client, developing treatment modules, and counseling families in behavior management techniques. The psychologist also functioned as a key member of the treatment team and assured adherence to the treatment philosophy and principles across the entire treatment program.

The rehabilitation program supervisor was responsible for the scheduling and integrity of all training and activity groups. In our program, a music therapist and an occupational therapist held this position at different times. With the assistance of a rehabilitation therapist, the rehabilitation program supervisor monitored nine training modules. First an occupational therapist, then a person with a bachelor's degree in psychology served as the rehabilitation therapist. The supervision of those who conducted the groups by these two ensured a standardized training procedure and on-time progress assessments. As members of the treatment team, the rehabilitation program supervisor and the rehabilitation therapist were able to provide highly specific data about module progress and client performance in organized activities to the rest of the team.

The unit managers on each unit were the direct supervisors of the case managers and were responsible for communicating treatment plans to them and ensuring that the plans were followed. The physical integrity of the unit was another responsibility of the unit managers, who ordered repairs to facilities and equipment, purchased supplies, and managed housekeeping. Both managers had personal responsibilities which included making case manager assignments (matching staff and clients), assigning module trainers and assessors, and assuring that all functions were covered. On a day-to-day basis, both unit managers were responsible for liasion with referral sources, screening potential clients, and supervising admission procedures. A person with an associate's degree and extensive institutional experience held this position on the residential unit; a person with a M.A. in gerontology and a background in social work was the unit manager on day treatment.

The unit director, who had a master's degree in gerontology and extensive administrative and mental hospital experience, had the responsibility for ensuring the administrative, legal, and supervisory integrity of the program. The unit director held the pivotal position in the management system of the program. With the exception of the psychologist, all the professional staff and the two unit managers were supervised by the unit director. This management system lent a cohesiveness and unity of purpose to our staff.

FUNCTION

During the first 24 hours after admission to the residential unit, or the first 14 days for day treatment, each client was interviewed and examined by the team physician. Barring the discovery of clearly inappropriate medications, the physician did not change the medications of the residential clients during an initial two-week period of observation. If untreated physical problems were found in the day clients, they were informed and told to seek treatment. Assistance in obtaining treatment was provided if needed. Also, day clients brought in all medications which they were currently taking for the purpose of identification and subsequent training regarding the nature and proper use of the medications as prescribed or directed.

Within 7 working days after admission to the residential unit, or 30 days for day treatment, the team convened for an initial treatment meeting. Thereafter, clients were scheduled for review every four weeks. Special treatment meetings were called as necessary.

On the residential unit, the team social worker obtained information regarding the physical and social support systems from the client during the first two weeks following admission to the program. A standardized social history and a modified version of the Environmental Deprivation Scale (EDS; Rehabilitation Research Foundation, 1977) along with referral information were primary sources of this information. The EDS was particularly useful in providing a great deal of information regarding *social* supports which is not obtained from other sources. If it was determined that the client had insufficient funds or no family to live with in the community upon discharge, application was made for supplementary sources of income.

The social work assessment was also accomplished by the end of two weeks on day treatment. The focus of this assessment, however, was on the extent and nature of existing community support systems. This included the client's knowledge and use of community resources and whether the client had a network of social supports (such as friends, relatives, church group). This information was used in formulating treatment plans.

The case managers completed a battery of initial assessments, including the modular assessments as described in Chapter 4 and a set of behavioral/psychosocial rating scales to be described more fully in Chapter 9. The modular assessments were used by the team to assign clients to specific modules. The behavioral/psychosocial rating scales included the Community Adjustment Potential Scale (Hogarty & Ulrich, 1972), the Nurse's Observation Scale for Inpatient Evaluation (Honigfeld, Gillis, & Klett, 1966), and the Social Adjustment Behavior Rating Scale (Aumack, 1962). They provided general information to the team as to a client's status. However, these latter instruments were used primarily for validation of the modular assessments (cf. Chapter 9) and program evaluation (cf. Chapter 10).

All of the staff observed the client during the initial two-week period, carefully documenting any behaviors which interfered with participation in the program or which could otherwise have caused problems. It was here that the BAF described in the preceding chapter was first put to use.

There were two types of treatment meetings on the residential unit. The first meeting, called the medication review, had as its purpose the review of the medical status of the client and the prescription or adjustment of medical treatments. The second meeting, called the treatment meeting, had as its purpose the review of the entire treatment plan of the client, including modular treatments, single case treatment, and the implications of the client's medical status and treatments. Progress and planning toward discharge were also reviewed. The reason for separating the treatment meeting and the medication review meetings was efficiency. Many elderly clients had one chronic illness or more of a variety of types, and complex medical discussions were required to deal with these problems. Although required for total treatment, such complexities went beyond the needs of the general treatment team. A summary of medical issues and the behavioral implications presented by a nurse was usually sufficient for the more general meeting. This two-meeting procedure also reduced the time the physician spent in meetings, and he did not usually participate in the implementation of behavioral treatments. However, the team did specifically request the presence of the physician on occasion.

During the medication review, the team physician presented briefly the client's background, reason for admission, current diagnoses and physical limitations, and current medications. The expected behavioral effects of these medications were also explained. As was noted in Chapter 4, the interface between the behavioral and pharmaceutical treatments was given considerable attention. Any particular behavioral difficulties which had been observed were discussed for possible pharmacological treatments. If a medication was prescribed or dosage altered to assist in achieving a behavioral change, the targeted behavior was recorded with the order. In some cases, decisions to prescribe medications to assist in behavior changes were delayed pending review by and additional information from the treatment team.

The second type of meeting, the treatment meeting, was attended by the entire team with the exception that the attendance of the physician was optional. In practice, the physician was most often represented by a nurse familiar with the client's medical condition. This meeting was held in later afternoon so that both the evening and the day case manager could attend. A case manager was responsible for presenting the current treatment plan for the client along with other information obtained from a variety of sources and observations. Modular assessments and information from behavioral analysis forms (BAF) were presented if they existed. Each team member who had had contact with the client also gave pertinent observations, including family contacts, placement-related information, current medications and health status, attendance at modules, and the like. The integrating factor of the team meeting, the element which allowed the team to work well together, was the empirical basis of the program. Usually there were sufficient data available to establish whether a presumed problem was really a problem, as well as whether specific environmental variables were related to (caused) the behavior. If sufficient data were not available, discussion was focused on what data were needed and how they could be obtained. The data-gathering assignments would be made and another meeting scheduled for several days hence to present the data and conclude the treatment plan. It is important to note that the meeting would be deferred to obtain data rather then concluded with incomplete data and a treatment plan which was *not* empirically based.

In day treatment, only the general treatment meeting was held because medical treatments of the client were not a team responsibility except in emergencies. This treatment meeting was similar to the one on the residential unit with the exception that discussions of community resources were much more frequent and immediately relevant to client treatment.

Clearly, a major responsibility of the treatment team was to develop and monitor comprehensive treatment plans. Indeed, that process will be the content of most of this chapter. An ancillary but equally important responsibility was that of identifying individual behaviors that required treatment.

Much of this book deals with the technology of changing human behavior. This technology concerns itself with the operations necessary to achieve specified behavioral results. The technology is exclusive of ethical considerations; its application is not. Those who decide what behaviors should be changed are making ethical decisions between the demands of the institution or society for conformity on the one hand and the right of the client to independence, personal freedom, and individuality on the other (Hersen, Eisler, & Miller, 1980). A function of the treatment team would be ethical arbiter, to make decisions about the desirability or undesirability of changing a behavior. Sensitive to this responsibility, the team established guidelines for making decisions. In order for a behavior to be targeted for change, one of the following conditions had to apply:

1. The behavior interfered with participation in the program.
2. The behavior interfered with placement in the least restrictive community setting.
3. The client requested treatment to acquire or extinguish the behavior.
4. The acquisition/elimination of the behavior would enhance the client's opportunities for enjoyment of life or optimize post-treatment adjustment.

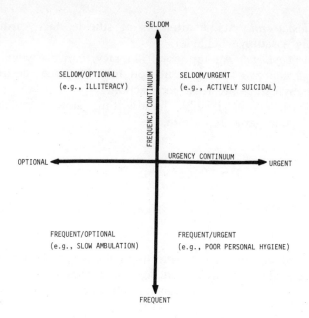

FIGURE 2. The classification of behaviors treated in the Gerontology Program.

Behavior which met one of these conditions was called problematic. Behavior which was inconsistent with all the conditions was not considered problematic.

As shown in Figure 2, behaviors relevant for treatment may be defined by dual continua, one representing the urgency of the problem and the other, the frequency of the problem in a population. The rapidity of action, expense, and effort directed to a problem are functions of its placement on this figure.

The modules were created for the behaviors which occurred with considerable frequency in our population. They have some urgency since they contribute to the quality of extrainstitutional life. However, they are not so urgent as to be immediately life-threatening or in other ways destructive. Behaviors which occur toward the low frequency end of the one continuum were usually treated by special SCBT methods developed at special, nonscheduled treatment team meetings. If the behavior was so severe as to require medical care or a more secure setting than could be provided by the unit, the client was transferred to an appropriate facility.

Examples of behaviors and medical conditions that could be placed in different quadrants in the figure are:

- *Seldom/urgent:* Active attempts at suicide, tachycardia, physically assaultive behavior.
- *Seldom/optional:* Agoraphobia, illiteracy, varicose veins
- *Frequent/urgent:* poor orientation to self, place, or time; poor personal hygiene, fecal compaction
- *Frequent/optional:* Illegible handwriting, slow ambulation, limited table game repertoire.

THE TREATMENT PROGRAM

TYPES OF TREATMENT

Modular and Single Case

Given the background for selecting behaviors to be treated, let us now consider those behaviors chosen for treatment. As discussed in Chapter 4, several areas of behavior deficits frequently found in institutionalized elderly have been identified as possibly jeopardizing community adjustment; training modules were developed which addressed these areas.

Briefly, these basic modules included training in personal hygiene, housekeeping, use of community resources and organizations, communication skills, self-esteem, and orientation to self, time and space. All clients who entered the program were assessed in order to determine which training modules were appropriate for each person.

Whenever confronted with a problematic behavior or behavioral deficit that could not be remedied by the modular training, individualized treatments (SCBT) were required. As Chapter 5 described, observations of behavior which fell within the purview of treatment guidelines but outside of modules were recorded on the BAF. After several day's accumulation of instances of the behavior (if it was not a rapidly escalating or dangerous behavior), the treatment team met to examine the data regarding frequency, rate, duration, time, location, antecedents, and consequences of the behavior. The team then designed an SCBT plan tailored to fit the exact parameters of the problem being displayed. At times the SCBT had as a target the elimination of a behavior judged to be detrimental. In other instances, the staff sometimes noticed a behavioral deficit, such as failure to generalize from a training module, and that became the focus of a treatment plan.

The Token Economy and the Milieu

The token reinforcement system used in our program was not a comprehensive token economy. Only a few privileges, no necessities, and some luxuries were available by token purchase. In exchange for attending and participating in the module (the primary method of obtaining tokens), clients could purchase coffee or tea at morning and afternoon breaks and purchase access to the cafeteria where they had a variety of foods to choose from. If they stayed on the unit, they could not exercise this choice because the cafeteria selected a tray of food and sent it over to the unit. There were also token stores on both units which were stocked with toilet articles, donated clothing, and occasionally items purchased specifically as reinforcers following a behavioral treatment plan request.

A very important element in the success of the program was the sophistication and high level of skill of the direct care staff. They received a 30-hour course (3 hours per week for 10 weeks) in behavioral techniques soon after they began working in the Gerontology Program. (All professional and managerial staff were given a shortened 10-hour version of this program before the direct care staff.) This course, which qualified for 4 hours of undergraduate credit at the University of South Florida, covered the basic theory and practice of behavior modification. As a result of such training, staff members rarely reacted inappropriately to undesirable behavior. The staff learned to dispense tokens and praise for appropriate behavior with professional timing and judgment. Training in what, when, and how to reinforce or extinguish client behavior made the development of SCBT plans much less frequent than might have been the case. Emerging problematic behaviors were not reinforced and more desirable, possibly competing behaviors were reinforced. When it was necessary for the team to deal with idiosyncratic or emergent problems, they were able to develop the treatment plan using behavioral language, knowing that they would be understood by the direct care staff. The case manager who presented the client's problem to the treatment team often had a workable suggestion as to how to treat the behavior.

Some standard approaches were derived from case managers' observing very similar treatment plans for similar behaviors; these observations made it possible for some SCBT plans to be developed and carried out all the way through resolution without going through the treatment team. For example, the standard approach to incontinence was restitution. All staff were aware that clients who soiled themselves were required to restore themselves and the environment to a clean state including washing, drying, and putting away the clothes and/or bed linens involved, mopping the floor, and cleaning the furniture.

The total environment of the units became, in the terminology developed by Patterson and Jackson (1980a), a therapeutic environment, that is, an environment in which the staff were engaged not only in life support functions (such as a typical nursing home or any general hospital) but also in continuous interaction with the clients in a manner to increase the likelihood of the occurrence of socially appropriate, independent behavior. Thus, the clients were exposed to far more training than the modules and the formally sanctioned SCBT interventions provided.

In addition to a highly trained staff, we had the good fortune to have been housed in a relatively new (1974), clean, spacious, and attractive physical setting. The food provided in the cafeteria was attractive, quite palatable, and varied, offering a daily choice of several salads, desserts, drinks, main dishes, and vegetables. These features were reinforcers for the clients to maintain their participation in the program.

Pharmacological Behavioral Treatment

A common dilemma in a behaviorally oriented treatment facility is whether to provide pharmacological treatment for behavior frequently labeled psychotic or to attempt to manage purely by the manipulation of antecedents and consequences. Of course, it is impossible to deliver pure pharmacological treatment unaffected by the environment in which it is administered. A wide, changing spectrum of antecedents is being presented continuously. Direct care staff are constantly strengthening or weakening behavior each time they interact or choose not to interact with a client following a circumscribed behavior. They choose to reprimand or ignore the client who is engaging in bizarre behavior, to help or not to help the client struggling to open a door, or to console or ignore a client who is crying or complaining about inconsequential matters. Staff members may make the wrong choices in such situations and reinforce bizarre, helpless, or complaining behavior. They then tend, over time, to become themselves discriminative stimuli for these types of behavior. The imperative question is not whether staff members are changing behavior but whether they are doing so in a direction consistent with the goals of the program and the treatment plan for the client.

When one chooses to treat a behavior pharmacologically, it is essential to do so in a setting which offers consistent control of the environmental antecedents and consequences in order to assess the effects of the chemical independently of environmental conditions. Otherwise, attempts by physicians to observe the sometimes subtle effects of biochemical agents on emotional or cognitive states are confounded inevitably by environmental influences.

The team believed that both behavioral procedures and medications were effective change agents. Therefore, the preference was to use a blend of the two in ways such that they would support each other. For example, procedures were devised on how to give an emergency injection for agitation without simultaneously reinforcing the agitated behavior. The team developed treatments of preference depending on which conditions were presented. The list to treat initially through behavioral procedures alone included obesity, insomnia, constipation, and mildly elevated blood sugar. Conditions which were initially treated both behaviorally and biochemically with gradual withdrawal of the biochemical agent, if that was possible, included high blood pressure (due to overweight, tension, or elevated sodium intake), unremitting insomnia, and agitation. Four types of behavior for which the preferred treatment was permanent biochemical-behavioral management were mood disorders, hallucinations, delusions, and assaultiveness.

To prevent confounding biochemical and behavioral treatment, the team preferred that the clients gain control of problem behaviors without the use of drugs when this could be accomplished practically and ethically. For this reason, except in an urgent situation, a biochemical treatment was never begun simultaneously with a behavioral treatment. A major concern was that if the two treatments were begun at the same time, knowledge as to whether the biochemical treatment was necessary would be difficult to gain.

If it was decided to treat a behavior biochemically and the biochemical treatment failed, SCBT were not initiated until the drug's half-life (the time needed for approximately one-half of the dose administered to become inactive) was past. During medication review the team physician set a time limit at the end of which he would review any changes in a targeted behavior. Data were collected on the frequency or duration of the behavior for presentation at the medication review meetings. On the basis of these data, the team physician determined whether further trials using medications were warranted. The following is a case example of this procedure:

Agnes had a long-standing, well-developed habit of rolling her tongue around in her mouth and protruding it once per second (diagnosed as tardive dyskinesia). After several months of attempting to control this grotesque behavior via biochemical means without success, the team decided to attempt to gain control behaviorally. This procedure was partially successful in that the rate of tongue rolling was reduced to four or five per 10 seconds (one half of the original rate), the intensity and magnitude of the movement were greatly reduced, and tongue protrusions had virtually ceased. When fitted with dentures, however, the continuation of tongue movement was manifest through the clicking of the dentures. Because of this noise, Agnes refused to wear the dentures.

When it was decided that a behavioral approach would be attempted before a biochemical solution was sought, the team physician avoided changing the client's medication unless absolutely essential in order not to confound the results of the behavioral treatment. For example:

Edna has spent eight years in a state hospital after breaking her leg. Initially she had gone into the hospital for medical treatment, and there was no documentation in her record about why she remained hospitalized for so many years or why she was on psychotropic medication. She had a movement disorder of chomping her jaw as if chewing a large object at a rate of 12 times per 10 seconds. Speculation that this might be exacerbated by her current moderate psychotropic dosage led to the gradual reduction and elimination of the medicine over a period of several months. Because this did not reduce her chewing behavior, a behavioral treatment plan was developed. Several weeks later, Edna developed severe delusional behavior. Despite the progress the behavioral treatment was demonstrating, psychotropic medication had to be reinstated. Thus, it was necessary to return to baseline and begin behavioral treatment all over again after she was restabilized on the medication. The work on the mouth movements was a preparation for dentures. The team had previously treated Agnes (see prior example) and obtained dentures for her which she had refused to wear.

Therefore it was decided not to risk such a refusal in Edna, and her jaw movement was treated preparatory to obtaining dentures. As with the tardive dyskinesia treated in Agnes, the rate of the chewing behavior was reduced to approximately one half of its original rate and the mouth movements became much less vigorous. She then obtained dentures and the mouth movements were almost unnoticeable. In Edna's case, the dentures helped reduce the magnitude of her jaw movements.

Because the program specialized in the elderly, a high incidence of physical illness was always present. For this reason, the team physician was a general practitioner rather than a psychiatrist. However, he had had many years of experience in observing the effectiveness of psychotropic medication with the elderly, and he had ready access to a staff of psychiatrists for consultation as needed.

The physical status of a great number of clients was debilitated. Many were heavy smokers, some of whom had developed chronic obstructive pulmonary disease. Obesity was also common, as were elevated blood sugar levels and elevated blood pressure. Complaints of constipation and diarrhea were very frequent. Many of our clients (22%) had a recent history of active alcohol abuse, and many suffered from chronic malnutrition. Almost all clients had dental impairment and dermatological disorders. Few exhibited even low-level regular exercise habits.

Because so many of these problems were appropriate for treatment using techniques of behavioral medicine, there was a significant effort to reeducate our clients who needed such training regarding the importance of diet, personal hygiene, exercise, and moderation in the use of drugs such as alcohol, nicotine, and caffeine. All clients were asked to attend 30 minutes of stretching exercises each morning. Tokens and praise were routinely administered for this activity. Those residents able to do so were reinforced for taking a walk in the evening. Clients on special diets (high fiber, low sodium, low calorie, or soft) were also taught why they were on a diet and how to recognize the food items they needed to maintain their diets in restaurants and at home.

Some of the clients who were known alcohol abusers and who met criteria for admission were referred to and attended an adjacent alcohol program. Although smoking was discouraged by restricting smoking times and by restricting locations (not in the bedrooms, bathrooms, or classrooms), rarely did the treatment team intervene in this behavior.

Clients who were expected to remain on medications were considered for independent placement when their performance on unit demonstrated that they had the ability, and the desire, to medicate themselves reliably. Medication training was employed to provide ongoing assessment of the clients' desire and ability to do so. It also provided ongoing training to maximize the clients' performance. A client was regarded as proficient in this area when the desire to administer his own medications was coupled with successful performance in taking medication as prescribed by the doctor and outlined on an index card. In addition, clients were told the purpose of each medication and received training on how to get prescriptions filled, how to obtain new prescriptions, and how to pay for them or get them free of charge.

INTEGRATING MECHANISMS

Three recording systems were used to communicate accurately on a daily basis the diverse and multiple treatments and client performance. Of course the treatment team itself was the major integrating mechanism, but it relied on data collected and transmitted by the following recording systems.

The Problem-oriented Record

A particular variety of the problem-oriented record (POR) developed by Weed (1970) has been in use by the Gerontology Program since its inception. In record systems which do not use POR, notes are entered in a client chart chronologically, by date and time. If one were interested in obtaining information regarding a client's progress in occupational therapy, for example, it would be necessary to peruse the entire chart and pick out the notes recorded after each occupational therapy session made by the occupational therapist. The original POR system required the development of a list of all problems, each of which was assigned a code number. All subsequent notes were referred to by the problem number to which they were related, making it possible to track all notes related to specific problems. In the POR system as used in our program, there was an initial problem list which defined an area for which treatment was to be given as in the original system. However, the system used by the Gerontology Program made tracking even easier by assigning each problem a discrete section in the chart, where all notes relevant to that problem and its treatment were entered with the date and the initials of the writer. In effect, the problem list was a table of contents for the treatment part of the chart and each discrete problem/treatment section was a chapter.

The POR system was a useful charting method for reasons other than organization of the chart. It prescribed a particular format for each progress note. Weed's (1970) original system required that for each problem there be recorded an S, the subjective report of the patient, an O, the objective observations of the problem, an A, the assessment or diagnosis of the problem, a P, the treatment plan prescribed, and an E, the education of the patient regarding the plan. The Gerontology Program developed a simplified version of "SOAPE" for writing notes pertaining to modules and SCBT treatment. It was a format of evidence, assessment, and plan (EAP) which fitted in well with a behavioral/modular approach. The evidence for a problem was an observed inability on the part of the client or observed problem behavior, the assessment was a modular assessment or evidence from a BAF, and the plan was to enter the client in the appropriate module or to develop an SCBT plan. For example, on a distinctly colored sheet of paper (to separate the lead sheets from the note which followed them) the following might be written:[1]

> *Problem*   Activities of Daily Living I deficit.
> *Evidence*   Client's hair and nails appear poorly groomed. Client has pronounced halitosis and offensive body odor.
> *Assessment*   Client scored 6/10 on the ADL I assessment.
> *Plan*   Enter client into ADL I training.

In addition to the problem list and the EAP format, the POR chart included the initial evaluation, treatment plan, progress notes, and termination note found in the conventional chart.

The Daily Observation Sheet

The daily observation sheet (DOS) was the major scheduling device for the individual client. The degree of individualization within the program made it necessary for each client to have his own schedule for each day. Each client had daily prescriptions and data recordings for any or all of the following: attendance at specific modules, specific accomplishments within modules, the nature of any SCBT plan, medical appointments, appointments with the social worker and others, tokens earned, tokens spent, and general observation by a variety of staff. Such a complex of information was not easy to keep track of. The DOS provided a single form to record many of these types of information, although it was deceptively simple in design. It was merely a sheet of paper with identification data at the top, and a few lines for special instructions, with the rest of the space divided into six columns. The first column indicated the time of day an event was to occur, the second column indicated the event, and the third column gave space for any special instructions relevant to the specific event. The fourth column was labeled "Observation" and was used for comments regarding the behaviors which actually occurred during scheduled periods. For example, the DOS might show that Mr. G. was scheduled for Communication at 10:30 A.M. He attended as ex-

---

[1]Due to different charting procedures of the medical staff, it was found to be expedient (though not ultimately desirable) to keep charting regarding medical orders and treatments in a separate section of the charts. The doctor and nurses used the original POR methods for these notes.

pected, volunteered to play a role, and earned a score of 30 points out of 42. For this he was paid six tokens. The next activity was lunch, after which he was scheduled for a short walk, and so on.

Having all this information on one form served multiple purposes. Perhaps the single most important key to its usefulness was the fact that it was completely *portable* and accompanied the client throughout the day. There was always someone responsible for observing and recording relevant activities in particular areas where clients were scheduled. This person always had the DOSs for those clients scheduled in that area. Therefore, the people observing any area always had immediately present a place to record behavioral information and token-system transactions. Furthermore, they always had immediate access to relevant brief instructions as written on the DOS.

It is true that much of the information regarding treatment plans was recorded in the charts and that the important behavioral observations also had to be recorded in the charts. Similarly, information about daily payments and expenditures of tokens was required to be recorded in a token balance book. Therefore, the DOS was duplicative. However, the importance of the DOS was in getting the information regarding treatment plans *from* the charts *to* the place where it was needed: the site of the treatment activity. The charts were too unwieldy to transport around all day, even if the leaders and observers of activities had time to read them on the spot. The DOS also served to make sure that the information got from the activity to the charts. Two major sources of information were routinely provided to the case managers for charting: (1) the DOSs for daily data and (2) the periodic module assessments. The DOSs were normally saved until the end of the week, at which time information from them was transferred to the charts, although significant events were charted as soon as possible. Token system recording was done daily to minimize problems of losses.

It is important to emphasize that the issue of communication to and from relevant staff was of special significance on the residential unit. There, the DOS served to overcome problems of communication *across shifts*, which is a difficulty encountered frequently in residential treatment operations. The case managers on each shift had assignments of specific clients, and they always received the DOSs for these clients upon reporting to duty. Thus, on all shifts they always had an up-to-one-hour, written report on the clients for whom they were responsible. In practice, the night shift filled out the scheduled activities for the day while the clients were sleeping. This started the whole process on a daily basis.

In addition to the fact that this information was provided to the *staff* by the DOS, much of the same information was also provided to the *clients* from this form. There was a daily morning review session in which case managers met with their clients and explained the schedule of the day. There was also a wrap-up session just prior to departure for day treatment clients and in the evening for the residential clients, in which all clients were informed of their accomplishments for the day and reminded of things they needed to continue to work on.

As can be seen from the above description of function, the DOS was a major communication tool and contributed greatly to a highly integrated treatment approach.

The BAF

The behavior analysis form (BAF) was the primary data collection device for emerging problematic behaviors. Whenever staff members observed a behavior which they judged to be possibly problematical, they recorded it in detail on the BAF. The BAFs were attached to the DOS and so followed the client through the day.

At each treatment team meeting held on a client, all the BAFs since the previous treatment team meeting were reviewed. These BAFs formed the basis for problem definition, often directed the treatment plan, and were used to track the client's response to any prior treatment plans. They were frequently useful to graph behavior based on the collected data.

A further function the BAF performed was to give the case manager who completed it an opportunity to analyze and examine his own handling of a client's problematical behavior. Thus, case managers who under "Consequences, Interpersonal Interaction," repeatedly found themselves writing "I argued with her" or "I told him to not do that" had an opportunity to improve their behavior management skills on their own without intervention from others.

DEVELOPING A TREATMENT PLAN

In order to gain information about treatment effectiveness, it was necessary to specify what constituted improvement. With few exceptions (outside strictly medical problems), improvement meant a change in the frequency of a behavior, either an increase or decrease, or the initiation of behaviors which had not been present in the client's behavioral repetoire. Thus, most data collection efforts were aimed at observing behaviors. These observations were different depending on whether the treatment was SCBT or modular training.

SCBT, Using Baseline Measures

Common diagnostic categories like depression or schizophrenia are not directly observable. They are a compilation of many observable behaviors such as crying, complaining, rarely smiling, and making statements about self-worthlessness. In order to verify treatment effectiveness, it is necessary to choose one or more of these behaviors as a target for change.

Several methods were used by the team to count behavior. Frequently a sampling procedure was used. Several 15-minute periods during the day were specified and a remote, unobtrusive observer was assigned to the person during those periods. The observations continued for the duration of treatment.

If the behavior to be targeted for change was relatively infrequent, occurring only occasionally during the day, then the treatment team relied on BAFs to determine the frequency of the behavior and the efficacy of treatment.

Once it was established that a client had a problem of frequency or severity sufficient to warrant attention, then a treatment plan was developed. Whether a problem needed treatment was a highly subjective determination, however. Zero incidence is the only acceptable rate of certain classes of behavior (assaultiveness, statements of intention to harm self or others, stealing, or wandering away from the facility, to name some of the most obvious). These are behaviors which severely jeopardize community living and are considered to be of the utmost urgency. It took only one incidence of these behaviors to warrant a treatment meeting and the development of a treatment plan.

For other behaviors, the tolerable rate or extent of problem varied widely:

Alice had been in a state hospital for 33 years before we admitted her. She had developed many eccentricities of dress and behavior which tended to make her highly visible when in public places such as restaurants and shopping malls. Her family and many clients objected to her accompanying them for these reasons. She was also extremely sensitive about her appearance and hostilely rejected any attempts to alter it. The treatment team collected a baseline description of her clothing ensembles in an attempt to define more precisely the high visibility features of her appearance. Samples of these ensembles included:

1. A pink, yellow, orange, and green floral headband, a light green wool V-necked jumper (no blouse), large hot pink purse, white anklets, navy blue sneakers, and a silver necklace.

2. Floral headband (same as in above example). Red, white, and blue blouse, gold wraparound skirt (open at one side where her white slip showed through), white anklets, navy blue sneakers, yellow dangle earrings, numerous bracelets and necklaces, and a large brown purse.

After collecting data describing her clothing for several days, the treatment team met to discuss the desirability of intervening. It was noted that attempts to praise more appropriate dress resulted in angry attacks by Alice. It was recommended that her family purchase a brightly colored ensemble (which she liked), including purse and jewelry, and offer to trade it for one which they particularly disliked. This ploy was successful and the strategy was to continue until her entire wardrobe was revamped.

The treatment team considered it tolerable for a client to complain to the nurse of physical problems other than emergencies once a day. Greater frequency than that began to be considered a problem. Missing one group a day was acceptable as long as it was not the same group each day.

Not infrequently during a treatment meeting, someone stated that they felt a given behavior was a problem for a particular client. Lacking any documentation, the staff were alerted to record all instances of that behavior. They often found that it occurred only infrequently. Thus, establishing a baseline not only allowed the team to determine the efficacy of treatment, but also to determine the need for treatment. In treatment programs that are not empirically based, treatment may be instigated upon impressions by staff members that a problem is more frequent or more severe than would be indicated by documentation if it were available. There were also times when one or two staff members became the discriminative stimuli for a deviant behavior. This resulted in their experiencing the behavior more frequently and thus seeing it as more of a problem than did the rest of the staff. Only the use of a recording device such as the BAF will accurately reveal the dimensions of behavior to allow accurate assessment of when, where, and to whom the behavior is a problem and what needs to be altered in order to reduce its frequency.

Using Standardized Assessments. As explained in Chapter 4, skills taught in modules were assessed before beginning training in each one. For the most part, these assessments were highly behavioral. In many instances, clients were asked to perform the skills to be taught. Some examples were: "Show me how you wash your hair" (ADL I); "What time is it?" (Personal Information Training); "Show me how to make a bed" (ADL II): "This person brought you hot soup when you were ill. How would you thank him?" (Communication Training); "Tell me some positive things about yourself" (Self-esteem). In the case of some modules, less direct methods of assessing response to treatment were chosen, such as the Life Satisfaction (Neugarten *et al.*, 1961) assessment in self-esteem training.

Regardless of whether the assessment was a behavioral one specifically designed for a particular module or was a generally used paper-and-pencil or rating scale, the issue remained the same. In order to document improvement, some measure of behavior before treatment was essential in order to show change toward some goal.

Determine the Type of Treatment

To speak of behavioral approaches to treatment as a unitary model is inaccurate (Hersen *et al.*, 1980, pp. 25–29). Wilson (1978) in his review of conceptual modules in behavior therapy identifies the following: applied behavior analysis, neobehaviorists' mediation S–R model, social learning theory, and cognitive behavior therapy. Although as a rule the treatment team relied on applied behavior analysis when developing treatment plans for isolated, undesirable behavior, other behavioral approaches have at times been used. Regardless of the behavioral approach chosen, the following criteria were applied to plans: (a) they had to be parsimonious, (b) generalization and maintenance had to be likely, (c) they had to have continuity and consistency, and (d) they had to be the least restrictive alternative. In detail, these criteria involve the following considerations.

Parsimony. The definition of parsimony relevant to the present discussion is that of economy in the use of means to an end. Expanding upon this meaning, the team strived for treatment plans which were simple, had the fewest elements necessary to achieve the goal, and worked as directly as possible on the target behavior.

An illustration of this concept is the example of Wanda:

> Wanda came to us after an extended hospitalization. She had many physical problems, including weakness as a result of remaining bedridden for weeks. She was accustomed to being pampered by staff. She complained about pains in her legs and unsteadiness when on her feet. Because of their concern about her ability to walk without falling, the direct care staff began to order food trays for her from the cafeteria. On one occasion, they even served her a meal in bed. The day after she received her meal in bed, she refused to go to the cafeteria at all, stating

that she preferred to eat on the unit. The treatment team met to discuss her that day. It was felt that this was a step toward returning to her earlier bedridden pattern. The treatment plan was: (a) no food trays were brought over from the cafeteria, (b) her token fee for attending the cafeteria was cancelled, and (c) the treatment team was to be notified if Wanda missed three meals in a row. She missed dinner that night, hurried over for breakfast early the next morning, and the problem was not observed again.

There were many alternatives to treating Wanda's refusal to walk to the cafeteria for meals. The staff could have ignored it and allowed her to eat by herself on the unit. They could have coaxed her, prompted her, or physically assisted her to the cafeteria. They could have ordered minimally palatable food trays from the cafeteria to be served on the unit or arranged for some highly reinforcing events for her in the cafeteria. However, they chose to let her go to the cafeteria for a normal diet and reinforce verbally all cafeteria attendance. This allowed Wanda to experience the natural consequence of refusing to eat: hunger. A primary advantage of the use of natural consequences as opposed to contrived consequences is that they are normally present in the environment. This should enhance the probability of generalization on discharge. Not infrequently with institutionalized clients, maladaptive behaviors, such as unwarranted dependency and physical retardation, may be iatrogenic in etiology. If so, the most parsimonious plan is to have the staff desist from reinforcing the undesired behavior. Not only was Wanda's refusal to eat treated directly and simply, but behavior management data which were likely to be highly useful to her eventual community placement were discovered.

A type of parsimonious treatment plan frequently used was to talk with a client about problematic behavior, why it was viewed as problematic, and what they could do instead. This was followed by having the entire staff make an effort to praise or thank the client for exhibiting the adaptive, replacement behavior (prompting it occasionally, if necessary) and ignoring the client when he or she was exhibiting the problematic behavior.

Maintenance and Generalization. For maintenance of many of the skills taught in our groups, we relied on what we assumed were inherent reinforcers. If clients became more skilled in accurate expression of feelings and thoughts, it was assumed that there would be more social reinforcers delivered from peers who were now able to enjoy socializing with them more fully. If they were able to reduce muscular tension, anxiety, or insomnia through the use of relaxation exercises, this should have reinforced the practice of these exercises. The direct care staff were also very alert to many behaviors which were considered adaptive and made an effort to reinforce clients for exhibiting them.

As we mentioned earlier in this chapter, failure to generalize and maintain improvements shown in training was cause for the development of a single case treatment plan by the treatment team. These issues were of special concern because we relinquished control of the client's behavior on discharge to his community placement, the stimulus complex where generalization was most desirable.

Opportunities to observe generalization of behavior to new stimuli did occur prior to discharge. Residential clients who chose to do so were taken weekly to a hairdresser and to a large shopping mall. Visits to the community, including picnics, trips to an ice cream store, fishing trips, and the like, were scheduled frequently. Residential clients also received visitors, which provided another opportunity to watch for generalization.

If generalization was observed not to occur, a description of the problematic behavior was taken to the treatment team for further consideration and treatment if indicated.

Irene had an 18-year history of repeated hospitalizations. She was extremely hostile when approached by staff to do anything. She was placed in the Communications Training group where she learned, among other things, to express anger appropriately. In ADL I, another group, she was asked to decline an offer of assistance in grooming as a role play. Instead of the type of appropriate response she had been taught in Communications Training, Irene yelled in a very nasty voice, "No, I don't want your goddamned help and don't bother me again." We astutely realized that there was a failure of generalization of Irene's appropriate angry behavior to the new (very similar) situation. As a result, the treatment team set up several individual practice and modeling sessions with Irene to attempt to increase the generalization of her newly acquired appropriate expressive skills.

If it was observed that clients interacted with their families or other visitors in an inappropriate manner, this too was reported to the treatment team. If these visitors or family were deemed to be an important variable in the client's postdischarge adjustment, we typically attempted to counsel the family in behavior management techniques which had already been established as successful with this particular client. Some of the most frequent and potentially destructive behavior patterns that families and friends were taught to manage included helplessness, complaining, enuresis, memory problems, negative attention-seeking, and dependency.

Continuity, Consistency, and the Least Restrictive Alternative. Some clients were found to be highly responsive to praise, others appeared to respond best when given a great deal of personal responsibility. On occasion, we had clients who were very responsive to authority and would do things only when told they must. Of course, each client's reinforcers had to be determined and utilized appropriately in order to motivate them to change.

Upon entrance into the program, initial exposure was always to the least restrictive approach. This approach consisted of describing what was expected in terms of unit rules and behavior. This was followed by prompting adherence to those rules and praising clients for behavior that we felt increased the probability of a successful community adjustment (such as adequate personal hygiene, adequate social skills, and increasingly competent and independent behavior).

If this least restrictive (in terms of personal freedom and dignity) approach did not result in, for example, regular bathing, we would attempt to identify some important reinforcers, other than meals or sleep, for the client and gain some control over one of them. Access to the reinforcer would be made contingent upon completion of the target behavior. For example, we might deny access to the cafeteria and limit meals to the unit until the client was acceptably clean. If the client continued to refuse to bathe, we offered him the choice of bathing himself or being assisted with bathing. When assistance was given, it was always in the form of graduated motor guidance. This meant that physical prompts were used to get the client to bathe himself, but only to the extent that these prompts were necessary.

It was rare that a client had to be physically assisted in bathing. In the event the client did need bathing, the staff member always used the least amount of assistance necessary to obtain completion of the target behavior. Occasional physical assistance was used only when the client would not initiate a bathing step with verbal and gestural prompts.

It was also rare for clients to exhibit serious aggressive behavior. There were few attempts at injuring others, with the aggressive behavior exhibited usually taking the form of loudness and/or threats to others. If aggressive behavior did occur, the client exhibiting the aggressive behavior would be immediately separated from the other clients by means of exclusion time-out. The client was allowed to rejoin the group when quiet for a period of time. Occasionally a medication was administered to assist the client in quieting down.

Also, the treatment team could convene at the first opportunity to review the client's aggressive acts and to provide an SCBT plan to deal with that client's specific aggressive behavior. If aggressive behavior occurred during the evenings or weekends when most of the treatment team members were absent from work, exclusion time-out with or without medication was a holding measure until such time as the treatment team would convene to form a more effective plan.

Unless aggressive behavior actually involved attempts to injure others, the least restrictive behavioral procedures were implemented before other more restrictive procedures were attempted. Least restrictive to most restrictive procedures were behavioral counseling, extinction (if appropriate), exclusion time-out, medication, and, on rare occasions, quiet training. If a client was determined to be a danger to either self or others, the client was appropriately transferred by legal action to a more secure program. A mechanism was in operation by which appropriate administrative personnel could be contacted on evenings or weekends to initiate such a transfer with little delay if it was necessary.

Coordination of Treatment

As with any residential treatment facility, ours had three shifts of staff plus weekend and holiday coverage. All staff were required to be aware of any ongoing single case treatment plans of any of 32 clients (usually 2–4 such plans were in effect on either unit at a time); thus, coordination was essential.

Across-Shift Coordination. During the treatment team meetings on both the units, the unit manager took notes which became part of the permanent record. These notes served several functions: they documented the fact that the team met to develop or update treatment plans, and they also served as a reference point for questions about client progress and as a vehicle for dissemination of the details of treatment plans to all shifts.

Treatment team meetings on the residential unit were deliberately held at a time when both day shift and evening shift personnel were available. Thus, the case managers from both of these shifts attended the treatment meeting. The day shift case manager was primarily responsible for seeing that treatment plans were properly conducted and for coordinating efforts among the staff on their shift. On day treatment, treatment meetings were held either before clients arrived or after they had left so that most staff could attend.

At the change of each shift, there was a brief meeting called "shift report." The case managers reported on the status of each of their clients. Information presented included new data from any source (such as visitors, laboratory reports, assessment scores, and new BAFs), any upcoming appointments, any successes or other positive events, and the details of any SCBT plans. Frequently, both when collecting baseline data and when carrying out treatment plans, it was necessary to assign staff to observe or interact with the client in a specified way. This was also accomplished at shift report; for example:

> Bill came to us from a state hospital. He had a 21-year history of manic-depression, uncontrolled by medication. When he was admitted to our program, he was at the peak of a manic cycle. Within a month, he began to deteriorate. He developed behavior which alternated hourly between stupor and bouts of assaultiveness and destructiveness. The treatment team put Bill on a DRO schedule requiring that small cubes of cheese (his elevated blood sugar level prohibited the use of candy) be given 4 times per hour contingent upon the occurrence of behavior other than throwing anything or tearing anything off the walls. Each cheese cube was accompanied by verbal praise. Within hours this behavior had greatly diminished, and it disappeared within a few days.

Such assignments were made at the beginning of each shift and usually covered an hour at a time. When it was necessary for all staff to interact in a highly standardized or structured manner, instructions were boldly written on the front of the DOS. Client responses to treatment plans were frequently reported at shift report, as were any modifications in the treatment plan.

In summary, treatment plans were disseminated through a written plan in the client's chart assigning the overall responsibility for coordinating the plan to one person, a verbal report at shift report meetings three times a day, and special intructions written on the DOS. In addition, a staff person was assigned to the client for specific observations or interactions on an hourly basis when this was required.

A meeting of all day treatment staff held at the beginning of the work day allowed for the verbal transmission of all such information as could occur in the shift report on the residential unit. Otherwise, day treatment used the same communication forms and methods as did the residential unit.

THE PROCESS OF DISCHARGE

Evaluation of the Client's Readiness for Discharge

There were three indexes used to ascertain the client's readiness for discharge. These may be grouped under the headings of program completion, resolution of referral problem, and behavior appropriate to the community placement of choice.

Program Completion. Clients completed the training program in one of two ways: by "graduating" or "plateauing." A client might enter all training modules and slowly but steadily progress through each, showing small increments of improvement on each monthly progress assessment. This would continue until the client graduated from all modules. More typically, clients would progress to a level higher than that at which they had begun, and in four to eight weeks their assessment scores would plateau and remain unchanged even with further training. In both instances, the modular training program was completed when further progress was not possible or not occurring. Assessment scores were used to indicate the skill level the client could probably achieve in community placement.

The essential determination was whether the client had received the maximum benefit from the program or whether continuation would result in further improvement in skills. Once it was judged that maximum skill development had occurred, the next steps toward discharge could proceed.

The type of modules the clients were able to complete and the level at which they reached a plateau provided valuable placement information. Since the components of the ADL series were designed to relate to different levels of placement, assessments of achievement in these modules were of particular value for placement. However, the scores were not followed to the exclusion of other evidence of abilities and available compensation for deficits. For example, completion of ADL III training was considered important for an independent living situation, but not absolutely essential.

> Wilma had cataracts, and although surgery had been performed, she was still very limited in visual acuity. She also exhibited some poor judgment and confusion. She did not perform well in ADL III. However, when allowed to return to her subsidized housing apartment for the weekend, she regularly showed up at the congregate meal facility and negotiated her way around the city without apparent danger. To support her poor memory, her medications were altered to a single nighttime dose, and each week her pills were placed in a pill dispenser marked with the days of the week. Her landlord agreed to check her pill dispenser once a week and refill it at that time. With these support services developed, the team agreed to discharge Wilma back to her independent community placement as she desired.

Information from activities on the units other than from modules was also used to plan discharge. The client's ability to medicate himself was an important piece of information. Obviously, if clients could not perform these activities for themselves, then the placement had to include someone who could. The resolution of SCBT problems also had to be achieved, in most cases, prior to discharge. If these could not be resolved, then a placement was required which could accept the presence of the problem behavior.

Resolution of Referral Problem. During the initial treatment meeting on each client, the team attempted to determine what behaviors the client was exhibiting in the community which led directly to his or her referral for treatment. Some major examples of these are assaultiveness, malnutrition, wandering the streets in confusion, talking to no discernible person, belligerence, staying in bed, running away, inappropriate sexual behavior, and inappropriate toilet behavior. Sometimes the behavioral difficulties the client was having while living in the community were stated on the referral. At other times, the nurse or the social worker would have to call the referral source (hospital staff, social agency, family, landlord, boarding home operation) in order to obtain a more specific description of the behavioral problem than that provided by the referral agency.

If the undesirable community behavior was not one explicitly addressed by a treatment module, the staff were alerted to complete BAFs for behaviors which resembled those which had precipitated referral. Behavior rehearsal was used to modify behaviors which did not normally occur on the unit; also, in some instances, staff were instructed deliberately to allow problem situations similar to those which had precipitated admission to develop and to record interactions around the target behavior on the BAF. The team would then meet when several instances of the behavior had occurred.

Helen came to the program from a hospital following a rash of friction-filled interactions with clients at the boarding home where she lived. She was a loner who rarely spoke to anyone, staff or clients, and never smiled. Her interactions with her three roommates grew increasingly hostile and suspicious. Instead of allowing her to change roommates, the staff completed BAFs on her complaints, her roommates' complaints, and all angry interchange overheard by staff. Instead of avoiding a roommate problem, the treatment team deliberately allowed one to develop in order to gain access to and treat the undesirable social behaviors.

Behavior Appropriate to the Community Placement of Choice. When considering the discharge of a client to the community, it is frequently advisable to match the eccentricities of the client to the tolerance of a given placement.

Some behavior is unacceptable in every community placement. This includes behavior discussed in more detail earlier in this chapter: assaultiveness, stealing, fire setting, starting false fire alarms, running away, destruction of property, enuresis, inappropriate sexual behavior, and grossly inappropriate eating behavior. Some tolerance can be found for such behavior as talking to people or objects not visible to others, poor grooming, sloppy eating habits, and belligerence. However, there are very few facilities which will accept such clients.

More subtle matchings occurred when a client who was affectionate and sociable was placed with a foster family which was affectionate and sociable. Or, in another instance, the team placed a socially isolated client in a large, impersonal boarding home which would make no demands on him for socialization.

When available, the family was always interviewed by a team member in order to gather background information on the client. If the client was going to live with the family, the psychologist frequently discussed with them the behavior they found most objectionable. She instructed the family members in behavior management skills. And she and the team developed an SCBT to attack the behavior to which the family objected while the client was still in residence at FMHI. It must be noted, however, that the majority of elderly clients did not have family or spouses with whom to live and that this lack of familial support may be considered as both a cause and a sequela of hospitalization among mental health clients.

PLACEMENT OF THE CLIENTS IN THE COMMUNITY

It must be emphasized at the outset of this section that the Gerontology Program, both by design and by lack of resources, included *no* clinical follow-up services of its own. Rather, all postdischarge services had to be provided by the social, health, and mental health facilities in the community where the client was to live. Discharge always included referrals to such agencies whenever required, and the client was informed of the benefits of such service prior to discharge.

It was not considered desirable to *design* the program to provide clinical follow-up because the residential unit was designed to model a program to be implemented in state hospitals; and state hospitals in Florida (and most other states) are neither staffed, funded, nor, very importantly *located* so as to be able to provide clinical follow-up. All state hospitals serve geographically large catchment areas poorly suited to allowing such follow-up. On the basis of the dissemination objective of FMHI, there would have been no purpose to our developing a system which could not have been implemented elsewhere.

With regard to resources, the residential unit faced the same issues as did the state hospital. Although we were located in a large metropolitan area, we served clients from all over the state; some were even placed out of state upon discharge. Resources to provide active clinical follow-up to such clients would have had to be great; and even if these were provided, there would have been the problem of our duplicating functions mandated to other agencies such as community mental health centers and aging services.

Reasons for not providing clinical follow-up in day treatment were similar to those for the residential unit. Again, we served clients from the catchment areas of three community mental health centers covering an extensive metropolitan area. A much richer staffing and travel budget would also have been required for day treatment to have done clinical follow-up.

With regard to the question of the day treatment program's being a model, the plan here was that the program as developed provided basic technology for treatment approaches useful with elderly mental health clients living in the community. These approaches could and probably should be employed not as an isolated service but rather within a broader context, such as that which would exist in a community mental health center and/or an agency on aging. These types of agencies would normally include a variety of clinical follow-up functions. Although FMHI did not provide such resources directly, they were available by means of referral to a variety of programs as was the case for the residential unit.

For residential clients, the team had the task of helping the client find a suitable place to live. The clinical social worker had the major responsibility for this function. In some cases, the clients themselves or their friends or relatives supplied appropriate living quarters. However, this occurred in the minority of cases (see Chapter 8 for detailed data regarding placements). In many cases, the clinical social worker had to apply for funds as well as apply through the local aging agency for housing for the individual.

The detailed information obtained by our program regarding the abilities, deficits, and peculiarities of the person referred made placement a much easier task for our own staff. It is worthy of noting that this same information also made the task of the referral agency much easier. Staff members from the local aging agency were often heard to comment about how enjoyable it was to work with referrals from our program, because of both the wealth of information available regarding the client as well as the considerable assistance and cooperation of our staff. Referrals to other agencies, such as community mental health, were also facilitated in a similar manner.

7

The Gerontology Evaluation System

David A. Eberly, Louis A. Penner,
and Roger L. Patterson

Introduction: Treatment and Evaluation
as an Integrated System

The foregoing chapters have described a treatment program and its component parts which are empirical in nature, that is, both individual treatment plans and intervention modalities are based on objective data on client conditions. Much of the effort and activity of the treatment staff is devoted to assessment of clients, measuring their performance, and observing and recording their behavior. These same data which have been collected for clinical purposes may also be used to evaluate treatment components and the Gerontology Program as a whole. This chapter describes how the evaluation system was developed by the staff and the rationale for the system, how the evaluation is done, and how it is an integral part of the overall treatment program. Chapters 8, 9, and 10 present the results of the evaluation. Chapter 8 provides basic descriptive data on the program clients, where they came from, how long they were in treatment, and where they went after discharge. Chapter 9 addresses the question of whether or not the modules worked. Were the clients actually learning the skills being taught? This question is answered by a series of experimental and quasi-experimental studies conducted on the modules. Whereas Chapter 9 evaluates the proximal or short-term goals of the program (namely client changes during treatment), Chapter 10 evaluates whether the program achieved its distal or long-term goals (the prevention of institutionalization and the deinstitutionalization of elderly clients) and whether the program materially effected the delivery of mental health services to the elderly of the State of Florida.

CLINICAL ACTIVITIES AND EVALUATION RESEARCH

The gerontology evaluation system (GES) was formulated on the premise that it was not sufficent merely to provide data on the program's efficacy, but rather that the data had to be of clinical relevance and be made available to the direct care staff for the purpose of improving the quality of the treatment that clients received. Most frequently program evaluation is viewed as a necessary evil, imposed upon the treatment staff by higher authority, and of little or no benefit to ongoing clinical activities or to client care (Kazdin, 1976; Weiss, 1972). To overcome these attitudes and for practical organizational matters, the evaulation system of the Gerontology Program was conceptualized from the onset as being an integral part of the treatment process. It was believed that there could be synergistic effect between the treatment process and the evaluation system; each might benefit from intimate involvement with the other. Clinical and operational requirements for data received equal priority with evaluation needs for policy decision making.

EVALUATION: CONCEPTUAL FRAMEWORK

The conceptual framework for the evaluation system was similar to that described by Kahn and Zarit (1974):

> The rationale of evaluation is twofold: first that it provides a scientifically rigorous method of determining the therapeutic efficacy, and secondly that these results can exercise a feedback into the system, modifying the clinical operations. Ideally such a system should lead to constant improvements in the area of care, reinforcing good programs and discouraging those programs which are poorer. (p. 223)

THE GOALS OF THE GERONTOLOGY EVALUATION SYSTEM: ANSWERING QUESTIONS

PROGRAM OPERATIONS: DESCRIPTIVE STATISTICS

The gerontology evaluation system was designed to address five basic evaluation questions. The first question was, how did the program operate? This question was concerned with the demographic characteristics of the clients served, what type of treatment they received, how long they stayed in the program, where they came from, where they went after treatment, and other descriptive data. This question did not address the effects of the program, but rather attempted to provide a comprehensive description of the clients served by the program and a description of the operation of the program. There were three reasons for being concerned with this. First, the Gerontology Program was conceived as a demonstration or pilot project which was to develop innovative treatment approaches for dissemination and implementation at other sites. Intelligent application of the program required that administrators of other programs be informed about the types of clients served, the treatment they received, how long the treatment lasted, and so forth. The second reason for the collection of these descriptive data was that they aided in the responsible and responsive management of the program. Finally, as a publicly funded program, from time to time we needed to provide summary reports on the program operation to higher administrative and legislative officials.

Basic Evaluation Questions

Although the descriptive data were valuable in their own right, they were also used as part of the overall evaluation of the effects of the program. This outcome or summative evaluation addressed four additional basic questions. First, were the modules effective in teaching the clients certain social and survival skills? Second, did the clients show changes in their general behavior over the course of treatment? Third, were the clients able to remain in the community after discharge? And finally, what was the relationship between changes during treatment (in both specific skills and general behavior) and postdischarge status?

In the language of program evaluation, the first two questions addressed short-term or proximate goals, the third question addressed ultimate or distal goals, and the final question concerned the relationship between the two types of goals (Weiss, 1972). In a phrase, these questions asked: Did the program work?

Social Validity

No attempt was made to assess the social validity of the program's ultimate goal: clients successfully living in a noninstitutional setting. Social validity was inherent in the goal, that is, the quality of life of an elderly person would be greater and the cost to society less if that person could be maintained in a noninstitutional community setting rather than a state hospital or nursing home. This statement of social validity may be considered a brash assumption, but the continuous push at both the federal and state levels for deinstitutionalization over the past 10 years lends credence to our statement about the social validity of this goal.

Impact

In addition to the specific evaluation goals mentioned above, we also sought to collect data on the impact of the program. Did the program change public policy? Had the program produced changes in the delivery of services to the elderly? And had the program contributed to the body of knowledge in gerontology? Although the GES was not designed to address these questions, the impact of the program is one dimension of evaluation and will be discussed in Chapter 10.

Clinical Feedback

In addition to creating a system which would provide meaningful answers to the above questions, the GES had a second, equally important goal. The sytem should provide feedback to the staff on the efficacy of treatment *and* provide the information which could be used in treatment plans. As Wiener (1950) established in his application of cybernetics to human behavior, effective behavior necessitates that "information concerning the results of . . . [the behavior] be furnished as part of the information on which to continue to act. This control on the basis of *actual* performance rather than *expected* performance is known as *feedback*" (p. 12). Further, in order for an organization to function effectively, its managers and staff members must receive feedback on the effects of the program operations (Katz & Kahn, 1978). If they do not, entropy will increase, "a universal law of nature in which all organizations move toward disorganization or death" (Katz & Kahn, 1978, p. 25). Therefore, a key element in the GES was the production of data which could be fed back to the direct service staff and be used to improve treatment and operations.

The Design of the GES: Theory and Practice

The design of the GES was greatly influenced by several practical and theoretical considerations. The following discussion of these considerations provides the background for the description of the GES design.

THE PRIMACY OF TREATMENT

In planning the GES, it was agreed that the collection of evaluation data would not interfere with the delivery of treatment to clients. The GES had to be built around the ongoing treatment program, and no client's treatment would be jeopardized by participation in the collection of data. The two basic reasons for this were professional ethics and program objectives. Clients admitted to the program were either in psychiatric treatment facilities or deemed to be at risk of institutionalization; they needed treatment and rehabilitation. On ethical grounds, treatment could not be deferred or withheld, nor could treatment be jeopardized or interfered with if it were to result in less than the best possible outcome for the client. Secondly, the program was to be a model, a pilot for future adaptation by others, and as such was required to demonstrate continuously a high level of service delivery. Although in some instances short-term experimental evaluations of some program components were conducted, in the main an experimental methodology with random assignment of clients to control and treatment conditions was not used by the GES as the basic mode of analysis.

EVALUATIVE RATHER THAN BASIC RESEARCH

Whereas the intent of basic research is to address theoretical issues, the goal for evaluation research is service and program application. Basic research is interested in testing some theoretical hypothesis; evaluation is interested in determining whether a program "works." The usual goal of basic research is to increase and modify the body of knowledge, and the manner in which such knowledge will be applied is not of immediate concern (Weiss, 1972). By contrast, the responsible evaluator fully expects that the evaluation will result in practical application. Although some basic research was conducted during the program, this was apart from the GES. Rather, the GES was directed at evaluative research with the primary objective to determine whether the program in actual operation really worked.

QUANTITATIVE RATHER THAN QUALITATIVE EVALUATION

There are a number of models or approaches to program evaluation. Some are based on subjective judgments of the quality of a program; others are based on empirical data. A brief review of several alternatives will explain why the GES was planned around an empirical data model.

Models of program evaluation can be examined along a continuum, with subjective, impressionistic judgments at one end of the continuum and empirical, experimentally derived inferences at the other end. At the subjective end an evaluator observes the program and reviews summaries of performance. The evaluator should be someone with expertise in the subject and should be looked upon as an acknowledged authority by those asking the questions. The evaluator then offers a subjective judgment as to program worth and merit. Although we rejected this approach as the basis of evaluating the program because of its subjective nature, we recognize the need to provide reports on program operation so that expert evaluators may submit recommendations to policy makers. It was believed that objective data produced by the GES could be summarized and, if necessary, presented to an external evaluator for consideration.

At about midpoint in the program evaluation continuum is the jurisprudence model of evaluation proposed by Levine (1978) and others. Here the evaluator presents conclusions about the program to a "jury of peers" in a manner analogous to court proceedings. The conclusions may be challenged by another evaluator and the jury may then present a "verdict." This design is based on the argument that over the years the Anglo-Saxon form of jurisprudence has shown itself to be a valid mechanism for arriving at some kinds of truth. Although appealing and again not requiring great resources and capabilities, this approach has two major shortcomings (Popham & Carlson, 1977). First, the advocacy trial technique often depends on the relative skill of the counselor (evaluator). Second, a program is seldom entirely innocent or entirely guilty, but rather a multivariate function with some excellent results, many modest accomplishments, and some failures. We rejected this evaluation design as a basic model but did recognize the importance and reality of the advocacy approach when concerned with impact on the service delivery system. This is particularly true when legislative bodies or state-level administrators must be persuaded of the worth of a program either for funding or for developing public policy. Therefore, as with subjective evaluations, the GES was designed to supply counselors/advocates/evaluators with the evidence they needed to contest opposing positions. However, the formal evaluation of the program did not rely on this model.

Another program evaluation model on the continuum is descriptive rather than truly evaluative (Stake, 1976; Stake & Easley, 1978). This approach, which is the traditional one of sociologists and anthropologists (Homans, 1950), provides a full "description of the program, its events, its effects, people's expectations, and their judgments of it" (Glass & Ellet, 1980, p. 215). There is much to recommend a descriptive design. For example, Gergen (1975) has proposed that certain descriptions of complex social phenomena may provide more faithful representations of these phenomena as they exist in the "real world" than would laboratory-based experimental investigations. Detailed program description is particularly valuable in the provision of feedback, in answering questions on process, in training other agency staff members, and in outcome evaluations which are based on comparisons with other programs. With regard to the final point, detailed descriptions can pinpoint the differences and similarities between programs which are being compared.

The basic problem with this approach is that the resources needed to implement it fully are considerable, a fact which is well recognized by sociologists and anthropologists. Having each staff member and client keep a detailed diary (not to mention training them in how to do so) was beyond the capabilities of the GES. Rather than compiling the exhaustive descriptive data required by this model, we sought to provide detailed summary data on the demographic characteristics of the clients, their pretreatment history, their behavior during treatment, and what happened to the clients for a 12-month period following discharge. These summary data provided a detailed description of the clients and the various treatment components and processes but did not describe all client and staff activities or nonstructured day-to-day occurrences and interactions.

Finally, at the opposite end of the evaluation continuum are the applied science models (Glass & Ellet, 1980). These models use the principles of scientific methodology (e.g., operational definitions, quantitative measurements, experimental/control comparisons, replication) and attempt to apply them to program evaluation. The design of the GES was most strongly influenced by this model and attempts were made to apply it whenever possible.

At the core of the applied science model is the issue of internal validity. A study is valid internally if the independent variable (or treatment modality) is the true and only cause of the observed effect on the dependent variable (client behavior) (Campbell & Stanley, 1963). Internal validity is the *sine qua non* in the investigation of any phenomenon. This is true whether the question of interest is conditioning a response in some lower organism or the efficacy of cognitive behavior modification in a treatment program for alcoholics. Just as a laboratory study which is not internally valid is worthless, program evaluation which lacks internal validity is also worthless.

In our view, an empirically based, scientifically rigorous methodology to determine if the program was reaching its proximal and distal goals was the most valid and useful evaluation technique. At the same time, in many cases the traditional experimental approach to the investigation of certain phenomena had to be modified as a compromise with operating an ongoing treatment program.

"Quasi" Rather Than True Experimentation

Several of the individual training modules were evaluated by means of true experimental designs, but a quasi-experimental approach was used to evaluate the overall program. *Quasi-experimentation* is a term coined by Campbell (Campbell & Stanley, 1963). It can be understood best by comparing it with traditional experimentation in which internal validity is achieved by using either random assignment of subjects to experimental and control conditions and/or the systematic administration of experimental and control conditions to the same set of subjects. These procedures provide the experimenter with control over the phenomena of interest. Control, in this context, refers to the ability to design an investigation such that alternative explanations of the results can reasonably be excluded from consideration (Cook & Campbell, 1979). For example, random assignment of subjects to groups may be used to control for the possibility that initial differences between the subjects could be responsible for differences in their behavior on the dependent measure. Quasi-experimentation strives for the same level of control (and thus internal validity) but does not rely on random assignment to conditions (or systematic manipulation of treatments) to achieve this end.

There were several reasons why a quasi-experimental approach was chosen for the evaluation of the Gerontology Program. First, as has already been discussed, the delivery of treatment to clients could not be disrupted. Treatment could not be withheld from clients for a prolonged period of time for the sole purpose of conducting a carefully controlled investigation of some program component.

Even if the laboratory paradigm could have been justified on programmatic and ethical grounds, there still would have been several arguments against its usage. There is some real question as to whether a laboratory investigation of complex behavioral phenomena represents the best means of understanding those phenomena. McGuire (1973) and Gergen (1975) have both argued that laboratory investigations may frequently distort the phenomena being studied by removing them from the context in which they normally occur. Therefore, the results, although internally valid, fail to provide a true approximation or representation of the phenomenon in the real world. Independent and dependent variables under experimental conditions may not be equivalent to treatment modalities and outcomes in an ongoing treatment program.

An alternative to the laboratory approach is the use of a control or comparison group to evaluate the immediate and long-term effects of the program. An example of this would involve the following procedure: A large group of elderly clients in need of treatment would be identified. Using random assignment, half of the clients would be placed in the Gerontology Program while the other half would be provided with the traditional custodial care form of treatment. The groups would be housed in facilities which, while separate, would be physically quite similar. The two groups would remain in the facilities for equivalent periods of time and would be released into the community simultaneously. Then the status of both groups after discharge would be determined.

Several practical, ethical, and methodological arguments can be made against this strategy. From a practical point of view, it would be impossible for us to identify a potential group of clients and randomly assign them to either a traditional treatment or the innovative program. The number of clients needed and the time and effort that would have been involved in the supervision of both groups would simply be beyond the capabilities of the program. From an ethical viewpoint, right to treatment and informed consent protocols conflict with random assignment.

Over and above these ethical and practical problems, there are some serious methodological weaknesses in this research strategy. Consider membership in the control group from the viewpoint of the client. He or she has been identified as someone in need of treatment but is told that the new, innovative treatment is either unavailable or will be delayed for some period of time. Cook and Campbell (1979) have suggested that such a procedure could have a serious impact on the behavior of the control group. More specifically, they proposed that withholding treatment could demoralize control group members and result in a decline in their level of functioning. This could produce a high rate of hospitalization for control group members. Differences between the two groups as to outcome might owe more to the effects of withholding treatment from one group than to the efficacy of the treatment provided to the other.

It is also possible that the control group may, in fact, receive considerable unplanned treatment. Cook and Campbell (1979) have argued that in some instances staff members feel obligated to compensate people assigned to a control group. This compensation takes the form of providing goods and services to control group members. In some instances these goods and services may approximate those being offered to the innovative treatment group. Cook and Campbell (1979) provided an example of this. In several evaluations of experimental educational programs for disadvantaged children (e.g., Head Start, Follow-Through), it was found that the supposed control or traditional treatment schools were, in fact, receiving considerable funds to compensate for the fact that they were not receiving the experimental program. Although this "compensatory equalization" is quite reasonable from a well-meaning administrator's point of view, it serves to invalidate the results of the evaluation.

Nathan and Lansky (1978) have suggested that because of these and other problems evaluation studies should compare different treatment procedures within the same facility. Such a procedure could provide adequate groups for comparison but would be expensive to implement.

The expense would result from the need to conduct two simultaneous programs in a manner such that clients in one program were not exposed to and thus "contaminated" by clients in another program. Even if total separation of the clients were possible, one would still have to control for differences in staff abilities and orientations between the two programs, since these differences rather than the content of the two programs might be responsible for any differences of the outcome measures. Ideally, control would be achieved by random assignment of staff to treatment programs. Also, as Nathan and Lansky (1978) point out, one would have to be sure that the amount and timing of the treatment the two groups received were equal. In Nathan and Lansky's view, these procedures are probably impossible to carry out. They recommend that, in lieu of comparing treatment programs in their entirety, one could evaluate the separate components of one treatment program. This was basically the approach adopted in the evaluation of the training modules in our program.

A quantitative, data-oriented approach was also taken in investigating the clients after discharge. That is, rather than relying on subjective impressions of the clients' level of functioning after discharge, we sought to examine the living situation of the clients and to administer validated measurements to determine client abilities and their level of functioning.

In summary, while the GES design was influenced by several

models of program evaluation, it was most strongly influenced by the applied science model. We sought to evaluate the program's effects by conducting statistical analyses of data generated by either experimental or quasi-experimental investigations of program components and program effects.

It should be noted that the GES did not attempt to assess the efficacy of the single case behavioral treatments which were used for individual client problems. To be sure, these interventions were an important part of the total treatment program. However, as Van Viervliet (1979) has noted, such interventions concern idiosyncratic problems and treatments and thus cannot be meaningfully combined for the purpose of program evaluation (these interventions are described in Chapter 5). It is acknowledged that these individualized treatments probably enabled certain clients to obtain optimum benefit from the modules.

Restriction and Limitations: Compromise with Reality

In addition to the issues of evaluation design, there were additional factors which exerted constraints on the system. These included: the equipment and funds available for evaluation, the personnel available, and the manner in which clients entered and left the program.

Resource Limitations

The Gerontology Program was quite restricted as to the amount of funds that could be used exclusively for evaluation efforts. No full-time research positions were funded, and there was no capital available for the acquisition of data-processing hardware or software. This latter problem was resolved by devising a data-processing system which was compatible with the computer facilities at the University of South Florida (which is adjacent to the Florida Mental Health Institute) and the Florida Department of Health and Rehabilitative Service's Data Center in Jacksonville. Data were entered into and returned from the latter system through a remote, interactive terminal at the Institute. Although the system was restricted to the program libraries and computer languages at these two locations, in practice this did not decrease the data storage and processing capabilities of the GES.

The lack of full-time evaluation or research positions was initially viewed as a major detriment to meaningful research; however, it developed into a blessing in disguise. Treatment staff had to be employed part of the time in data collection, reduction, and encoding. This involved all staff in evaluation and resulted in a research orientation toward program performance that could not have been achieved if the staffs for evaluation and treatment had been separate. The principle operating constraint was on the quantity of data that could be collected since all data collectors also had client treatment responsibilities. Here again what appeared to be an impediment turned out to be a benefit. Data could not be collected just for the sake of data collection, but rather a parsimonious approach was required because of limited staff time. This meant that the data collection system, individual experiments, and evaluation designs had to be planned in detail prior to recording data, administering instruments, or making observations. In practice, this led to directed evaluation research with purpose and meaning rather than *post hoc* analyses of data collected without designs.

The human resources available were not experienced, professional evaluation staff but rather the direct care project staff. In addition, the nature of the client population, the personnel system for state civil service positions, and the proximity of a university campus with alternative employment opportunities all contributed to a relatively high turnover rate among subprofessional and paraprofessional personnel. With the professional positions, a chronic shortage of nursing personnel in Florida resulted in a high turnover among registered nurses and LPNs. This meant that the GES had to be designed so that it could be operated and maintained by personnel with little or no evaluation experience and with no formal training in research techniques or methods. Various instruments and forms could be taught in a matter of hours and did not require prior professional training or experience. Here again this constraint turned out to be a benefit. Measurement techniques which required sophisticated clinical judgments could not be entered into the GES. Although the system might be faulted for not including these measurement techniques, the characteristics of our staff resulted in the formation of a system that utilized extremely simple instruments for data recording and encoding. As an additional benefit, the instruments could be utilized by agencies with staff who had little or no training in clinical research areas, program evaluation, or the use of computers. Of course, clinical judgments were included in the clients' individual records. Also, standardized clinical diagnostics (e.g., DSM II classifications at admission) were included in the data base used by the GES.

Just as the characteristics of the staff dictated the type of input data, they also dictated output from the system. One must remember that a basic objective of the GES was to provide feedback to the direct care staff. This feedback would be meaningless if it could not be understood and used by the staff members in their interactions with the clients. The simplicity of the input data was complemented by the simplicity of the output data. In practice, this created the feedback mechanism that the GES sought to provide. By keeping the output from the system simple, we were able to make the utility of the system clear to the staff and, perhaps more important, provide data which was useful clinically.

An Ongoing Treatment Program

The final constraint on the design and operation of the system was due to the realities of operating an ongoing treatment program. The program was required to provide services to elderly clients on a continuing basis. Further, the state mandated that the program maintain its client population at or near capacity. This meant the clients were admitted to the program as soon as there was space available, and this generated a sporadic, nonuniform admission rate. At the discharge end, professional and ethical standards dictated that clients be discharged when they would no longer benefit from the program and could be placed in less restrictive living situations. In addition, all clients voluntarily participated in the program (human research subjects, informed consent) and could exercise their right to leave the program whenever they desired. This produced considerable variability among the clients in terms of length of stay. Since by design the clients progressed at their own rate through the training modules and only received training in those areas in which they showed skill deficits, qualitative differences were introduced in treatment as well as quantitative differences. These differences between clients would have made comparisons between groups of clients difficult to interpret. Within each group there would have been clients who entered the program at different times, had different module training experiences, and had been under treatment for varying lengths of time. These differences among clients within each group also would have existed between the groups. It would have been fallacious to assume that length of time in treatment, amount of prior training in other modules, and length of time in a particular module would have had no impact on a client's performance in that module.

One solution to this problem of comparison between groups of clients would have been to compare cohorts of clients, groups of clients who entered the program at the same time (e.g., the same week or month) and who were given the same type of treatment. Although this procedure would have solved the problems of differences in length of stay and differences in treatment, it had two major deficiencies. First, it would have reduced the numbers of clients available for any comparison (admissions averaged about six clients a month for both residential and day treatment units); and second, it would have violated our principle of developing individual treatment plans based upon each client's particular behavioral deficits (or excesses). The smaller number of clients in each cohort would have reduced substantially the power of the statistical analyses to the point at which inferences could not have been made about the actual treatment effects of the program. With elderly persons there is considerable variability in health, behavioral repertoire, cognitive function, and social environment, far more so than is found in the adult population as a whole. This between-subject variance has the effect of reducing the sensitivity of the statistics to treatment effects. In the absence of covariate or "blocking" techniques, it is necessary to use large sample size. The dilemma is obvious: to have groups of subjects large enough to obtain significant results, a large variance among subjects in terms of prior conditioning, learning, or maturation must be accepted.

The solution to the design dilemma was to form cohorts or treatment groups according to the length of time in treatment rather than by calendar dates. For example, measurements could be taken on all clients (or subjects) after each had been in treatment for four weeks, under the assumption that the most critical independent variable was the length of stay in the program. Of course, collapsing across subjects by time in treatment assumes that there were no significant changes in program variables during the total calendar period when clients were in treatment. As is described in Chapter 9, the validity of this assumption was tested and proved to be valid as related to the programmatic variables being examined.

Another problem which had to be considered was that the program had to provide simultaneous treatment to two different populations in two different situations: a hospital population in a 24-hour 7-days-a-week residential unit and a community living population in a 6-hour, 5-days-a-week treatment unit. Resource limitations prevented separate programming, treatment, or evaluation of these two different groups. Therefore, we had to treat these two groups as the same but also had to identify them so that comparisons could be made between residential and day treatment clients, recognizing that there might be significant differences in the populations, the treatment effects, and, of course, in postdischarge outcomes.

Design Specifications: A Summary

Having determined the purposes and objectives of the GES and having recognized the real constraints and the available capabilities, we were able to specify the characteristics of a feasible system. These characteristics were grouped according to three broad questions: (1) what data shall be collected on clients, (2) how will the system be operated, and (3) how will the data be managed? The specifications are listed below as answers to each of these questions.

Client Data Collection

Data on clients should be collected along three axes simultaneously, that is, a time dimension, a treatment modality or intervention dimension, and client demographics. This specified that data must be acquired on clients: (1) prior to treatment, (2) at admission, (3) during treatment, (4) after treatment. For each planned or programmed modality or intervention, there had to be a measurement prior to, during, and after treatment, and these measurements had to be amendable to aggregation, summation, or tabulation across clients and across time in treatment. Collapsing the data across clients enabled us to have a sufficiently large sample to provide a base for inferential statistics, and collapsing across time enabled us to make assumptions about the effects of maturation or history.

For example, we could collapse the intake assessments on clients admitted during the first six months of the program and compare them with similar assessments during the last six months of the program, with a year's intervening time period between the two samples to determine whether the client population entering the program had changed over the two-year period during which clients had been admitted. We could also collapse across all first progress assessments after four weeks of training, for example on the ADL I module, and have a sufficiently large sample size to offset the high degree of variance normally found in an elderly population. And finally, we could collapse across client demographics such as age, sex, or county of residence to determine whether there were differential treatment results according to demographic variables.

System Operation

The realities of operating a treatment program with limited evaluation resources defined the operating requirements of the system. They were:

1. Data were to be collected by treatment staff.
2. Data were to have clinical value in order to motivate and involve the staff.
3. The quantity and frequency of data would not be so great as to conflict with treatment requirements.
4. Responsibility and authority for data collection were to be structured to ensure collection prior to treatment, periodically during treatment, and periodically after treatment.
5. Monitoring and control feedback loops were to be established to assure adherence to data collection schedules, since the heart of the statistical evaluation hinged on being able to collapse across *time in treatment.* (A missed assessment could not be collected 2 weeks later since the client might have received an additional 2 weeks' treatment and the data then could not be collapsed across all clients who had had, for example, 8 weeks of treatment.

These operating requirements established the formal organization to operate the GES.

Data Management

Here, again, the realities of limited resources together with the availability of great data-processing capability specified the data management requirements of the GES. They were:

1. The data management staff was to be minimal, probably limited to part-time graduate assistants.
2. All data processing would be done either with the HRS Data Center in Jacksonville via Remote Job Entry Terminal or with the University Data Center on the adjacent campus.
3. There would not be physical possession or retention by the Gerontology Program of data storage discs or tapes. These would remain at the data centers.
4. To ensure against loss of data, data card decks were to be retained by the Gerontology Program.
5. All data to be processed were to be punched on Hollerith cards with a master deck and working decks.
6. Data manipulation and analysis were to be limited to the programming available at the data centers.
7. System design and software development were to be limited to that which could be done by part-time graduate assistants under the guidance of the program directors.
8. Since the primary source of data is the client population, and

since it would not be possible at the outset to determine exactly what data would be collected on how many clients, the basic data set would be by client, using an individual client identifier as the file label.
9. Real time, on-line data processing and retrieval would not be possible; therefore, data would be batch-processed, the processing interval being a function of the amount of data collected and the assessment intervals.

In actual practice, none of the above requirements proved to be onerous and the capabilities of the two data centers were more than adequate to meet the needs of the GES.

System Description: Subsystems and Organization

Four Interdependent Subsystems

The Gerontology Evaluation System was composed of four interdependent subsystems: (1) intake, (2) progress, (3) follow-up, and (4) data processing. The first three subsystems were defined by client progress through the program; the fourth, the data processing subsystem, was the common bond in that it coded, stored, and processed all data collected by other subsystems. The four subsystems were interdependent in that there was a natural sequence of data flow between them and each was concerned with the same basic data set. Diagrammatically, the four major subsystems may be represented as shown in Figure 3. The two-way arrows between the data processing subsystem and the other three subsystems represent the feedback and the control and monitoring loops. The factors which made these subsystems separate entities rather than one system were that different staff members were involved in the data collection and supervision and that the time of data collection and batch processing varied. The data coding, processing, and storage subsystem was under the program and project directors, with staff involved in this subsystem reporting directly to the program directors. The intake subsystem actually consisted of two teams, one for the residential unit and the other for the day treatment unit, with the rehabilitation therapies program supervisor participating as a member of both teams. The progress subsystem consisted of both teams and the rehabilitation therapies program supervisor functioning as one organization, sharing responsibilities, but under the overall scheduling of the program supervisor. The follow-up subsystem consisted only of the day treatment team and the data processing group. The detailed organization

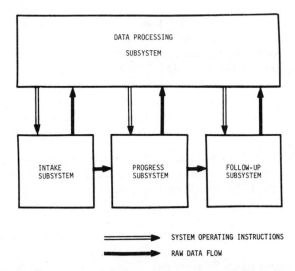

FIGURE 3. The four major subsystems of the Gerontology Evaluation System.

and operation of each of these subsystems, their interdependence, and the provision of the essential feedback loops are discussed in the following section.

THE DATA PROCESSING SUBSYSTEM

The data processing subsystem was the operational brain of the GES. As part of the program director's office, the broad functions of this subsystem were: (1) system development, design, and control, (2) system operation and scheduling, and (3) system records and archives. The function of system development, design, and control involved the design of the codebook for all data to be entered into computer storage, the issuance and document control of all instruments and forms, developing and disseminating all system procedures and standards, and the design of all programming and control routines necessary for access and utilization of the computer systems employed.

The subsystem operation and scheduling involved the maintenance of the client admission chronological logbook; the maintenance of the client assessment tickler file (a reminder of when progress or follow-up assessments should be conducted); the issuance of assessment requests; the collection, verification, and correction of data; the coding of data, the supervision of keypunch operations; the batch processing of data; and the preparation and publication of monthly, quarterly, and special reports.

The subsystem records and archival function involved the maintenance of a client file which included all of the original instruments used to assess the client (only summary scores were entered into the client's chart) and the social history interview form. All data collected on postdischarge follow-up interviews were also entered into these client files. It was possible, therefore, to return to the original data should there be a need either to verify information or to conduct some analysis on data that had not been entered into computer storage. This function also involved the maintenance of the basic data set on punched cards. Since we did not have direct control over the storage of information by the computer centers, that is, we did not retain physical possession of data tapes and data discs, it was possible that data might be lost by inadvertent erasure or program error. This did in fact happen more than once. Therefore, the data processing subsystem had to maintain the data set by keeping a punched card archive. In operation this meant that two cards were always punched; one for the working deck, and the other for the security archive deck.

The data processing subsystem employed three people, one full-time and two part-time. The full-time position was that of data collection coordinator (DCC), a position filled by a direct care staff member who wished to learn about evaluative research (four different people held this position during the two-year period of Phase II). The part-time positions were filled by graduate students. One graduate student, who worked approximately 25 hours a week, was responsible for the development of the code book and the computer entry routines. As the program progressed, he assumed responsibility for computer processing of all data and analyses. He also prepared the periodic and special reports. The other part-time position was filled by various graduate students, averaging 10 to 15 hours a week. The principle assignment was the coding of data for keypunching and the maintenance of the client research files.

The operation of the data processing subsystem was initiated when the data collection coordinator received notice of admission of a client. On the basis of this notification, the DCC would open a client file by assignment of a case number (the FMHI client number), enter a card in the tickler file, and issue an initial assessment request. The assessment request went to the appropriate unit manager, the clinical social worker in the residential project, and the social service worker in the day treatment project. The unit managers would assign the assessments to direct care staff, and the social workers would schedule interviews with the newly admitted clients. Upon completion of the assessments and interviews, the forms would be returned to the DCC. After translation to coding sheets, the raw data forms would be filed in the clients' research files.

It should be noted that the basic data set was organized by client, that is, both the raw data and the data punched on cards were stored under a client file number. This meant that whenever a client entered the program a new file had to be started. However, it also meant that as a client completed a program, was discharged, and completed follow-up, a file could be closed. Thus, the average length of stay plus the 12-month postdischarge follow-up established the number of active client files, about 120. If some other variable, say modules, had been used as the basic method for organizing the files, all files would have had to be kept open until the last client had completed the follow-up. Organization of the basic data set by client also permitted us at any time to summarize the performance, as well as demographic characteristics, of all the clients who had completed the program as of that date. By cross-reference of client numbers with admission and discharge dates, we were also able to group clients according to the length of time that they were in the program. As we pointed out earlier in this chapter, the capability of grouping clients into cohorts by time period is an essential requirement for the quasi-experimental design as employed to evaluate the program.

Either by attendance at the initial treatment team meeting, by conference with the rehabilitation therapies program supervisor, or by review of the treatment plan, the DCC learned which modules the client would be attending. At the end of the third week of modular training, the DCC issued a request for assessments of the client in the appropriate modules together with assessments of general behavior using the psychosocial instruments. This process was repeated in four-week cycles, progress assessments being requested at the end of the third, seventh, eleventh (and so forth) weeks of treatment. These progress assessment requests were directed to the appropriate direct care staff member. The DCC did in fact maintain the assessment schedule, making sure that clients were assessed at the proper time intervals in their training/treatment program. This permitted us to summarize data across clients, again an essential requirement to perform module and program evaluation.

The DCC was notified by the unit managers when a client was going to be discharged. Upon this notification, the DCC issued a discharge assessment request which followed the same administrative route as the initial assessment request. In practice, if a client had received a progress assessment within the two-week period prior to

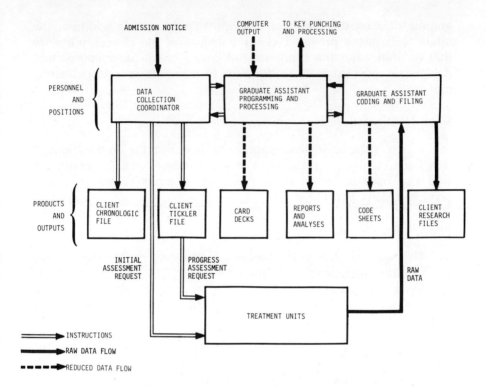

FIGURE 4. The operation of the data processing subsystem.

discharge, the last progress assessment was used as the discharge assessment. The last progress assessment was also used as the discharge assessment when the client's discharge could not be anticipated (for instance, voluntary withdrawal from the program or emergency hospitalization for physical health problems).

The operation of the data processing subsystem is schematically presented in Figure 4. This shows the flow of completed instruments back to the DCC. If the DCC did not receive the instruments as stipulated in the assessment request within one week, the appropriate unit manager or social worker was contacted to supply the missing data. In this manner, the timely flow of information was monitored and expedited.

THE INTAKE SYSTEM

From an evaluation viewpoint, the purpose of the intake subsystem was to capture data on the client's condition at the time of admission (as baseline) as well as to obtain historical and demographic data on the client for descriptive purposes. In addition, the intake subsystem provided client information for clinical purposes that did not enter the computerized data system. More specifically, data were collected on five different instruments or sets of instruments:

Social History Interview

This was the basic demographic and historical file on the client. It was filled out by the social worker based on the intake interview. It was also used to collect medical history in terms of mental health services received in the past.

Physical Examination

This was the start of the basic medical record on the client. Only the admitting diagnosis was entered in the GES. The results of the admitting physical as performed by the program physician and nurse were supplemented by laboratory reports and kept in the client's chart.

Module Assessments

During the first week following admission, the clients were assessed as to their skill level in the various modules, using the standard module assessment procedures and instruments. These assessments were performed by the direct care staff, who had been trained to conduct modular assessments.

Environmental Deprivation Scale

The instrument used to record the client's environmental support system was a modified form of the Environmental Deprivation Scale (EDS) (Rehabilitation Research Foundation, 1977). The scale was completed by the social worker on the basis of a behavioral interview conducted during the first week following admission. EDS scores were entered in the GES and the raw data were useful in the placement planning process.

Global Behavior/Psychosocial Rating Scales

These instruments were administered by direct care staff who were in the best position to evaluate clients' overall behavior, usually the case manager. They consisted of the NOSIE-30, the CAP, and the SABRS (refer to Chapter 9 for descriptions and references on these instruments) and were based on observations during the first week in treatment.

A copy of the social history interview form, the reports on the physical examination, and the scores on module assessments, EDS, and the global behavior ratings were entered into the client's chart. These became the data base for the initial treatment team meetings. The original of the social history interview form, the admission diagnosis, and the original instruments administered for module assessments, EDS, and the global scales were transmitted by the unit managers to the DCC. After coding, these became the initial documents in the client's research file.

Figure 5 schematically depicts the intake subsystem. It should be noted that all the data generated by this subsystem were not incorporated in the GES. Much of the data were used for clinical purposes only and were retained in the client chart on the treatment unit.

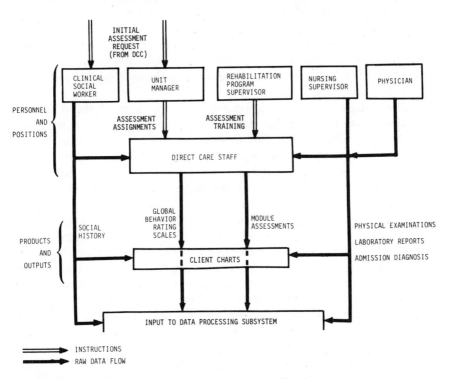

FIGURE 5. The operation of the intake subsystem.

The Progress Subsystem

The progress subsystem collected periodic data on the modular performance and general behavior of clients. This was the subsystem employed to ensure that clients were assessed during every fourth week. As was pointed out earlier in this chapter, the assessment of each client on a regular schedule based on the length of time in treatment was an essential requirement for evaluation of modules. On the basis of the client's tickler file, the DCC issued each Friday an assessment request for each client who had been in treatment for three weeks since the initial assessment or the previous progress assessment. The form of this request was identical with the initial assessment request; however, the request was only for the psychosocials and the modular assessments for modules in which the client was enrolled. The request went to the unit managers, who assigned specific direct care staff to conduct the assessments. The DCC had to verify which modules the client was attending with the rehabilitation program supervisor who, in turn, had to be sure that the unit managers assigned individuals who had been properly trained in conducting the assigned modular assessment. The importance of this training was to maintain interobserver agreement (reliability) which had been established for the various modular assessments based upon *trained* observers (cf. Chapter 9 for a discussion of these reliability measurements for each of the modules).

The progress subsystem operated in the same fashion as the intake subsystem except that data were not requested of nor supplied by the social workers or the nursing supervisor. Diagrammatically, this system functioned as depicted in Figure 5 but excluding the clinical social worker, the nursing supervisor (R.N.), and the physician. All raw data forms were forwarded to the DCC for coding and then filing in the client research file.

Discharge assessments were also processed in the same fashion by the progress subsystem. However, discharge assessments were initiated by the DCC on the basis of discharge notification from the unit managers, not upon the basis of the tickler file. The DCC made the decision as to whether the last progress assessment would be used as the discharge assessment or whether a final discharge assessment would be requested. The decision was based on how much time had elapsed since the previous progress assessment and how much time was left prior to discharge in which to conduct an assessment. If the previous progress assessment had been conducted within the past two weeks, it was believed that the client's condition had probably not changed sufficiently to warrant another assessment series. If the client was to be discharged in less than three working days hence, it was believed that there would not be enough time to conduct the assessment. Outside of these limits, the DCC would issue a discharge assessment request.

THE FOLLOW-UP SUBSYSTEM

The purpose of the follow-up subsystem was to acquire data on the clients for one year following discharge from the treatment program. Three types of data were to be acquired: (1) general assessment of the client's living situation and environmental support system, (2) a direct assessment of the client's functional level in the areas of the behavior skills taught in the program, and (3) an evaluation of the client by a significant other as to the client's well-being and social adjustment. To acquire these data, the following instruments were administered at one month, three months, six months, and one year after discharge:

The Environmental Deprivation Scale

This was administered to determine whether clients were building and maintaining an environmental support system.

Activities of Daily Living Assessments

In follow-up, clients were assessed in ADL skills up to the level in which they had received training, that is, if they had only received ADL I training they were only assessed in ADL I; in ADL I and ADL II if they had received training in both; or in ADL III if they had been trained in all three levels. The assessment instruments used in the field were modified from those used while the client was in training, since the administration of all three ADL assessments would consume too much time and since some of the items (washing clothes or preparing meals) would not normally occur during a follow-up interview. In those matters in which a client could not be observed performing the target behavior, the interviewer had to depend on verbal examination of the client.

Personal Information Training (PIT) Assessment

This instrument was identical to the one used in modular training and was the first administered by the interviewer since it tested for orientation to time, place, and self. If the client was unable to respond appropriately to this questionnaire, the interviewer was able to modify the interview schedule depending on the client's degree of confusion or lack of memory.

Self-esteem Assessment

The Life Satisfaction Instrument (see Chapter 9 for a discussion and reference on this instrument) self-administered rating form was employed to gather data on self-image and satisfaction with the living situation. In the event that a client could not execute the instrument (unable to read, write, or comprehend the written questions), the interviewer read the instrument to the client, checking the response selected by the client.

Significant Other Report

The NOSIE-30 (see Chapter 9 for a description and reference on this item) was given to the individual specified by the client as being most familiar with the client's postdischarge living situation. The interviewer explained the NOSIE-30 form to the significant other at the start of the follow-up visit, asked that it be filled out during the time the client was being interviewed, and obtained the completed instrument at the end of the interview.

Client Evaluation of the Treatment Program

This form was used to obtain "consumer satisfaction" data. It consisted of four questions with space for written answers as well as a "yes" or "no" answer. The questions asked if the clients believed the program had helped them, if any particular staff member had helped them, whether they preferred the program to staying at a state hospital (not applicable to all clients), and what had happened to them during the program. If the client was unable to execute the questionnaire, the interviewer read the questions and wrote the responses.

Abridged Social History Interview

This form was used to gather information on the living situation and environmental support system.

Operationally, the DCC initiated the follow-up subsystem upon receiving notice that a client was going to be discharged. He removed the card from the client tickler file, and after noting on it in which calendar months the four follow-up interviews would occur, he placed it in a follow-up tickler file. He notified the day treatment unit manager of the impending discharge because the day treatment unit supplied the direct care staff who conducted the follow-up interviews. There were two reasons that follow-up interviewing was assigned to day treatment. First, the day treatment unit had direct care staff who regularly made trips throughout the immediate catchment area to screen clients for admission to the unit (most residential clients were admitted from psychiatric in-patient hospitals, and therefore the residential staff were not traveling throughout the catchment area, but only visiting a few hospitals). Often follow-up interviews and screening interviews could be accomplished on the same trip. Second, the day treatment staff usually had no direct care responsibilities after 2:30 in the afternoon and many of the interviews could be scheduled after the day treatment clients had left for home.

A schematic of the follow up subsystem is presented in Figure 6. The first task of the staff who were assigned to follow-up (they were known as follow-up specialists in this role) was to contact the clients *before discharge* and talk to them about the follow-up procedure. For this reason, one staff member was assigned to follow up all residential unit clients and another, all day treatment clients. In this way they identified with the clients before discharge and in practice were usually informed of pending discharges before the DCC received the

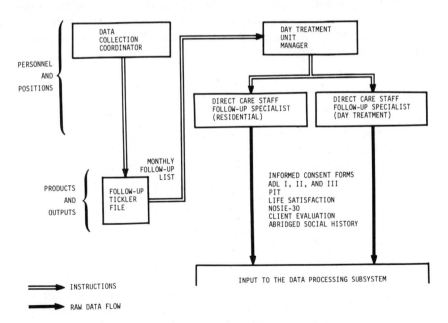

FIGURE 6. The operation of the follow-up subsystem.

official notification. Because a relationship with the client was established prior to discharge, there was a greater probability that the client would agree to participate in the follow-up. The follow-up specialist attempted to obtain a signed consent form from each client and whenever feasible an authorization to contact a designated significant other to fill out the NOSIE-30. In the event that a signed consent form could not be obtained or the client refused to participate in follow-up, the client was still called by telephone or visited at the one-month follow-up date and again asked to sign the consent form and the authorization form. Two consecutive refusals were required before a client was dropped from the follow-up list. In practice, about 10% of the clients (9 in the residential unit and 14 in the day treatment unit) refused to grant permission for follow-up, but only seven refused interviews after discharge. Since most who signed consent forms prior to discharge agreed to continue with the full one-year follow-up, the effort expended prior to discharge to persuade clients to participate was worthwhile.

Each month the DCC would prepare a list of the clients scheduled for follow-up during that month and forward it to the day treatment unit manager. On the basis of this list, which contained addresses and telephone numbers, the follow-up specialist would make telephone calls and schedule the follow-up interviews. If clients could not be reached by telephone, the follow-up specialists made the interview trips anyway, hoping to be able to conduct the interview even without a definite appointment. Repeated trips and telephone calls were made to try to locate and schedule follow-up interviews.

The Data Base

The data base of the GES, which was organized by client, consisted of the data collected by the three subsystems, namely intake, progress, and follow-up. The basic method for reducing the raw data, transforming it into a form amenable to high speed manipulation, and storing it was to code and punch the data onto Hollerith cards. Our objective was accuracy through comprehension and understanding by the inexperienced data coders and key punch operators, and therefore we did not try to achieve maximum card-packing densities, but rather used simple coding formats.

As soon as a client had been admitted and the intake processing and initial assessments had been completed, the code sheet for the demographic and diagnostic card was completed. Code sheets were initiated for the other cards but could not be completed until all the progress and discharge assessments had been administered. Code sheets were held until there was a batch ready for punching, usually once a month but no less frequently than at the end of each calendar quarter. Code sheets on follow-up data could not be completed and punched until the client had completed the 12-month follow-up period. In fact, therefore, there was not a continuous flow of client data into the GES on each client; rather the flow was episodic. First the historical and demographic data were entered shortly after admission, then the progress and performance data shortly after discharge from the treatment program. Although these procedures had the disadvantage of not providing real-time feedback for managerial and clinical application, they were much more efficient than coding and punching cards as each incremental piece of client information was acquired. In addition, the coding and punching on an episodic basis had the advantage of reducing the number of times that data had to be transferred and reprocessed, thus lessening the probability of error. Accuracy was also increased by eliminating the time pressures which are inherent in real-time or short-response feedback systems. Yet, a major objective of the GES was to provide feedback to improve both project operations and clinical services. How this was achieved despite the episodic and batch processing of client data is explained in the following and final section of this chapter.

The Total System: Data Acquisition and Feedback

The above sections of this chapter have described the four subsystems that comprise the gerontology evaluation system from the viewpoint of the acquisition of data for evaluation purposes, not from the viewpoint of providing feedback to clinicians and managers. As we pointed out earlier, the provision of feedback was a major objective of the GES; yet for reasons of efficiency and because of lack of resources, automated processing of data was done on a batched and episodic basis, with progress data on clients not being available until the client had been discharged from the program. Obviously such data arrived too late to be of clinical use. To reconcile the conflict between efficiency of processing and the need for feedback, a distinction must be made between data which were computer-processed and data which were manually processed. Computer-processed data had a relatively long turnaround time: from one to three months on demographic and historical data, the entire length of stay in treatment for a client's progress data, and for at least one year after discharge on follow-up data. On the other hand, manually processed data could be available in 24 hours (an assignment for night shift staff on the residential unit was to transcribe raw data collected during the day to client charts, while on the day treatment unit data could be transcribed after the clients left for the trip home or in the mornings before they arrived). In practice, therefore, computer-processed data were used to provide feedback on low-frequency functions such as shifts in referral sources or admission rates, and manually processed data were used to provide feedback on high-frequency functions such as individual treatment.

The overall operation of the GES is presented in Figure 7, which schematically depicts both the data acquisition and the feedback channels. The data acquisition starts with the assessment requests from the data processing subsystem to the other three subsystems, as explained above. It continues with the forwarding of raw data which is coded and punched and converted into the three basic files: demographic, progress, and follow-up. Feedback channels occur when some of the raw data is manually entered on client charts which are reviewed by the treatment team members and when reports are

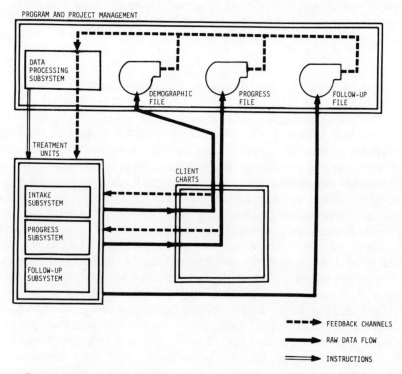

FIGURE 7. The overall operation of the Gerontology Evaluation System.

prepared from the computer-processed data from the three basic files. Low-frequency reports which were based on computer printouts were quarterly reports on project performance, quarterly reports on client demographics, *ad hoc* evaluations of modules, and *ad hoc* evaluations of general behavior scales. High-frequency reports which were based on manually transcribed data were client assessments, monthly census, admissions and discharges, and the monthly follow-up on client living situation.

These two types of feedback confirmed the rationale of the evaluation system to "determine the therapeutic efficacy . . . [and] to improve the level of care" (Kahn & Zarit, 1974). For example, *ad hoc* evaluations of modules enabled us to drop those modules which did not significantly increase client skill levels and to strengthen those which proved to be effective. Similarly, we were able to eliminate redundant instruments, increasing staff time for client intervention and individual treatment. From a clinical perspective, the greatest feedback benefit came in the form of both reinforcement of method and substantive content. Each assessment score was recorded in the client's chart on a raw data flow sheet. These sheets were filed in the client charts along with the problem statement (using a problem-oriented record format) of the deficit that called for the client's being enrolled in that particular module. Every fourth week, as the treatment team reviewed an individual client and went over the problem list, there was the latest assessment of the client's progress toward resolving the problem. Thus, as each case manager reviewed a client with the treatment team, there was reinforcment of the basic program methodology and, as Wiener expressed it "control on the basis of *actual* performance rather than *expected* performance" (Wiener, 1950). The following chapters present the results of this type of evaluation feedback for the program operations, the program components, and the program as a whole.

8

Client and Program Characteristics

DAVID A. EBERLY AND LOUIS A. PENNER

INTRODUCTION

From the first admissions in December 1975 through March 1981, the Gerontology Program had provided treatment to 840 clients. Who were these clients? Where did they come from? How long were they in treatment, and where did they go after treatment? The first step in evaluating a treatment program, and for that matter in planning one, is to define the population which was served by the program. This chapter attempts to do just that, namely to describe the clients of the Gerontology Program. It is concerned with the demographic characteristics of the clients, the type and length of treatment that they received, and their discharge destination. In addition, it provides answers to two simple but very basic evaluation questions. First, did the program treat the population it was designed to serve, that is, were the clients representative of the targeted population? And, second, was the sample of clients used for empirical evaluation of the program representative of the total client population treated?

PROGRAM AND CLIENT CATEGORIES

Before describing the clients and addressing the basic evaluation questions, it is necessary to define the categorization scheme that was used to classify periods of the program and types of clients. On a calendar basis the program was divided into three phases:

- *Phase I.* Development, organization, and initial treatment, 20 months—December 1975 to August 1977
- *Phase II.* Treatment, training, and initial evaluation, 24 months—August 1977 to July 1979

- *Phase III.* Treatment, dissemination, and evaluation, 24 months—August 1979 to July 1981

During Phase I, the treatment, operational, and administrative components of the program were being developed, tested, and refined; and, although clients were being served, there was not sufficient temporal stability to conduct a systematic program evaluation. During Phase II, there was apparent programmatic stability and consistency, and the data collected during this phase are used in the following two chapters to evaluate the immediate and long-term effects of the program. During Phase III, the last phase, major effort was directed toward dissemination and evaluation. Trainees from other facilities participated in residency programs on the treatment units, and the program provided consultation for and supervision of replications at state hospitals and community agencies. It should be noted, however, that across all three phases, treatment was being provided and that the basic treatment rationale and behavioral methodology were consistent.

Within the Phase II period, a further time-based division was necessary. As pointed out in Chapter 7, and as will be described more fully in Chapter 9, a prerequisite for the application of the quasi-experimental evaluation design was the classification of clients into temporal cohorts. Two cohort groups were defined within the Phase II time period: Group I, which consisted of clients admitted from August 17, 1977 through March 23, 1978 and Group 2, clients admitted from March 24, 1978 through December 1, 1978. One of the basic evaluation questions, to be addressed in the following section, is whether there were differences between the clients in Group 1 and Group 2, whether these groups differed from all Phase II clients, and whether they were representative of the total client population served during all three phases.

Two additional classifications of clients are important for both evaluative and operational considerations. First is a distinction by type of treatment, that is, residential inpatients or day treatment outpatients. Obviously these two groups differ in amount of treatment, one being in the program 24 hours a day, 7 days a week, and the other being in the program approximately 6 hours a day, 5 days a week. As will be discussed in the next chapter, there were differences between these two treatment groups as to both their initial and discharge behavior and their skill levels. The second distinction is between research clients and those who were not included as part of the research data base. As noted in the previous chapter, clients participated in the program on a voluntary basis. As might be expected, a certain number of clients withdrew from the program after very short periods of treatment and others were discharged for medical reasons to medical/surgical hospitals shortly after admission. There were several options for dealing with client attrition in the evaluation of the program. One was to consider only those clients who completed the program as valid research subjects. Only clients who were formally discharged to an appropriate placement would be included in the data base. This option would have excluded many clients who had 3 or more months of treatment but who had not reached their maximum skill attainment level (and had yet to be placed appropriately) at the time they voluntarily withdrew. Such a procedure would have biased the results so that almost all research subjects were successes, that is, no one would be considered a valid research subject unless they met the criterion for success, namely a preplanned discharge to a non-institutional community setting. Instead of this criterion, it was decided to define *attrition* operationally as those clients who withdrew from the program voluntarily or who were discharged from the program in 4 weeks or less from the date of admission. Any client who had not received a 4-week, first progress assessment was considered a dropout, a case of client attrition, and was not considered a valid research subject. This criterion selection was influenced by the opinion of the clinical staff, who believed that a client would have to participate in treatment for at least four weeks to derive any benefit from the program.

The numbers of clients admitted to the program by category are presented in Table 2. It indicates the temporal as well as the treat-

TABLE 2. Clients Admitted by Category

	Total program[a]	Phase II only	Group 1	Group 2
Residential clients admitted	401	141	46	47
Day treatment clients admitted	439[b]	134	39	45
Total clients admitted	840[c]	275	85	92
Less than four weeks in program	−123	−48	−17	−15
Valid research subjects	717	227	68	78

[a]From December 1975 through March 1981.
[b]Includes 40 day treatment clients admitted to a special alcohol treatment project; not included in Phase II or Groups 1 and 2.
[c]Unduplicated count; excludes readmissions.

ment categories and shows the effects of attrition, leaving the numbers of valid research subjects.

Demographic and Historical Characteristics

Comparison of Client Categories

Table 3 presents summary statistics on the temporal classifications of clients, namely the total client population, Phase II clients, and clients of Groups 1 and 2. It also contains summary statistics on their psychiatric hospitalization history and gross measures on the type of treatment they received in the program. These statistics of the four temporal classifications were compared in a series of statistical analyses. These analyses failed to disclose any statistically significant or clinically meaningful differences between the four classifications.

TABLE 3. Summary of Demographic, Historical, and Treatment Characteristics of Temporal Classification of Clients

	Total program	Phase II	Group 1	Group 2
Number of clients	840	275	85	92
Demographic data				
Mean age (years)	67.2	67.4	67.1	67.8
Sex				
Male %	39.3	38.9	37.6	39.1
Female %	60.7	61.1	62.4	60.9
Married with living spouse %	20.7	19.6	16.5	24.4
High school graduates %	18.8	16.4	14.1	12.4
Tampa Bay residents %	78.2	84.4	83.5	79.4
Treatment history				
Mean prior months of hospitalization	19.1	17.3	10.8	21.4
Mean number of prior hospitalizations	2.0	2.0	2.0	1.7
Program treatment				
Admission diagnosis psychotic %	42.1	37.2	44.9	38.6
Residential treatment %	47.7	51.3	54.1	51.1
Voluntary competent %	89.5	89.0	88.1	85.6

Thus, the clients described in the remainder of this chapter, namely Phase II clients, and the clients of Groups 1 and 2 used for the empirical evaluations described in Chapters 9 and 10, appear to be representative of the total client population served by the program. Similar comparisons were conducted between clients from Phases I, II, and III, and the results of these analyses were the same. No statistically significant differences were disclosed between these three groups of clients.

COMPARISON WITH TARGET POPULATIONS

Thus, it would appear that the data base developed from Phase II clients was representative of all clients served by the program. The next basic question is whether the client population was representative of the targeted population, the group of clients whom the program was designed to serve. Of course, the staff applied the client admission criteria, and in that sense the population served had to be the targeted population. Yet even in the application of criteria, judgment is not always perfect and exceptions can be made. For example, although a criterion for admission was an age of 55 years or older, three clients under 55 were admitted (one at age 52 and two at age 53). In all three cases special extenuating circumstances were judged to warrant waiving the admissions criteria. Similarly, it can be argued that the criterion of "being medically stable and not in need of skilled nursing care" was violated in those cases in which clients had to be discharged to medical/surgical hospitals for physical illnesses which had their origin prior to admissions, for instance, undetected carcinomas.

A more difficult question is whether the program's clients were representative of the groups whom the program was intended to serve, namely elderly institutionalized inpatients and those living in the community but deemed at risk of institutionalization. The only way to answer this question is to measure the two populations either by survey or by direct observation and then to compare them statistically with the group brought into treatment (the alternative approach would have been to select clients randomly from the two populations at risk, but, as has been pointed out in Chapter 7, this was not possible). Obtaining reliable and valid data on these two populations has been beyond the scope of the Gerontology Program and therefore comparisons can be made with only those data which are already available, and these data are quite limited, being restricted to age, sex, and race. Figure 8 displays the age distribution of clients of the residential and day treatment units as compared with the age

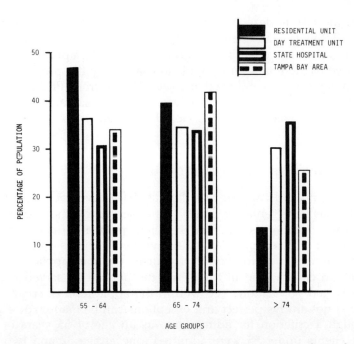

FIGURE 8. Age distributions of day treatment, residential treatment, and state hospital clients and elderly residents of Tampa Bay area.

distribution for patients over age 55 in the state hospitals and in the greater Tampa Bay area—the area in which the program is located. It should be noted that although approximately 47% of the residential clients fall in the 55–64 year age group, only 30% of the hospital clients do. On the other end of the distribution, only 14% of the residential clients are in the above 74 years group, while more than 35% of the hospital clients are in the upper age bracket. Thus, the clients served by the residential unit cannot be considered representative of the elderly population within the state hospitals. The principle explanation for this discrepancy is that a large percentage of the over 65 population in the state hospitals are, in fact, nursing home patients who require skilled or intermediate nursing care and therefore were excluded from the residential treatment program by the medical criterion. However, until the geriatric hospital population is assessed, a project currently underway, we can only state that clients admitted to the residential unit were not representative in terms of age distribution of the elderly, hospitalized population.

Statistically, there is no significant difference between the age distribution of day treatment clients and the hospitalized population or that of people 55 years of age and older in the Tampa Bay area.

TABLE 4. Distribution of Populations by Sex[a]

	Residential unit	Day treatment unit	State hospitals	Tampa Bay area
Female %	61	61	54	55
Male %	39	39	46	45

[a]All populations are 55 years of age and older.

This may be interpreted to mean that day treatment clients were representative of the target population. However, it should be noted that the day treatment unit was intended for the at-risk elderly residing in the community. The age distribution for the Tampa Bay area is for all residents, not just those at risk of institutionalization. Here again the available data do not permit us to draw definite conclusions, and we can only say that the day treatment population appears to be representative of the age distribution found in the elderly population in the community.

Table 4 presents the proportion of elderly males and females in the treatment units, state hospitals, and in the Tampa Bay area. As indicated in this table, there was no difference between the residential and day treatment units. There was, however, a difference between the program clients and both the hospitalized population and elderly Tampa Bay area population, with little difference between the latter two. We can offer only a tentative explanation as to why the percentage of female clients in both residential and day treatment was higher than that in the other two populations. It has been our experience that elderly women are more aggressive than elderly men in seeking out services and in expressing their needs. It may be that this produces a self-selection bias when screening clients at psychiatric hospitals for admission into the residential unit and in the referral system for admission to the day treatment unit.

The only other data readily available for determination of whether the client population was representative of the target population are racial data. Table 5 represents the racial distribution of clients

TABLE 5. Distribution of Populations by Race

	Residential unit	Day treatment unit	State hospitals	Tampa Bay area
White %	93.6	92.5	88.1	90.8
Black %	6.4	7.5	11.9	9.2

182

CHAPTER 8

by treatment unit, of the hospitalized population, and of the Tampa Bay area residents. There are not statistically significant differences in these data, and we can assume that with regard to race that the clients admitted to the program were representative of both the hospitalized and the Tampa Bay area. The nonsignificantly higher percentage of black residents in the state hospitals than in the program was probably due to the demography of the areas from which

TABLE 6. Demographic Characteristics of Phase II Clients

	All clients	Day treatment	Residential treatment
Number of clients admitted	275	134	141
Sex			
Male %	38.9	38.8	39.0
Female %	61.1	61.2	61.0
Age			
Mean age	67.4	69.4	65.5
Age range	52–90	55–90	52–89
Marital status			
Single %	7.8	5.4	10.0
Married %	19.6	23.1	17.1
Separated %	5.9	6.2	5.7
Divorced %	26.3	24.6	27.9
Widowed %	40.0	40.8	39.3
Education			
None %	1.5	1.6	1.4
1–4 years %	9.2	6.4	11.3
4–8 years %	25.6	28.0	22.7
9–12 years %	23.3	24.8	21.3
High school graduate %	16.4	12.8	19.7
Vocational/technical school %	11.4	13.6	9.5
Some college %	6.5	8.0	5.1
College graduate %	5.8	4.8	7.3
Monthly income			
None %	8.6	4.8	12.1
$ 0–100 %	2.3	2.4	2.2
$101–150 %	8.9	8.0	9.8
$151–200 %	15.9	12.8	18.9
$201–250 %	21.4	23.2	19.7
$251–300 %	10.5	10.4	10.6
Over $300 %	32.3	38.4	26.5

the program drew its clients. The program's clients came primarily from the Tampa Bay area and a state hospital about 100 miles southeast of the Florida Mental Health Institute. The percentage of blacks in the state as a whole is somewhat greater than the percentage in the Tampa Bay area and the catchment area served by the "feeder" hospital.

PHASE II CLIENTS

The demographic characteristics of the Phase II clients are presented in Table 6. Statistical analyses were conducted to compare the differences between residential and day treatment clients. There were no significant differences between the two treatment groups on the variables of sex, marital status, education, and income level. They did differ in age. The residential clients were significantly younger than the day treatment clients, t (274) = 3.81, $p < .005$. Figure 9 shows that the distribution of age within the two groups also is markedly different. The reason for this difference is not readily apparent. It could not be explained on the basis of difference in the populations from which the clients were admitted. Recall that the difference between the two populations from which the day and residential clients were drawn was small. One possible explanation is that the degree of impairment or the rate at which dysfunction occurs as a function of aging is

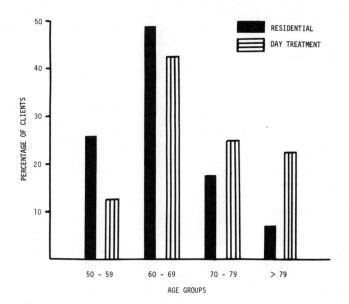

FIGURE 9. Age distributions within day and residential treatment units.

higher or more rapid for clients with psychiatric hospitalization histories than for those without such illnesses. As is indicated in the following section, there was a significant difference in the psychiatric treatment histories between residential and day treatment clients. A larger number of residential clients had previous psychiatric hospitalizations (95%) than did day treatment clients (39%), and the average length of prior hospitalizations was also greater among residential clients. Another possible explanation is that the program's admission criteria and procedures served to introduce a selection bias in the age of the admitted clients. As noted earlier, one of the admission criteria was that the client must be free of any medical/physical problem that would require one-to-one care. Also, because participation in the program was voluntary, clients must have been willing to transfer from the facility where they presently lived to the institute. It may be that those elderly institutionalized clients who fell in the lower part of the age distribution (e.g., 55–65 years) were more likely than their older counterparts (e.g., 70–80 years) to meet the physical/medical admission criteria and more willing to accept transfer to a new facility (because they were less dependent and institutionalized). This resulted in the admission of residential clients who were younger, on the aver-

TABLE 7. Psychiatric Histories of Phase II Clients

	All clients	Day treatment	Residential treatment
Mean stay in months	17.3 (months)	14.1	20.4
S	50.2	52.4	48.0
Range	0–396	0–396	0–361
Number of clients	263	130	133
Number of prior hospitalizations			
Mean	1.97	.88	3.05
S	2.86	1.94	3.21
Range	0–25	0–17	0–25
Number of clients	266	132	134
Admitting diagnosis			
Psychotic	94 (37.2%)	18 (15.7%)	76 (55.1%)
Nonpsychotic	159 (57.8%)	97 (84.3%)	62 (44.9%)
Legal status by admission			
Voluntary	254 (92.4%)	133 (99.3%)	121 (85.8%)
Involuntary	5 (1.8%)	—	5 (3.5%)
Court ordered	13 (4.7%)	—	13 (9.2%)
Unknown	3 (1.1%)	1 (0.7%)	2 (1.4%)

age, than the institutionalized elderly population from which they were drawn and younger than the day clients.

The psychiatric histories of Phase II clients are presented in Table 7. The two groups differ to a much greater degree in their psychiatric history than they do in their demographic characteristics. The average length of prior hospitalization was 6 months longer for the residential clients than for the day treatment clients (20.4 months versus 14.1). However, this difference was not statistically significant due to the large variation in the length of prior hospitalization among the clients in both groups. Figure 10, a frequency distribution of prior hospitalization by treatment groups, illustrates the considerable difference between the groups in length of prior psychiatric hospitalization. The two groups did differ significantly in the number of prior hospitalizations, t (132) = 6.68, p < .01. The average number of prior hospitalizations among the residential clients was three times as great as that of the day treatment clients. The two groups also differed in their admitting diagnoses, χ^2 = 141.75, p < .0001. Whereas 16% of the day treatment clients were diagnosed as psychotic at admission, 55% of the residential clients were. In terms of their legal status at admission, another indirect measure of their psychiatric history, there was also a significant difference between the groups as to voluntary versus involuntary or court-ordered, χ^2 (1) =13.1, p < .001.

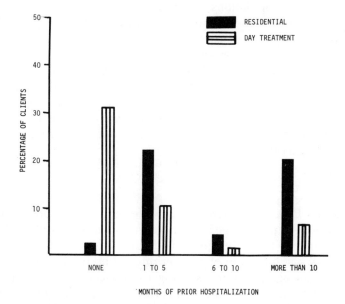

FIGURE 10. Length of prior hospitalization within day and residential treatment units.

In summary, we can conclude that there were some meaningful statistical differences between residential and day treatment clients admitted during Phase II of the program. Although the only demographic differences were in the average age and age distribution, there were significant differences in their psychiatric treatment history, their admission diagnoses, and their legal status. We cannot be sure why the two groups did differ, but we can assume that the two treatment programs were addressing different at-risk populations. This leads us to believe that there are meaningful differences between the elderly institutionalized population and the population deemed at risk of institutionalization but still residing in the community.

ADMISSION AND ATTRITION

During the two-year period of Phase II, 275 clients were admitted to the program, 134 to day treatment and 141 to residential. Forty-eight of these clients were discharged or voluntarily withdrew from their treatment units in 4 weeks or less after their date of admission. These clients were lost as research subjects so that Phase II experienced a 17½% subject attrition rate. Analysis of admission and attrition is useful for both descriptive and evaluative reasons. Related to admissions are referral sources which in turn relate to the basic question of the populations being served. Related to both admission and attrition rates is the question as to whether the program practices and procedures changed as a function of time. As was discussed in the previous chapter, consistency of practice across time is an essential requisite for the application of the evaluation designs employed. Equally important with measuring consistency is the question of whether there were systematic, programmatic variables or special client characteristics which could be associated with the 17½% subject attrition or with admission practices. These questions are addressed in the following sections.

REFERRAL SOURCES

During Phase II, clients were referred to the program by 19 different governmental agencies in addition to many different private referral sources. The latter group is defined as individuals or agencies that are not a subdivision of a governmental body, nor employed by a governmental agency, nor receiving categorical funds for the provision of mental health services. Governmental agencies are categorized into mental health centers operating under federal and state

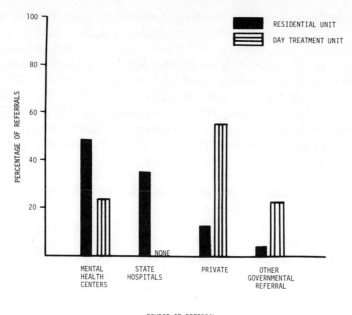

FIGURE 11. Referral sources for day and residential treatment units.

guidelines for comprehensive community mental health centers, state hospitals, and "other governmental." This latter category includes such agencies as Veterans Administration hospitals and the Community Action Agency, the Senior Resource Centers, and county health departments, all of which receive either federal or state funding for the provision of services to the elderly clients.

Figure 11 presents the distribution of referrals across the four basic categories by type of treatment. As this figure illustrates, the referral sources for residential and day treatment clients admitted during Phase II were quite different. Statistical analysis indicates that the differences are significant, χ^2 (3) = 83.30, $p < .001$. The differential use by residential and day treatment units of state hospitals and private referral sources is the cause of this significant χ^2. No clients were admitted to day treatment from state hospitals, while private referrals accounted for 55.2% of admissions. The converse was true for residential admissions: 35.5% came from state hospitals and private referrals accounted for only 12.1%. In addition to providing outpatient and day treatment services, most of the mental health centers also operate inpatient facilities. These facilities (called Baker Act Receiving Centers) are mandated by Florida statute to provide inpatient psychiatric evaluation prior to admission to state hospitals.

Of the 48.2% referrals to residential treatment from mental health centers, 44.7% were from such psychiatric inpatient facilities. Only five (3.5%) of the referrals from mental health centers were not inpatients at the time of referral. The Baker Act Receiving Centers chose the residential treatment program as an alternative to hospitalization at a state institution. Of the 23.1% referrals to day treatment from mental health centers, 11.2% (16 clients) were from Baker Act Receiving Centers and had been discharged to community living situations with the expectation that they would receive day treatment support from the Gerontology Program.

Another difference between the two treatment units is the location of referral sources. All day treatment clients were referred by sources operating in Hillsborough county, the county in which the Institute is located. Residential clients, on the other hand, were referred from sources throughout the state, although the majority of referrals came from the immediately adjacent four-county area and the closest state hospital, which is about 100 miles away.

These differences in referral sources tend to confirm that the two treatment groups were addressing different populations. As planned, the residential treatment unit was receiving clients from psychiatric inpatient facilities; the day treatment unit was relying on community referrals and admitted no patients from the state institutions.

RATES OF ADMISSION

An examination of the number of clients admitted per month disclosed that the rate of admission was fairly constant across the two-year period of Phase II. July was the month with the fewest admissions, with only 4% of the 275 clients being admitted. The largest numbers of clients were admitted in March (11.5%) and in January (10.5%). The percentage of clients admitted during the other 9 months differed by less than 3% from an average of 8.2% per month. The lower rates during the summer and higher rates during the fall and winter were typical of the seasonal pattern of admission to mental health services in the state of Florida.

To determine whether the rates of admission were comparable across the 24 months of Phase II admissions, two types of analysis were used. First, calendar periods of time were compared with number of admissions. This showed that during the 4 months of 1977 in which Phase II was in operation (16.7% of Phase II), 18.2% of Phase II clients were admitted; during the 12 months of 1978 (50% of Phase II), 51.3% of the clients were admitted; and during the 8 months of 1979

(33% of Phase II), 30.5% of the Phase II clients were admitted. The comparability of the actual admission percentages with the expected percentages derived from months of operation indicates that the rate of admission was constant across Phase II. The second method for determining linearity was to regress cumulative admissions on months of operation. This regression line is shown in Figure 12 for both residential and day treatment. If these lines were completely straight, there would be a uniform rate of admission across both treatment units. They depart from linearity because of seasonal fluctuations, a fixed client capacity which makes admissions a function of discharges, and varying numbers of working days per month. Correlation analysis indicates that, despite these stochastic processes, admissions are highly correlated with time, the Pearson correlation coefficient being 0.998 for residential and 0.997 for day treatment. Average admissions per month as calculated from the slope of the regression line were 6.4 for residential and 6.3 for day treatment. We can conclude that, as indicated by admission rates, there was a remarkable degree of consistency in both residential and day treatment during the 24 months of Phase II.

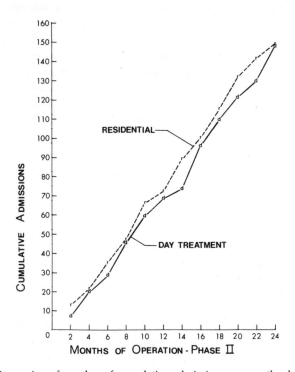

FIGURE 12. Regression of number of cumulative admissions on months during Phase II.

ATTRITION

For the program as a whole, 48 clients (17.5%) withdrew voluntarily or were discharged prior to the completion of the first progress assessment (usually by the end of the 4th week following admission). Fifteen of these were residential clients and 33 were day treatment. There is a significant difference in these attrition rates by treatment group, χ^2 (1) = 6.73, p < .05. There are two reasons for this difference in attrition: the first is related to differences in screening/admission practices between the two groups, and the second is related to the difference in the relative ease of voluntary withdrawal. Since admission to residential treatment involves a change in residence, often over considerable distance, the residential unit carefully screens almost all clients at their place of residence, usually a psychiatric hospital, prior to admission (this includes screening trips to the state hospital, as mentioned in earlier chapters). Effort is expended to try to ensure that a client who is relocated will stay in the program and benefit from it. On the other hand, day treatment does not involve disruption or relocation of existing residence. Therefore, the day treatment unit practices "trial" visits by prospective clients. When these trial visits extend beyond one week, the client is admitted formally even though both staff and clients may be unsure as to continued participation. As a result, the more stringent screening procedures employed for residential admissions will tend to reduce attrition due to inappropriate client selection, whereas the more casual procedures of day treatment will result in higher attrition. The ease of discharge or voluntary withdrawal from day treatment is obvious: a client need only stay home. In contrast, to withdraw or be discharged from residential treatment is a more difficult and complex matter. Other living arrangements must be made, personal belongings packed and transported, and formal documentation of discharge and release executed.

Even though subject attrition was small, it is still important to determine whether the clients who left the program during the first 4 weeks differed significantly from those who remained and were considered as research subjects. Possibly, program outcome evaluation would be biased by excluding the short-term clients. Therefore, the demographic characteristics and the psychiatric histories of the two groups were examined.

Table 8 compares the demographic characteristics of the clients who remained in the program more than 4 weeks with those who were terminated prior to their first progress assessment. Statistical analyses of these data failed to produce any significant differences

TABLE 8. Demographic Characteristics of Attrition
and Treatment Groups

	Four weeks or less	More than four weeks
Number of clients	48	227
Sex		
Male %	50	36.6
Female %	50	63.4
Race		
Black %	8.3	6.6
White %	91.7	93.4
Age		
Mean	65.7	67.8
Variance	8.7	8.1
Range	52–90	53–84
Marital status		
Single	11.6	7.0
Married	20.9	19.8
Separated	7.0	5.7
Divorced	18.6	27.8
Widowed	41.9	39.6
Education		
None %	2.8[a]	1.3
1–4 years %	11.1	8.8
4–8 years %	13.9	27.4
9–12 years %	22.2	23.5
High school graduate %	25.0	15.0
Vocational/technical school %	5.6	12.4
Some college %	5.6	6.6
College graduate %	13.9	4.9
Income		
None %	14.3[b]	7.7
$0–100%	2.9	2.3
$101–150%	14.3	8.1
$151–200%	8.6	17.1
$201–250%	14.3	22.5
$251–300%	2.9	11.7
Over $300%	42.9	30.6

[a]Only 36 of these clients provided information on educational levels.
[b]Only 35 of these clients provided information on income levels.

TABLE 9. Psychiatric Histories of Attrition
and Treatment Groups

	Four weeks or less	More than four weeks
Number of clients	48	227
Length of last prior hospitalization (months)		
Mean	7.2	19.1
S	25.2	53.53
Range	0–132	0–396
Number of prior hospitalizations		
Mean	0.87	2.19
S	1.02	3.06
Range	0–4	0–25
Admitting diagnosis		
Psychotic %	32.4[a]	37.9
Nonpsychotic %	67.6	62.1
Legal status at admission		
Voluntary %	.94	92
Involuntary %	0	2
Court ordered %	4	5
Unknown %	2	1

[a]There were admitting diagnoses on only 34 of these clients.

between the two groups. We can conclude that there were no demographic variables that caused early withdrawal.

Comparisons of the two groups' psychiatric histories is presented in Table 9. The clients who remained in the program had a significantly longer length of prior hospitalization than did the clients who were terminated, $t (263)^1 = 2.25$, $p < .01$. They also had a significantly greater number of prior hospitalizations than did those who left, $t (261)^1 = 5.15$, $p < .001$. A χ^2 analysis failed to disclose any difference between the two groups on admission diagnosis or on legal status at admission. The most likely reason for the difference between these two groups' psychiatric histories is that 69% of the attrition was with day treatment clients. As we pointed out earlier in this chapter, day treatment clients have less lengthy and less frequent psychiatric hos-

[1]The degrees of freedom on these two t tests differ because some clients did not provide data on their psychiatric histories.

pitalizations in their history than do residential clients. However, at least in terms of psychiatric history, the comparison indicates that the clients who withdrew from the program or were discharged in the first 4 weeks were less chronic than those who remained. If there is any bias in eliminating the short-term clients from the research sample, it is in the direction of keeping the clients with the greater degree of chronicity, who are therefore the more difficult clients to rehabilitate.

Treatment and Outcome

The final section of this chapter deals with the gross treatment outcomes for the clients, namely, the length of time they were in treatment and their discharge destinations. Detailed analyses of what happened to clients in treatment and what happened after they were discharged from the program are presented in Chapters 9 and 10.

Length of Stay

The average length of stay in the program for all 275 clients admitted during Phase II was 16.6 weeks. The average for day treatment clients was 16.2 weeks and for residential clients, 17.0 weeks. These figures include those clients who were not considered to be valid research subjects since they were terminated or voluntarily withdrew prior to receiving the first progress assessment. Excluding these short-term clients, the length of stay for the total remaining 227 clients averages 19.4 weeks—20.8 weeks for day treatment and 19.0 weeks for residential clients. Statistical analysis failed to disclose any significant differences between the lengths of stay of the two groups.

Figure 13 illustrates the length of stay distribution for the two treatment groups broken into blocks of less than 4 weeks, three 8-week treatment blocks, and then more than 28 weeks. The length of stay distribution of residential clients is fairly normally distributed about the mean of 17.0 weeks. The distribution for day treatment clients, however, is quite flat, with the less than four weeks accounting for the largest percentage of the clients in this distribution. These differences in length of stay between the two groups may be attributed to the basic difference in the operating schedules and selection process of the two treatment units and are typical of differences found between inpatient and outpatient programs. In the former there are definite, operational outcome goals, namely, the discharge of the client to a community residence or a return to home. In the

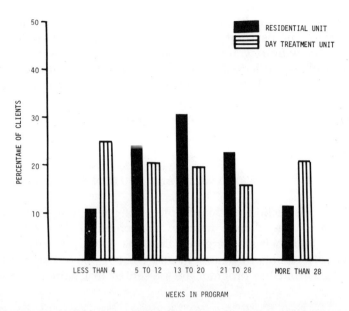

FIGURE 13. Length of stay for day and residential treatment unit clients.

latter, although the outcome goal may be verbalized, it is much more difficult to operationalize when a client who is living at home has been sufficiently rehabilitated to remain at home without further day treatment. In addition, since there is no disruption in residence, many day treatment clients and their families look upon the program as a useful and socially beneficial way for the elderly to occupy themselves, even though there may no longer be a clinical reason for their participation. For this reason, there is not as much pressure from clients or from significant others for discharge as there is in the case of residential clients.

CLIENT OUTCOMES

Table 10 presents the discharge destination of the clients of Phase II. All the categories of discharge destination are self-explanatory except for "Independent Living." This category covers all living or residential destinations wherein there is no licensed operator or paid care provider. It includes living with spouse or family, living with friends, or living by oneself. Three of the six categories were considered "failures" by the program staff. These were medical/surgical hospitals, psychiatric hospitals, and nursing homes, all of which were considered to be institutional in nature. The other three categories were considered "successes."

As Table 10 shows, the majority of clients were successes, being discharged to noninstitutional community settings. Although all types of institutional discharges are considered failures, it should be noted that only 6.2% of all clients were discharged to psychiatric hospitals, 3.7% of the day treatment clients and 8.5% of the residential clients. The other two failure categories—medical/surgical hospitals and nursing homes—were usually discharges for medical reasons. Either the client was in need of skilled nursing care or required medical/surgical procedures necessitating hospitalization. These matters were beyond the control of the program staff and therefore should not be considered failures of the treatment and rehabilitation program.

Of special interest is the finding that there is no significant difference between the two treatment groups as to discharge destination. The slightly higher discharge rate to psychiatric hospitals of residential clients (8.5% versus 3.7% for day treatment clients) is consistent with the previous findings presented in this chapter that the residential clients have a history of greater length and frequency of psychiatric hospitalization. The lower percentage of residential clients going into independent living (50.4% versus 64.2% for day treatment clients) is indicative of the previous finding that fewer residential clients than day treatment clients are married with a living spouse. In general, it is representative of the fact that institutionalized clients, such as those admitted to the residential unit, have on the average less well developed social support systems than do clients living in the community.

TABLE 10. Discharge Destinations of Phase II Clients

	Total	Day treatment	Residential treatment
Number of clients	275	134	141
Medical/surgical hospital %	5.5	5.2	5.8
Psychiatric hospital %	6.2	3.7	8.5
Nursing home %	5.1	5.2	5.0
Total	16.8	14.1	19.3
Independent living %	57.1	64.2	50.4
Boarding home %	22.5	18.7	26.2
Foster home %	3.6	3.0	4.3
Total	83.2	85.9	80.9

Except for these minor differences in psychiatric hospitalization rates and the percentage discharged to independent living (and neither of these differences was statistically significant), the discharge destination of the two treatment groups was remarkably similar. Despite the fact that all the residential clients were deemed to be in need of residential inpatient treatment at the time they were admitted, they did not differ as to discharge destination from their day treatment peers at the time of discharge. This would suggest, in a very preliminary fashion, that the residential program may have been successful in achieving its goal of returning previously institutionalized elderly to the community. The next two chapters lend further empirical support to this conclusion.

9

The Evaluation of Program Components

Louis A. Penner, David A. Eberly,
and Roger L. Patterson

This chapter addresses a rather simple and straightforward question. Did the clients learn the skills they were taught in the modules? Prior to presenting the data relevant to this question, it is necessary to discuss the psychometric properties of the assessments associated with each of the modules. Obviously, if these assessments did not possess some degree of reliability, then any changes they indicated in the clients' modular skill levels would be meaningless. Because many of the assessments used were created especially for the program, it was also desirable to determine the construct validity of these assessments wherever possible. The following section presents these data.

Reliability and Validity of Measures

Reliability of the Measures

All module assessment instruments were administered before a client entered the module and at 4-week intervals for the period of time a client remained in the module. These 4-week assessments provided the data for an estimate of the test–retest reliability of assessments. The word *estimate* is used intentionally because assessments were taken in the course of an ongoing treatment program, and thus during the 4-week intervals between the assessments, the clients received training. Strictly speaking, test–retest reliability is determined by the correlation between two measurements differing only in the time they were administered. However, in the present case, the

197

measurements differed not only as to when they were taken, but also in the amount of training a client had received at the time of measurement. Prior work had indicated that most of the training effects in the modules occurred within the first 4 weeks of training. Therefore, in order to minimize the effects of training on estimates of the temporal stability, the correlations between assessments subsequent to the first 4 weeks of training were used, namely correlations between the first progress (4-week) and second progress (8-week) assessments. Because a large percentage of the clients did not require 8 weeks of training in each of the modules, this decision resulted in some test–retest reliability estimates' being based on fewer clients than were actually trained.

In some of the modular assessments, it was possible to obtain another estimate of reliability, the degree to which observers agreed in their assessments of the clients. When available, the interobserver agreement on the modular assessments will be reported.

ACTIVITIES OF DAILY LIVING I (ADL I)

This assessment was comprised of 10 items concerned with basic personal hygiene skills. The items were scored on the basis of client self-reports confirmed by staff observations whenever possible. The correlation between the first and second progress assessment of 16 clients was .53 ($p < .05$).

Two raters independently observed the assessments of six clients in ADL I. They agreed in their scoring on 93% of the clients' responses (exact agreement method: Repp, Dietz, Boles, Dietz, & Repp, 1976).

ACTIVITIES OF DAILY LIVING II (ADL II)

ADL II was assessed via a 10-item instrument which measured the clients' skill and knowledge in the areas of laundry, money management, nutrition, housekeeping, and use of the telephone. Because of a coding problem, the 4-week correlation for ADL II was lost and a special determination of this assessment's temporal stability had to be conducted. Over a 10-day time period, the correlation between clients' assessments scores was .91 ($n = 15$, $p < .05$).

Two independent observers rated five clients on the ADL II assessments. They agreed in their scoring on 94% of the responses made by the clients (exact agreement method: Repp et al., 1976).

ACTIVITIES OF DAILY LIVING III (ADL III)

The assessment of ADL III consisted of a 34-item test of knowledge in the areas of budgeting, community resources, meal planning and preparation, and housekeeping. The 4-week correlation for this module was .83 ($n = 24$, $p < .05$).

PERSONAL INFORMATION TRAINING (PIT)

PIT was assessed with a 10-item scale which measured the clients' memory skills and ability to orient themselves to time and place. The correlation between assessments taken 4 weeks apart was .75 ($n = 22$, $p < .05$).

Two raters independently observed the assessments of nine clients in PIT. They agreed in their scoring on 100% of the clients' responses (exact agreement method: Repp et al., 1976).

COMMUNICATION TRAINING

The assessment of the communication of pleasure was based on the ratings of the client's role-playing behavior in six different areas (e.g., facial expression, use of hands) and one overall rating of the client's performance. A client could receive a score ranging from 1 to 6 in each category, producing a maximum total score of 42. Exactly the same procedure was used for the assessment of the communication of displeasure. The correlation of the two sets of scores taken 4 weeks apart for the communication of pleasure was .60 ($n = 76$, $p < .05$); it was .62 ($n = 76$, $p < .05$) for displeasure.

Four raters observed the performance of 21 clients in the Communication Training module. The average interobserver correlation was +.88 ($p < .05$).

CONVERSATION TRAINING

The clients were assessed in conversation skills by a staff member observing them while they sat in a day room area. Staff members observed the clients for 30-second intervals and recorded whether or not they were talking to another client. The 4-week interval correlation was .55 ($n = 78$, $p < .05$).

The recordings of the occurrence of conversation by two raters were compared by the exact agreement method (Repp et al., 1976). Agreement of 95% was achieved by these raters.

Self-esteem Training

Three different assessments were used in Self-esteem Training. They were: (1) a modified version of a 20-item self-report question-naire on Life Satisfaction by Neugarten, Havighurst, and Tobin (1961); (2) a modified version of Rosenberg's (1965) 10-item self-report questionnaire of self-esteem; and (3) a simple count of the number of positive and negative self-statements the clients made in response to questions about what had happened that made them feel good or bad about themselves and their lives. The 4-week interval correlation for the Life Satisfaction questionnaire was .75 ($n = 45$, $p < .05$). The correlation was .71 ($n = 45$, $p < .05$) for the Rosenberg Self-esteem questionnaire and .53 ($n = 45$, $p < .05$) and .45, ($p < .05$) for the positive and negative self-statements respectively.

Validity of the Module Assessments

The data on the validity of several module assessments come primarily from a study conducted by Patterson, Penner, Eberly, and Harrell (1982). This study used Campbell and Fiske's (1959) multitrait, multimethod technique to determine the construct validity of the ADL I, Conversation Training, Communication Training, and Personal Information Training assessments. A complete description of this study is beyond the scope of this chapter, but briefly the procedure was to intercorrelate the initial assessments of 143 clients in the modules and on the behavior rating subscales of the NOSIE-30 (Honigfeld et al., 1966) to form Campbell and Fiske's multitrait, multimethod matrix. These subscales (which will be described more fully below) were selected because they measure the same areas as the module assessments. (For example, the NOSIE-30 Neatness subscale addresses the same type of behaviors as the ADL I assessment.) After determining that all the measures had acceptable test–retest reliabilities (cf. sections on reliabilities on the modular assessments and NOSIE-30), the correlations between the two different techniques of measuring the same behaviors were examined. These convergent correlations were all substantial, from $r = .41$ to $r = .57$, and well within the range suggested by Campbell and Fiske for establishing the construct validity of a measurement technique. These convergent correlations were also, in the main, greater than the discriminant correlations (i.e., correlations between different traits measured by the same techniques). Thus, for all four of these modular assessments, it was established that they met the criteria for construct validity set forth by Campbell and Fiske.

There are also construct validity data on the assessments used in

TABLE 11. Intercorrelations of Assessments Used in Self-esteem Training[a]

	Life satisfaction	Self-esteem	Positive self-statements	Negative self-statements
Life satisfaction	—			
Self-esteem	.46 (54)	—		
Positive self-statements	.27 (76)	.29 (64)	—	
Negative self-statements	−.21 (76)	−.46 (64)	.34 (76)	—

[a]The numbers in parentheses indicate the number of clients on which correlation is based. All correlations shown are significant ($p < .05$).

Self-esteem Training. The correlations of these assessments are presented in Table 11.

As Table 11 shows, all the measurements are significantly correlated with one another. Although the correlations vary in size from .21 to .46, they are significant, and all but one are in the expected direction. The exception is the correlation between positive and negative self-statements. Theoretically, this correlation should be negative, but it is positive. This raises some serious questions about the validity of the self-statement measures. It would seem reasonable to propose that both are measuring how verbal the clients were as well as their level of self-esteem. On the other hand, the Life Satisfaction and Self-esteem questionnaries both seem to be measuring the clients' feelings about their self-worth and the quality of their lives.

In summary, the assessments of ADL I, Communication Training, Conversation Training, and PIT were all determined to be construct valid. The questionnaires concerned with life satisfaction and Self-esteem Training assessments seemed to measure both self-esteem and how verbal a client was. The construct validity of the ADL II and ADL III assessments was not investigated.

GENERAL BEHAVIOR RATING SCALES

Three general behavior rating scales were used in the evaluation of the Gerontology Program to gain information on the validity of the module assessments *per se* and to aid in the interpretation of the changes in the skills of clients. These scales were used also as part of the evaluation of the overall program, presented in the next chapter, as well as for clinical purposes.

The procedure of data collection for the behavior rating scales was the same as that used for the module assessments. All clients were rated on these scales by their case manager during the first week they were in the program and rerated by a staff member every 4 weeks thereafter. These 4-week assessments were used to estimate the temporal stability of the general behavior ratings. Since these rating scales have not been described previously, we will present a brief description of each of them.

The Nurse's Observation Scale for Inpatient Evaluation (NOSIE-30)

The NOSIE-30 was developed by Honigfeld, Gillis, and Klett (1966) as a sensitive measure of a clients' on-ward behavior and changes in that behavior over time. It consists of six subscales derived by means of an orthogonal factor analysis. Items on each subscale are rated on a five-point Likert scale in terms of how frequently the client displayed the behavior described in the item over the past three days.

The first subscale is called *Social Competence*. It contains five items which address memory deficits and general intellectual competence. The *Interest* subscale contains five items concerned with conversational and interpersonal skills. The next subscale is *Neatness* and is comprised of four items which address the client's personal hygiene and clothing skills. Whereas the first three subscales concern positive aspects of the client's behavior, the last three concern negative aspects of behavior. Ratings of irritability and impatience are derived from the five items in the *Irritability* subscale. Evidence of psychotic behavior (e.g., hallucinations) is assessed in the four-item *Psychosis* subscale. Finally, there is the *Retardation* subscale, which contains three items and concerns how *physically* retarded the client is.

Community Adjustment Potential Scale (CAP)

The CAP was developed by Hogarty and Ulrich (1972) and contains 16 items. The first 10 items are concerned with a client's interpersonal skills and intellectual competence. The remaining 6 items ask the rater to make judgments of how well the client would function in a community setting. Each of the items is rated using a five-point Likert scale.

Social Adjustment Behavior Rating Scale (SABRS)

The SABRS (Aumack, 1962) contains 33 items and like the first part of the CAP addresses conversational/interpersonal skills and intellectual competence. Clients are rated on a true/false basis as to whether they display the 33 behaviors described in the scale.

TABLE 12. Estimates of the Test–Retest Reliability of the General Behavior Rating Scales Instrument[a]

Subscale	Reliability
NOSIE-30	
Social competence	.71
Social interest	.67
Neatness	.78
Psychosis	.59
Irritability	.71
Retardation	.63
Community Adjustment Potential	.73
Social Adjustment Behavior Rating Scale	.76

[a]All correlations are based on 108 clients and are significant ($p <$ .05).

RELIABILITY

As with the modular assessments, the correlations between the first and second progress assessments (i.e., the 4- and 8-week assessments) were used to estimate the temporal stability of the behavior ratings. The correlations between the first and second progress assessments for the NOSIE-30 subscales, CAP, and SABRS are presented in Table 12.

As Table 12 shows, five of the eight correlations are above .70 and only one (the NOSIE-30 Psychosis subscale) is below .60.

There are also data on the interobserver agreement for the NOSIE-30 subscales. As part of their 1981 study, Patterson *et al.* had four judges independently rate the behavior of 11 clients on the six NOSIE-30 subscales. For all subscales the average interobserver correlation was greater than .70.

VALIDITY

The general behavior rating scales that were employed have been validated by their authors. The clients of the program were considered to be sufficiently similar to those used in the validation of the scales not to require independent validation.

DID CLIENTS LEARN SKILLS TAUGHT IN THE MODULES?

Three different designs were used to determine whether the clients were learning the skills taught in the modules. The first two were true experimental designs and the third was the quasi-experimental, institutional cycle design described in Chapter 7. These three designs were used in consort to determine the efficacy of the training modules. That is, no one research design was capable of fully evaluating the training modules, but by combining the strengths of each of the designs we were able, we believe, to achieve a valid evaluation of the modular training.

Research Designs Employed

Within-Subjects Experimental Design

For two of the modules we were able to conduct experimental investigations which employed within-subject designs. The Personal Information Training module was evaluated through a version of multiple baseline procedure, and the Conversation Training module was evaluated with an ABAB reversal design. An explanation of these types of designs was presented in Chapter 5.

Between-Subjects Experimental Designs

Two of the modules (Communication Training and Self-esteem Training) were evaluated through an experimental/control group design. In this type of design subjects are randomly assigned to a treatment (experimental) or control group and the pretreatment and posttreatment measurements of the two groups are compared. According to Campbell and Stanley (1963), this type of design is a true experimental design which controls for all the factors which would jeopardize the internal validity of a study.

Both the within- and between-subject experiments enabled us to eliminate the possibility that *history* and/or *maturation* were responsible for the changes observed in the modular skills. *History* refers to specific events over and above the treatment which could produce the same effects as the treatment (e.g., improved medication). *Maturation* refers to changes within the subjects which occur as the product of the passage of time (e.g., growing older). In the within-subject designs, treatment is systematically administered to a group of subjects (either by dividing treatment into subunits or administering and withdrawing treatment). It is highly unlikely that some external event or the simple passage of time could produce effects which would be comparable to the effects produced by the actual treatment. In the between-subjects designs, random assignment is used to control for history and maturation. Since clients were randomly assigned to a module or control condition and measured at the same points in time, history and maturation should have affected them equally. Thus, any difference between the two groups on the posttreatment measurement must be attributed to treatment rather than history or maturation. These two types of designs also control for the possibilities that changes in the measurement procedures, selection of clients, or attrition rates among the clients receiving the treatment could have produced the observed effects.

These designs provided a valuable first step in the evaluation of a program component. They could not be used, however, to provide a definitive evaluation of a program component. The fact that treatment effects could be demonstrated with these designs did not mean that, *in practice*, clients were changing as the result of a training module. The manner in which a module was conducted as part of the day-to-day treatment of a client may have been quite different from the manner in which it was conducted during its experimental evaluation. As Cowen (1978) has pointed out, in treatment programs there is often considerable slippage between a treatment component as it is conceptualized by program coordinators and as it is actually carried out by the program staff. Thus, it was also necessary to evaluate program components as they were actually conducted, that is *in vivo* rather than *in vitro*.

The Institutional Cycle Design

The *social validity* of a program component could not be evaluated by using the within-subject and between-subjects designs. *Social validity* refers to the societal impact of some treatment modality. Does the treatment produce a change which is socially meaningful or important (Wolf, 1978)? Since these experiments were time-limited and may not have reflected treatment as it occurred on a day-to-day basis, they could not provide the data to determine the social validity of a program component. Because of these factors, it was necessary to use a third approach to evaluate the program components, the institutional cycle design. This is a quasi-experimental design, which "does not use random assignment to create comparisons from which treatment-caused change is inferred" (Cook & Campbell, 1979, p. 6). This design, which was mentioned in Chapter 7, and the reasoning underlying its usage are particularly suited to questions of evaluating ongoing treatment programs. The basic logic of this design is to look for treatment effects in one group of participants who undergo exactly the same treatment at a later point in time. To illustrate this design, consider a hypothetical training module, Module A. During the first week of a client's stay in the program and before treatment in Module A begins, a client receives a modular assessment. On the basis of the initial assessments, clients who require training in A are assigned to the module. They receive three weeks of training. Training continues during the 4th week, but during this week the client also recevies the first progress assessment in Module A. If criterion is reached, the client "graduates" from the module. If not, the client continues training. Every 4 weeks the client receives an additional progress assessment (i.e., second, third, fourth progress assessment). After clients graduate from the module, they are no longer assessed in it. Immediately prior to discharge from the program, clients receive a discharge assessment in the module. This pattern of data collection (i.e., intake, progress and discharge assessments) is repeated for all clients enrolled in the module. Although clients enter and leave the module at different times in the calendar year, all clients' assessments in a module are comparable with respect to how many weeks of modular training each had had before the first, second (and so forth) progress assessments. Thus, it is possible to group clients together on the basis of how much training they had received in a module. This grouping process continues until a sufficient number of clients have gone through the module to permit meaningful data analysis. The analysis of changes across assessments provides the first test of the efficacy of the module.

At some point in the course of conducting Module A, the first group of clients is ended and a second set of clients starts participating in the module. The data collection procedure is identical to that used with the first set. The two groups differ only in when the clients entered the module. For example, the first group could be comprised of clients who entered the module between January and June 1981, the second group clients who entered the module between July and December 1981. The intake, progress, and discharge assessments on the first group are analyzed against those of the second group. The changes across assessments within each group and for the groups combined are also investigated. In the interest of clarifying the design as we used it, a schematic representation is presented in Figure 14. Although this example utilizes a module which began when clients entered the overall program, in practice this design was used also to evaluate advanced modules, those which began after a client had completed the basic modules.

In terms of internal validity, this design can control for history. The initial, progress, and discharge assessments of the two groups are compared. If the initial assessments of the two groups are comparable and both groups show comparable changes from initial to progress

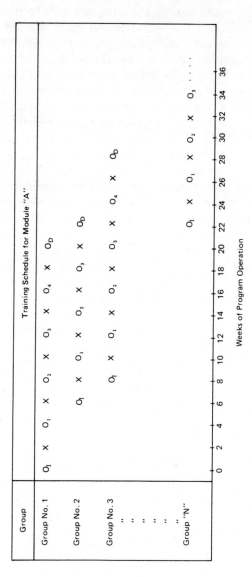

FIGURE 14. Schematic representation of institutional cycle design as used by the Gerontology Program.

and progress to discharge assessments, then one can reasonably conclude that the outcomes are not attributable to history. If history were
responsible for the observed outcome, then the specific event or series
of events that was causing the outcome would have had to occur
twice at two different times and would have affected the two groups
in an identical fashion. Although this is possible, history is a much
less plausible explanation of the results than a replication of the
program effect. Even if the initial assessments of the two groups are
not comparable, comparable amounts of change within each group
would strongly argue against history as an explanation of the obtained effects. Indeed, this second case may provide a stronger argument for the effects of the program, because comparable or parallel
changes can be replicated with two groups that were different when
they started the program.

      This design also controls for selection. Selection effects can occur
when there are biases in assignment to experimental and control
groups (sampling error). In such instances, differences between the
groups on the dependent measure may be due to the initial selection
or assignment differences (Cook & Campbell, 1979). In the institutional cycle design, there are within-group (e.g., initial assessment
versus discharge assessment) comparisons as well as between-group
comparisons (e.g., initial for the first group versus discharge for the
second group). Although differences in the latter comparison could be
attributed to selection, differences in the former comparison could
not. That is, a significant within-group change cannot be attributed to
selection. If this change occurs in both groups, then both history and
selection can be discounted as causes of the observed effect.

      The greatest weakness of this design is its inability to control for
maturation. In the present instance, the term *maturation* is used to
refer to the general impact of the Gerontology Program on its clients.
It is possible that simply being in the program rather than modular
training could produce positive changes in clients. Recall that many
clients came to the program from severely deprived environments in
which they may have had little or no contact with other people. By
contrast, the Gerontology Program provided the elderly clients with
the chance to interact with others in a positive and supportive social
setting. The change in environments alone could conceivably have
produced improvement in clients. For example, the simple fact that a
client must interact with the staff and other clients on a day-to-day
basis may have resulted in an improvement in personal hygiene
habits through modeling, peer pressure, or subtle reinforcement of
positive behavior by staff and other clients. Since modular training
began almost as soon as the client entered this new environment,

there was no way to separate this general program effect from the effect of modular training. For example, many of the clients come from institutions where there is strict separation by sex on male and female wards with little or no interaction between the two. If a client improves in ADL I skills, is it because of the training or because of a desire to appear more attractive to the opposite sex?

In view of this potential confusion, it was deemed advisable that whenever possible an experimental investigation (which controls for this kind of maturation) be conducted. If the results of an experimental investigation of a module supported the results of the quasi-experimental study, then we would have much greater confidence in the conclusions drawn from the latter type of study.

From a program evaluation viewpoint, this quasi-experimental design has two major strong points. First and foremost, it permitted us to collect evaluative data on the modules without disrupting the normal procedures for training clients. This served the purpose of obtaining ecologically valid data on the modules because data were collected as part of the actual clinical treatment of clients. Second, as will be discussed in the next chapter, it provided data which can be used to determine the social validity of particular program components as well as the entire program.

The Experimental Evaluation of Modules

Experimental investigations were conducted on Communication, Conversation, Personal Information, and Self-esteem Training modules. Each of these is described below.

Communication Skills Training

The purpose of this experiment (Patterson, Smith, Goodale, & Miller, 1978a) was to determine whether the Communication Skills module was effective in teaching the clients how to express pleasure and displeasure. As discussed in Chapter 4, the lack of appropriate and effective expressiveness in social interactions is believed to be a fairly common problem among elderly clients. This module was intended to remedy this deficiency.

The basic method in this study was to assign clients randomly to either the Communication module or the Conversation module in which clients were reinforced for talking to others and compare the two groups in their ability to express pleasure and displeasure.

The rationale for using the Conversation module as a comparison for specific training effects of the Communication module was that such a comparison group controlled for several variables. First, all clients were enrolled in the same program. Second, clients in both groups attended a group activity of about the same length on the same days. Third, clients in both groups received social and token reinforcement. Last and most important, clients in both groups were reinforced for interacting socially; in fact, the conversation group was required to interact much more than the communication group. Thus, if improvements in expressiveness could be caused by any of these variables, such improvements should occur in both groups. Conversely, any improvements in expressiveness found to be greater for the communication groups could be claimed with some confidence to be due to the specific training procedures.

Training Procedures. The training procedure for the communication group was the same as that described in Chapter 4, with the exception that this group received 6 weeks of training on the expression of pleasure first, followed by assessments; then six weeks of training on the expression of displeasure, followed by assessments. The training of conversation group was like that described in Chapter 4.

Assessement Procedures. The assessment instrument was the Communication Behavior Rating Scale (BRS) as previously described. However, the actual assessment procedures for the experiment differed from the routine module assessments. A group of four raters who did not know the clients was obtained to make the experimental ratings. These raters received training with the BRS so that they were able to achieve average interrater correlations of .88 on preexperimental role-playing trials. The raters never attended any training sessions for any group, but instead made ratings from videotapes of the actual client role-plays. Thus, the raters did not know which clients were in which group. Prior to any training, clients in both role-played and were videotaped for later rating. Videotapes were made in exactly the same way of all subjects role-playing after those in Communication training had been trained to express pleasure and again after these latter subjects had been trained to express displeasure. Thus, blind ratings by reliable raters were available of both experimental and comparison subjects before training and again after the experimental group had been trained on each of two types of expression.

Analyses and Outcomes. The data were analyzed by means of a 2 × 2 × 3 mixed-model analysis of variance. Communication skills was operationally defined as the average of the four observers' ratings on the behavior rating scale of the clients' expression of pleasure and displeasure. The analysis of variance addressed three questions. First, did the clients who participated in communication training display better communication skills than the clients who participated in the coversation reinforcement group? Second, did the clients show any differences in their ability to express pleasure and displeasure? And finally, did the clients show improvement in their communication skills across assessment periods? The data relevant to these questions are presented in Figure 15.

Figure 15 shows the total communication skills ratings (i.e., pleasure and displeasure combined) for the two groups. Although the two groups did not differ prior to training, the communication group was rated significantly higher than the comparison group on the total score after training. Overall, the communication training group received higher ratings of communication skills than did the conversation group, F (1, 16) = 7.58, p < .05. This was true for the expression of both pleasure and displeasure. That is, despite the fact that the first 6 weeks of training in the communication group only involved the expression of pleasure, these clients were rated higher in both pleasure and displeasure than were clients in the conversation groups. There was also a significant group (i.e., communication or conversation) by assessment interaction, F (2, 32) = 4.55, p < .05. Although the two groups did not differ in their pretraining ratings, the communication group's later ratings were significantly higher than those of the conversation group. The average increase for the communication group was 24.91 points; it was 7.42 for the conversation group. Thus, whereas all clients showed improvement in communica-

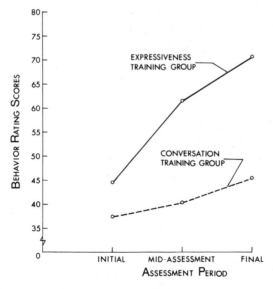

FIGURE 15. Total scores on the Behavior Rating Scale for two groups in the Communication Training experiment.

tion skills, the increase in the communication group was over three times as great as the increase in the conversation group. Closer inspection of this difference disclosed that it was primarily due to the dramatic increase in the ratings of the communication group from the pretraining to the 6-week assessment.

Finally, it was possible to obtain an estimate of the extent to which the effects of communication generalized beyond the formal assessments. After the training was completed, clients in both groups were asked to approach a client or staff member on the unit and express either pleasure or displeasure with that person (depending on how they felt about the person). These interactions were rated by trained observers. The members of the communication training group ranked significantly higher in this *in vivo* assessment than did members of the comparison group.

Conclusions. The results of this study provide rather strong evidence for the efficacy of the Communication Skills Training module. Clients who underwent this training were much better at the expression of affect than were the clients in the conversation/comparison group. Further, the effects of this training generalized to another response. Although the clients initially received training only in the expression of pleasure, after 6 weeks their expression of displeasure also improved. Not only did the behavior taught generalize to another response within the role-playing situation, it also generalized to another location, from the role play of the classroom to the social area of the unit. That is, clients who received communication training were better able to express pleasure and displeasure in their day-to-day interactions with others than were members of the conversation/comparison group.

Conversation Training

The goal of the conversation training was to increase the frequency with which clients engaged in informal, social conversations with one another. Two interrelated experiments were conducted to determine the efficacy of the training procedures (Patterson, Smith, Goodale, & Miller, 1978b).

To recapitulate briefly, in conversation training clients are instructed to remain in the social area of their treatment unit and to converse with another client. Clients are required to do this for about 1 hour a day. During this period, observers are assigned the task of watching and recording the behavior of four to six clients each. Observers monitored their assigned clients for a series of six 5-minute periods. The observers recorded whether the clients were conversing (i.e., talking with someone close to them) during the second half of each minute they were observed. At the end of the total observation period, clients received feedback from the observers as to the frequency of their conversing and both token and social reinforcement for engaging in conversation.

Experiment I. The first experiment was conducted on seven residential treatment clients. An ABAB reversal design was employed. The ABAB reversal design obtains baseline behaviors in the first A condition, followed by the reinforcement of the target behaviors in the first B condition. After a period of time, reinforcement is withdrawn and the client returns to the baseline condition (Second A). Finally, the reinforcement is reinstated in the record B condition. In this experiment, the clients were simply observed and their behavior recorded during the first baseline condition. After 5 days of baseline, the treatment condition was introduced. In this condition, clients received verbal feedback on their performance, token reinforcement, and praise. After 17 treatment sessions, the baseline condition was reintroduced followed by the second treatment condition. Figure 16 presents the percentage of intervals with conversation averaged across clients. As this figure shows, this percentage was higher during the treatment conditions than during baseline conditions. During the ini-

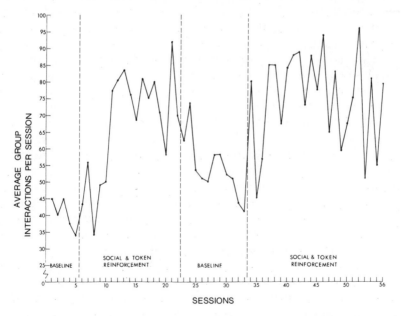

FIGURE 16. Average group interactions per session of the residential Conversation Training group during repeated baseline and repeated experimental conditions.

tial baseline period the clients conversed during an average of 40% of the recording intervals; 67% during the first treatment condition; and down to 55% during the second baseline period. In the second treatment condition, they were conversing during an average of 75% of the intervals.

Experiment II. The second experiment had two purposes: first, to replicate Experiment I with day treatment clients and second, to determine whether social reinforcement and feedback in the absence of tokens were each effective in increasing the frequency of conversational behavior. This latter goal was deemed important because in some settings in which conversation training might be beneficial it might not be possible to establish a token economy. The clients used in this experiment were five individuals randomly selected from the day treatment population.

In the first portion of this experiment, baseline conversing was observed for 7 sessions each on consecutive days followed by a treatment condition of 15 daily sessions in which the clients received feedback and social reinforcement (verbal praise) but no tokens. Then the clients returned to the baseline conditions for 8 days. In the second treatment condition, feedback, social reinforcement, *and token reinforcement* were introduced for 18 days and then the clients returned to the baseline condition for 10 days. At the conclusion of the collection of the final baseline data, the experiment was terminated and the clients were placed in the regular conversation training module for continued treatment.

It should be pointed out that from a strict technical point of view, Experiment II should be considered as two studies conducted consecutively on the same subjects. The first study employed an ABA design and the second an ACA design. The actual interactive effects of the two treatment conditions could not be studied without a more complex design, but this study was not intended to investigate the *relative* efficacy of the two treatments. Rather, we wanted to determine the efficacy of the first treatment condition (social reinforcement and feedback only) in increasing conversation as well as that of the second treatment condition (social and token reinforcement). Figure 17 presents the results of the second experiment. Under the baseline condition, the day treatment clients spent 55% of the intervals talking. This percentage is somewhat higher than the 40% found for the residential clients. The level of conversing in the treatment conditions was comparable, 71% in the social reinforcement and feedback condition, 74% in the combined condition. Note that these percentages are quite close to the 75% observed in the second treatment condition among the residential clients. However, the final baseline was some-

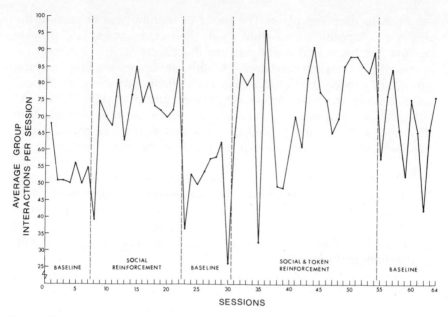

FIGURE 17. Average group interactions per session of the day treatment Conversation Training group under the baseline and two experimental conditions.

what unstable, and there appeared to be a tendency toward extinction for unknown reasons. The overall average during this baseline period when there was no reinforcement dropped to 60% of the intervals with conversation.

The results of these two experiments indicate that the procedures used in conversation training can greatly increase the frequency of conversation among both residential and day treatment clients. Also, among the day treatment clients it was found that social reinforcement and feedback alone were effective in producing an increase in conversation. However, since these data were collected within the treatment setting, we could not at this point determine whether the procedures employed would result in the generalization or maintenance of conversation skills. Quasi-experimental data relating to generalization and maintenance are reported later in this chapter.

Personal Information Training (PIT)

This study (Johnson, Frallicciardi, & Patterson, 1977) was conducted early in the development of this module. Its goal at that time was to determine whether clients who had received a medical diagnosis of organic brain syndrome (OBS) could learn to orient themselves as to time and place. The mode of training was to present the clients with specific information about their environment and provide positive reinforcement contingent on the clients' giving a correct response to a question pertaining to this environment. The teaching procedure consisted of questioning each client, providing praise and touch if he or she gave the correct answer, and prompting the correct answer if it were not given (tokens were not used as reinforcers in this study). Prompting procedures included saying, or partially saying, the correct answer as well as showing the client written materials.

The clients used in this study were four men between the ages of 59 and 71. All were from the day treatment program. They were selected on the basis that they had had either a primary or secondary diagnosis of OBS and had moderate to severe deficits in the areas of personal data, time, and place orientation and knowledge of significant others in their lives.

The design employed in this study was a variant of the multiple baseline design. The information to be taught was divided into four areas: (1) personal data (PD), which consisted of the client's name, address, telephone number, age, and date and place of birth; (2) significant people (SP), the names of relatives, friends, doctor, and case manager at the Florida Mental Health Institute; (3) Time (T), the time of day, time of the week, month, and year, and the identification of the next major holiday; and (4) location (L), where the client was at that time, the city, state, and region of the country he lived in. For all the clients, their baseline performance was determined by asking them the 21 questions which covered these four areas each morning for 5 days prior to the onset of training. Then the training began. The four categories were taught sequentially (i.e., first personal data, then significant people, etc.). Each category was taught until at least 80% of the clients achieved 80% correct responses without prompting for two consecutive days. Performance was measured by asking the questions on all four categories immediately after a training session.

During the first training session, clients received training only in personal data. After training in this category, the clients' performance in this and the three other areas was measured. If the training in this category was effective, clients' performance in it should improve, while their performance in the three other areas should remain at the baseline level. The reader will note that this design provides a control for the effects of history and maturation. If factors external to the training (such as a medical treatment or family interventions) were producing improvement in one category, then improvement in all four categories should take place simultaneously. Similarly, if the passage of time was a significant factor (i.e., maturation effects), then the client should also show improvement in all four categories simultaneously. If, however, improvement took place only in the category being trained, then these explanations of improvement could be excluded.

The average of the percentage of correct responses for four subjects during baseline and after each category of material was taught appears in Figure 18. This figure shows that on the average answers to each category improved after it was taught. Also, with one exception, the performance on each category did not improve until it was taught. The exception was that responses regarding significant people improved when personal data was taught. An indication of the magnitude of the improvement due to training is given by the fact that the mean baseline performance of all subjects was 53.7% correct, but the mean performance for all subjects for the measures on each category taken immediately after each category was taught was 73.3% correct. The data for each of the subjects taken individually showed

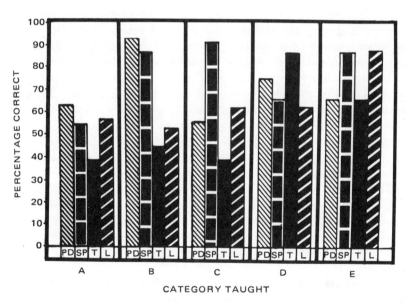

FIGURE 18. Mean performance of four subjects in Personal Information Training as a function of category taught at a specific time. Section A shows baseline performance. Section B shows performance after only Personal Data (PD) was taught. Section C shows performance after training in both PD and Significant People (SP). Section D shows performance after training in PD, SP, and Time (T). Section E shows performance immediately after training in all four categories, including Location (L).

the same general pattern as Figure 18. Subject 1 improved on each category after it was taught and did not improve on any other categories until it was taught. Subjects 2 and 4 improved on each category after it was taught and did not improve on any other category until it was taught, with the exception that both PD and SP improved when only PD was taught. Subject 3 improved on PD, SP, and T after only PD had been taught, but otherwise showed improvement on each of the other categories after it was taught.

Statistical confirmation for the observed effectiveness of treatment was obtained by use of a sign test (Siegal, 1956). The logic of this analysis was that under the null hypothesis of no treatment effect the performance of all subjects considered individually on a particular category taught at a particular time would not be better than their individual performance on other categories not taught at that time. Conversely, the experimental hypothesis was that if the treatment was effective each subject should perform better on each category immediately after it was taught than on the other categories. The sign test indicated that the null hypothesis could be rejected at the .01 level of significance.

These data and analyses indicate that the clients were acquiring information during the training periods and retaining it until immediately after the end of training. A second, related question in this study was the extent to which the information the clients acquired was retained after training. We were able to obtain follow-up data on how well two of the clients retained the information 4 and 12 weeks after training. The first of these clients showed very good retention at 4 weeks. His scores in the four categories at baseline had averaged 49.5%, but at the 4-week follow-up, he achieved 84.5% correct. The 12-week follow-up assessment still showed considerable retention for this subject, with 76.3% correct.

The follow-up results for the second client were not quite so good. His average score at baseline was 61.3%, at four weeks, 73.8 percent, and at 12 weeks 66.5%. However, an encouraging result with this subject was that he scored 100% on significant people on both follow-ups, whereas he had achieved only 65% on this category during baseline.

The results of the study, while not definitive, were encouraging. They indicate that the techniques employed in the Personal Information Training module were effective in enabling some clients with OBS diagnoses to reacquire important personal information. These findings led us to implement the PIT module formally and evaluate it further, as is reported in the next section of this chapter.

Self-esteem Training Module

The purpose of this study (O'Sullivan, Eberly, Patterson, & Penner, 1979) was to determine whether behavioral techniques could be used to improve the clients' self-esteem and satisfaction with their lives. This question was investigated by means of the following procedure. Clients who passed the PIT assessment at admission or after training (i.e., who were not in need of Personal Information Training) were randomly assigned either to the Self-esteem module or to a group which involved the clients in social leisure activities. The latter group of clients constituted the control group. Twenty-four clients were assigned to each group and remained in the experiment for at least 8 weeks.

Self-esteem Training. The Self-esteem Training lasted 8 weeks. The group met three times a week for an hour. The basic procedure in the module was to get a client to make public positive statements about himself (e.g., "I'm a generous person"), to have other clients support this self-statement by examples such as "I saw him/her give John a magazine Friday," and then to provide reinforcement in the form of praise and tokens for these positive self-statements.

A session began with the trainer stating the purpose of the module—to increase the clients' self-esteem. Then the trainer would ask a client to make a positive self-statement. The statements made would tend to be rather general, and the trainer would mildly challenge the client to support the positive self-statement with a specific behavioral example of the positive attribute. Since it was believed that peer support was an important component of this module, the trainer would then ask other group members to make positive statements about the client who had just spoken. Clients who did so were reinforced with praise by the trainer. While this process was going on, an observer stationed in the back of the room recorded the number of positive self-statements each client made and the number of positive statements each client made about another. At the end of the session, the trainer recorded on the recording sheet the positive contributions each member made and reinforced the clients with praise and tokens.

Comparison Group. At the same time the self-esteem training was being conducted, the comparison group clients were taking part in the social leisure group. Clients in this group engaged in activities such as arts and crafts, table games, and music appreciation. The social leisure group also met three times a week for 8 weeks.

It was originally intended that all clients in the two groups would switch group assignments at the end of 8 weeks (i.e., Self-esteem clients would go into the social leisure and vice versa). However, because of discharges from the program, few of the clients received both the full 8 weeks of Self-esteem Training and social leisure activities.

Assessments. Three different assessments were used. All were conducted outside the Self-esteem module or social leisure group. Clients in both groups were assessed prior to training and after 4 and 8 weeks of training. The test–retest reliabilities of the assessments were presented in the previous section.

The measure of self-esteem was a modified version of Rosenberg's (1965) Self-esteem Scale. The scale is a 10-item self-report scale in which respondents indicate whether they agree or disagree with a series of statements about their opinions of themselves. Although all 10 items were included in the modified version, some of them had to be modified for our clients. This was because pilot work had indicated that many of the clients had difficulty understanding statements which contained a negative or double negative. Therefore, all statements which contained negatives were rewritten into simple declarative sentences. Some typical items from the scale were "All in all, I tend to feel that I am a failure" and "On the whole, I am satisfied with myself." The scale is scored such that the lower a respondent's score, the higher the level of self-esteem.

Life satisfaction was measured with a modified version of Neugarten *et al.*'s (1961) Life Satisfaction Scale. This is a 20-item self-report scale in which respondents indicate whether they agree or disagree with statements about themselves and their lives. Although the scale was developed for an elderly population, pilot work disclosed that statements which contained negatives, as with the Rosenberg, confused our clients. Therefore such statements were rewritten. Some typical items from this scale were "My life could be happier than it is now" and "As I look back on my life, I am fairly well satisfied." Scores were summed across items. On the Life Satisfaction Scale the higher the score, the higher the respondent's level of life satisfaction.

The final assessment was developed specifically for this module. In a structured interview clients were asked: (a) "Could you tell me the things that you like about yourself and your life right now?" and (b) "Could you tell me the things that you don't like about yourself and your life right now?" It will be recalled that the number of positive and negative statements the clients made were positively correlated. This indicated that the verbosity of some clients may have influenced the number of statements they made. Therefore, rather than using frequency counts of positive and negative self-statements as a separate dependent measure, we had to devise a method which would control for this "talkativeness" factor. The number of positive self-statements minus the number of negative statements was used.

Results. The scores on the self-esteem scale were analyzed with a 2 × 3 mixed-model analysis of variance. The between-subject variable was group (experimental versus control); the within-subject variable was assessments (initial, 4-week, 8-week). In this and the other two analyses an alpha level of .10 was set for all main effects and interactions. A least significant difference (LSD) level was used for the *post hoc* comparisons of means.

The self-esteem scores of the experimental and control groups did not differ. The F ratio for assessments was a significant, F (2, 92) = 4.05, $p < .05$. The LSD test disclosed that the self-esteem scores at the conclusion of training were significantly higher than the scores obtained prior to training. Finally, there was a significant groups by assessments interaction, F (2, 92) = 2.36, $p < .10$. The LSD test disclosed that while the two groups did not differ in their first two assessments, the experimental group evidenced significantly higher levels of self-esteem at the completion of training than did the control group. This difference was the result of a continuous improvement across assessments among the experimental clients while the control clients did not change.

The average life satisfaction score of the experimental clients was significantly higher than the score of the control clients, F (1, 46) = 3.06, $p < .10$. The LSD test disclosed that the final assessment of life satisfaction was significantly higher than the pretraining assessment. Although the interaction term was not significant, planned comparisons did reveal differences in how the two groups changed. Prior to training the two groups did not differ, but on the 4-week and 8-week assessments the experimental group's average score was significantly higher than the control group's. Whereas experimental clients improved across assessments, control clients did not change.

On the self-statements measure, the average score of the experimental group was significantly higher than the average score of the control group, F (1, 46) = 5.26, $p < .05$. The F ratios for assessments and the group by assessments interaction were not significant. The examination of cell means through the LSD test disclosed that while the two groups did not differ prior to training, the experimental group had significantly higher scores on this measure than did the control group at the 4-week and 8-week assessments.

The results of this study provide fairly strong support for the efficacy of Self-esteem Training. On all three measures the experimental group showed significant improvement and the control group did not change. Thus, we can conclude that the modular teaching approach can be used to modify elderly clients' level of self-esteem.

THE EVALUATION OF THE MODULES USING THE INSTITUTIONAL CYCLE DESIGN

The evaluations of the training modules using a modified version of the institutional cycle design (Campbell & Stanley, 1963) are presented in this section. As the reader may recall, the major strength of this design is that it permits the evaluation of an ongoing program in a manner which controls for most of the factors that might jeopardize internal validity.

The primary goal of these evaluations was to determine whether clients learned the skills which were taught in the modules. An important component of this evaluation was to rule out the possibility that changes (if found) were peculiar to a specific set of clients or period of time. Therefore, the assessments from two groups were used in the evaluations of the modules. The first group of clients was comprised of people who entered the program between August 17, 1977 (the start of Phase II of the Gerontology Program) and March 23, 1978. The intake, progress, and discharge assessments taken on these clients were summed to provide a sufficient number of clients for parametric statistical analyses. The second group was comprised of clients who entered the program between March 24, 1978 and December 1, 1978.[1] The assessments of the members of the second group were also summed.

Since clients in the day and residential components differed both in their characteristics and their time in treatment, members of the two groups were separated on this basis also. This permitted an examination of differences and similarities in how the day and residential clients acquired skills and changed behaviors. For all clients, there was an initial and discharge assessment on each module, and for those who received training in the module, at least a first progress assessment. An examination of clients' performance in the modules disclosed that a large percentage of them reached the criteria for graduation from the module after 4 weeks of training, that is, by the first progress assessment, and subsequently withdrew from the training. For this reason, initial, first progress, and discharge assessments

---

[1]March 23 was selected as the dividing point in an attempt to have approximately equal numbers of clients in each of the two groups. The December 1, 1978 cut-off date for the record group was prior to the end of Phase II, and therefore the total number of research clients in the two groups (177) is less than the total for Phase II clients (227).

were used.[2] Thus, each module was evaluated by means of a 2 × 2 × 3 mixed-model analysis of variance. The classification variables were Group 1 versus Group 2 (based on when clients entered the program), day versus residential treatment (based on program component), and assessments (initial, first progress, and discharge). The alpha level for all main effects, interactions, and planned comparisons of cell means was set at .05. In these analyses, the following questions were addressed: First, overall, did clients show significant improvement in their modular skills (as measured by the modular assessments)? Second, did clients differ initially or in their rate of change as a function of when they entered the program? And, third, did day and residential clients differ initially or in their rate of change in the modular skills?

For several of the modules, we employed a second evaluation procedure. Each modular assessment had been examined and clinical professional judgment applied to set a criterion score for successful completion of that module, whenever feasible. (This was needed in order to decide when a client was no longer in need of training in that module.) For those modules which had such graduation criteria, we examined the number of clients who had reached them.

Activities of Daily Living I (ADL I)

This module attempts to teach clients the rudiments of personal hygiene, proper dress, and proper eating habits. Skills in the modules are assessed with a 10-item instrument yielding a score between 0 and 10. The assessment has moderate test–retest reliability and good inter-observer agreement and appears to be construct valid (cf. section on reliability and validity).

One hundred seventy one clients received initial ADL I assessments and 67 of them (39%) needed training in this module. Of these 67 clients, 54 (80.6%) had valid initial, first progress, and discharge assessments. Overall, the clients showed significant improvement from their initial to first progress assessment, while the first progress and discharge assessments did not differ. Day and residential clients did not differ significantly, but there was a significant main effect for (time-based) groups. The planned comparisons revealed that clients

[2]Although the time period between the initial and first progress assessments was 4 weeks for all clients, the interval between the first progress and discharge assessments varied as a function of how long a client remained in the overall program. For some clients in some modules, the interval was as short as 4 weeks; for other, it was 12 to 16 weeks. Because of this variability, caution must be exercised in the interpretation of change (or the absence thereof) between the first progress and discharge assessments.

who entered the program after the dividing date had significantly lower initial scores than did the clients who entered before this date. Despite their initial difference, both groups showed significant initial to first progress assessment improvement and did not differ in their rate of improvement, that is, the group by assessments interaction was not significant. In other words, the effect obtained with Group 1 was replicated by Group 2 (we will return to the group differences shortly).

Although the analysis of variance indicated that significant change had occurred, we were concerned to know whether this reflected true improvement in ADL I skills or merely an artifactual improvement. To be more specific, it was possible that the significant difference may have been due to the clients' learning how to score well on the assessment instrument and/or rater biases. We were able to obtain independent evidence that the improvement found in this analysis probably reflected a real change in the skills taught in ADL I.

As noted earlier, clients were rated on the Neatness subscale of the NOSIE-30 during the same weeks they received their assessments in ADL I. These ratings were made independently by someone other than the person who administered the ADL I assessment. Patterson *et al.* (1982) have found that the Neatness subscale and the ADL I assessment appear to be addressing the same set of behaviors. If the changes found by the ADL I assessment scores were generalizing beyond the specific assessment, then there should be a significant correlation between the change in clients' ADL I assessment scores and changes in their NOSIE-30 Neatness subscale ratings. To test this, a change score from initial to first progress assessment on the ADL I assessment and the Neatness subscale was computed for each subject and the scores were correlated. The correlation was $+.53$, which was significant ($p < .05$). This correlation was then compared to the correlations between changes in ADL I and changes on the other NOSIE-30 subscales. The ADL I–Neatness correlation was significantly greater than the correlations between ADL I and the five other subscales.

Achievement of Criterion. The criterion for successful completion of ADL I was 9 of the 10 items correct. Of the 54 clients who entered this module and who had valid initial, first progress, and discharge assessments, 27 (50%) met this criterion. Eighteen left the program before completing training in the module, and nine (16.7%) failed to reach the criterion despite 12 or more weeks of training.

In interpreting the effects of ADL I training, two issues must be addressed. The first is the difference between the (time-based) groups. Although the two groups showed similar acquisition curves, the initial differences between them raised the possibility that either clients or assessment procedures had changed across time. As noted earlier, the dividing date was chosen in order to generate equal numbers of clients in the groups. It did not reflect the true calendar midpoint during the evaluation period. In order to determine whether there was a systematic change across time in the ADL I initial assessments, date of entry into the program was regressed onto the clients' initial ADL I assessment scores. If there was a systematic time-dependent relationship, there should have been a negative correlation between entrance date and initial ADL I assessment scores, that is, clients who entered earlier should have had higher scores. The correlation was nonsignificant. Thus, the difference in the initial scores of the two groups does not appear to be due to systematic changes in the clients admitted or to the manner in which they were assessed. Rather, it appears to be an artifact of the dates used to define the two groups.

A more serious problem in the interpretation of these data is the possibility that maturation rather than training was responsible for the improvement found. There is a possibility that clients' ADL I skills would have improved significantly even in the absence of modular training. Certainly, in the course of 4 weeks the staff and other clients could have engaged in behavior which imparted the personal hygiene, dress, and eating habits to the clients enrolled in ADL I. This possibility causes caution in claiming that modular training was the sole reason for the improvement in these skills; however, the modular training does provide the most logical explanation for the improvement in personal hygiene skills.

Activities of Daily Living II (ADL II)

ADL II is an advanced module for clients who have graduated from ADL I. It was intended for clients who planned to live in supervised environments after discharge. The 10-item assessment instrument measures skills in the areas of laundry, money management, nutrition, housekeeping, and use of the telephone. The assessment has high temporal stability and interobserver agreement.

Clients do not enter ADL II before they have reached criterion in ADL I. Of the 88 clients who received initial assessments in ADL II, 29 also had first progress and discharge assessments. The small number of clients in the ADL II evaluation was primarily due to the fact that many of the clients entered this module relatively late in their stay in the program and were discharged before they received the first progress assessment.[3]

Clients did not differ as a function of when they entered the program or whether they were in the day or residential treatment component. The clients showed a significant improvement in their scores from the initial to first progress assessment.

Achievement of Criterion. In the judgment of the staff who developed the module and the assessment, 90% of the items correct on a progress assessment represented successful completion of the module. Of the 88 clients who received initial assessments in this module, 40 required training in it, and 29 of them were in the module for at least 4 weeks. Of these 29, 10 (34.5%) reached criterion, 16 left the module before completing training, and 3 (10.3%) failed to reach criterion despite 12 or more weeks of training.

There are several considerations which make the evaluation of ADL II difficult. The first of these is the inability of this design to control for maturation effects. Clients could have acquired the ADL II skills in the absence of any specific training. In order to gain some information about this alternative explanation, we conducted an additional analysis. As we noted before, clients entered this module after they had completed ADL I training or achieved ADL I criterion on initial assessment. This resulted in considerable variability between clients in terms of how long they were in the program before they entered ADL II. If length of time in the program *per se* was responsible for the changes we found, there should be a significant positive correlation between time in the program and initial ADL II scores. When this correlation was computed, it was negative (and nonsignificant). That is, the longer clients had been in the program, the *lower* their initial scores tended to be. This finding does not totally exclude maturation as an explanation of the changes found, but it does make this alternative explanation somewhat less likely.

A second problem is the lack of any independent confirmation of the validity of the changes obtained in the ADL II assessments. Unlike ADL I (and some of the modules to be presented later), there was no independent rating of the skills taught in ADL II. Thus, the possibility cannot be excluded that the improvement observed was artifactual rather than real. Although this ambiguity exists, the validity of the ADL II changes found may be based on the fact that the

---

[3]Approximately 25% of the clients who entered ADL II were discharged within 2 weeks of their progress assessments. For these clients, the first progress was also entered as their discharge assessment. Caution must be exercised, therefore, in considering first progress–discharge assessment differences.

assessment is a rather straightforward test of the clients' skills in certain areas and that independent observers showed extremely good agreement in their ratings of the clients' performance.

Finally, the fact that only 35% of the clients enrolled in the ADL II reached criterion must be considered. The reason for this low percentage does not appear to be a failure in the modular training, but rather the fact that 55% of the clients enrolled in this module left the program before completing training. Participation in the program is voluntary and clients can withdraw whenever they or their family desire. Thus, it does not appear appropriate to use the absolute percentage of clients reaching criterion as an index of this module's effectiveness.

Activities of Daily Living III (ADL III)

The ADL III module is intended for clients who will be living independently after discharge. Clients entered this module after completing ADL I training or reaching ADL I criterion through assessment. The assessment instrument in ADL III consisted of 34 items which measure the clients' knowledge and skills in the following areas: budgeting time and money, community resources, meal planning and preparation, home safety, and housekeeping. The assessment has test–retest reliability of .83.

Of the 61 clients initially assessed, 39 had valid first progress and discharge assessments. (As with ADL II, most clients enter ADL III late in the treatment and many of them are discharged before they complete training in this module.)

The analysis of variance disclosed that there was a significant increase from the initial to first progress assessment and from the first progress to discharge assessment. These changes are presented in Figure 19.

There were no differences as a function of whether clients were enrolled in the day treatment or residential units or when they entered the program.

Since there was no independent investigation of ADL III which controlled for maturation, it was necessary to conduct an additional analysis. A correlation was computed between length of time in the program and initial ADL III assessment scores. The rationale behind this analysis is the same as that for ADL II. This correlation was not significant. Thus, it would not appear that length of time in the program *per se* can explain the improvement in ADL III scores.

Achievement of Criterion. The criterion for successful completion of this module was 31 out of the 34 items correct. Of the 41 clients who

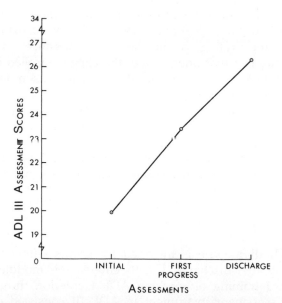

FIGURE 19. Effects of modular training on ADL III skills.

entered this module, 11 (26.8%) achieved criterion, 10 (24.4%) failed to reach criterion despite 12 or more weeks of training, and 20 (48.8%) left the program before completing ADL III training.

As with ADL II, there was no independent confirmation of the improvement observed on the ADL III assessments. However, the assessment instrument was a knowledge test and there was little room for rater bias to distort the clients' scores. A more serious question about this module's efficacy is why so few clients reached criterion in it. Unlike ADL II, where only 10% of the clients who remained in the module failed to reach criterion, in ADL III almost 25% of the clients could not reach criterion. Given the significant improvement clients showed on the modular assessments, it may be the criterion for success was too high. That is, clients were profiting from the ADL III training but were unable to reach the success criterion set by the staff of 91% correct.

Personal Information Training (PIT)

The primary goal of this module was to train clients in ways to orient themselves to self, time, and place. PIT skills were assessed with a 10-item instrument. This assessment, as previously noted, is reliable and construct valid.

Of the 168 clients who received initial PIT assessments, 68 (40.5%) required training in this module. Of these, 65 (95.6%) had valid initial, first progress, and discharge assessment. The analysis of variance disclosed that, overall, clients' scores improved significantly from their initial to first progress assessment. First progress and discharge assessments did not differ.

There were not any overall differences between day and residential clients, but there was a significant assessments by program, that is, day versus residential, interaction. This interaction is presented in Figure 20. The cause of the significant interaction was the difference in the rate of improvement between the initial and first progress assessments. Residential clients' rate of improvement in this time period was significantly greater than the rate of improvement for the day treatment clients. Despite the difference in *rate* of improvement, both groups showed the same pattern of change. That is, both groups showed significant improvement from initial to first progress assessment.

There was also a significant groups by assessment interaction. The clients who entered after March 23, 1978 showed significantly greater improvements from initial to first progress assessment than did the clients who entered before this date. However, both groups

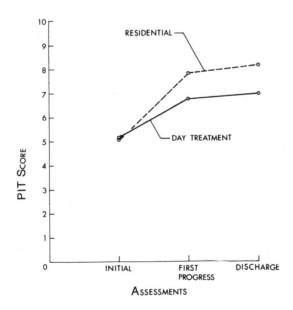

FIGURE 20. Effects of modular training on Personal Information skills for day treatment and residential treatment clients.

showed the same pattern of change. Irrespective of when they entered the program, clients improved significantly from initial to first progress assessment.

Achievement of Criterion. Criterion for successful completion of this module was set at 80% of the items correct. Of the 67 clients who actually entered this module, 43 (64.2%) reached criterion, 8 (11.9%) failed to reach criterion despite 12 or more weeks of training, and 16 (23.9%) left the program before reaching criterion.

The first issue which must be considered in evaluating this module was the groups by assessment interaction. A regression of entry date onto initial PIT scores failed to disclose any significant time-dependent relationship. Thus, there does not *appear* to be any systematic change in the clients or assessments procedures across time. We must acknowledge, however, that clients who entered the program after the dividing date started at a lower level in PIT and improved more rapidly than did the earlier clients. The difference is one of magnitude rather than pattern of change. That is, both time-based groups showed significant improvement from their initial to first progress assessment. History may explain the difference in rate of change between the groups, but it cannot explain why both groups showed significant change. This more reasonably can be attributed to the modular training.

The program by assessments interaction was also due to a difference in magnitude rather than pattern of change. The residential clients started at a lower level but improved at a greater rate than did the day treatment clients. Within both groups there was significant improvement from the initial to first progress assessment.

This improvement appears to be due to the training rather than to maturation. In the multiple baseline study, presented earlier, simple time in the program was controlled for and clients showed improvement in PIT skills as the result of the modular training.

Finally, the data on achievement of criterion indicate that the PIT training was effective for most of the clients enrolled in it. If the clients who left the program before completing training are excluded, then 85% of the clients enrolled in PIT reached the criterion for successful completion of the module.

Communication Training

This module attempted to teach how to express pleasure and displeasure effectively and appropriately. Communication skills were assessed with seven 6-point rating scales. The first six dealt with specific aspects of the clients' verbal and nonverbal behavior; the last scale is an overall rating of how well the clients displayed pleasure or displeasure. Scores can range from 7 to 42 points. Separate assessments were conducted for pleasure and displeasure. As noted earlier, these assessments are reliable and construct valid.

Of the 167 clients who received initial Communication Training assessments, 131 (78.4%) required training in the module. Of these, 116 (88.5%) had valid initial, first progress, and discharge assessments.

Pleasure. The analysis of variance disclosed that clients' assessment scores increased significantly from the initial to first progress assessment and from the first progress to discharge assessment. The analysis also disclosed a significant program (i.e., day versus residential) by assessments interaction. This interaction is presented in Figure 21.

As this figure shows, the initial assessment of the residential clients was significantly lower than that of the day clients. However,

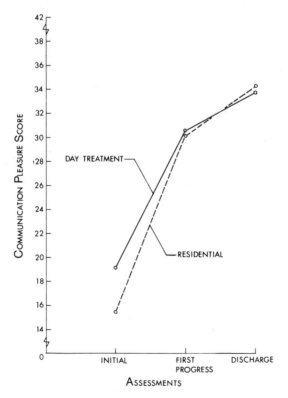

FIGURE 21. Effects of modular training on Communication (of Pleasure) for day treatment and residential treatment clients.

the rate of improvement between initial and first progress assessments was much greater for the residential than for the day treatment clients. By the first progress and discharge assessments, the two groups did not differ.

Displeasure. The same 116 clients were included in the evaluation of the displeasure component of this module. As with pleasure, there was a significant improvement from the initial to first progress assessment and from the first progress to discharge assessment. The day and residential clients did not differ in the rate at which their communication of displeasure scores improved.

Achievement of Criterion. In this module the criterion for success was an overall rating of 35 or more in the expression of both pleasure and displeasure. Of the 131 clients who entered this module, 70 (53.4%) reached criterion, 44 (33.5%) failed to reach criterion after 12 or more weeks of training, and 17 (13%) left the program before training could be completed.

The analyses of both pleasure and displeasure indicate a steady rate of improvement in communication skills across assessments. These findings are consistent with the findings of the experimental investigation of communication training presented earlier. This would suggest that it was the modular training rather than maturation which was responsible for the improvement in the clients.

Although the day and residential clients differed in their rate of improvement from initial to first progress assessments, both groups did show significant improvement. Thus, what differentiated the clients was the magnitude of change rather than the pattern of change. The data on achievement of criterion suggest that most of the clients who remained in the module were able to reach criterion. If the dropouts are excluded, 61.4% of the clients were able to reach criterion.

Conversation Skills

In this training, clients were prompted to converse, provided with an opportunity to do so in the day room of their unit, and received reinforcement for their performance. The assessment of conversation skills consists of observing a client for five 30-second periods during a 30-minute observation made at a time other than during the training group and recording whether the client is speaking to someone. The assessment score is the sum of the ratings the client receives for the five 30-second periods. This assessment had good temporal and interobserver reliability and is construct valid (cf. earlier section on reliability and validity).

Of the 167 clients who received initial assessments in conversation, 128 (76.6%) had valid initial, first progress, and discharge assessments. (The 23% attrition rate is attributed to clients' being absent on the days when assessments were conducted and/or leaving the program before a discharge assessment could be conducted.)

The analysis of variance disclosed that the clients' scores did not change significantly from initial to first progress assessment, but there was significant improvement from the first progress to discharge assessment. There was a significant main effect for program. Inspection of the clients' scores at each assessment period disclosed that while day and residential clients both showed significant improvement, the scores of the day treatment clients were invariably higher than those of the residential treatment clients.

Because the behaviors used to assess conversation skills were so specific (whether the client was talking during the 30-second observation period), evidence of generalization of the improvement in conversation skills was sought. Correlations of initial assessments disclosed that the assessment of conversation skills was most strongly correlated with three behavior rating scales, the Interest subscale of the NOSIE-30, the CAP, and the SABRS. All three of these scales contain items which deal with conversational skills. The correlation between changes on the conversation assessment and changes on these three scales was examined. (Since the significant change in conversation skills occurred between the first progress and discharge assessments, change scores were examined over this period.) Although the correlations were small (they ranged from .25 to .29), all were significant and in the predicted direction. Further, these correlations were larger than any of the other change score correlations and comprised three of the four significant correlations obtained. The fourth significant correlation was a negative correlation with the NOSIE Retardation subscale, that is, increases in conversation scores were associated with decreases in the retardation rating, which indicates that the client was becoming more physically active. Although this relationship was unexpected, we can offer a *post hoc* explanation of it. It would appear at least reasonable to propose that clients who displayed an improvement in their conversation skills (i.e., they talked more) also became more physically active. Indeed, an increased willingness to engage in conversation with others may be the reason for the decline in the retardation ratings.

Any conclusions about the efficacy of conversation training must take the results of the experimental study, presented earlier, into account. In that study it was shown that the reinforcement procedures used in conversation training were effective in changing the clients' behavior. The effect obtained in the experiment could not be attributed to history or maturation. Thus, we have reason to believe that the results of the quasi-experimental evaluation of conversation training can be best explained by the reinforcement procedures used in the program.

Self-esteem Training

The purpose of this module was to improve the clients' self-esteem. Three measures were used to evalute this module: the Rosenberg (1965) Self-esteem scale, Neugarten et al.'s (1961) Life Satisfaction Scale, and positive and negative self-statements made by the clients. As noted earlier, all three measures are reliable, and the Self-esteem and Life Satisfaction Scales appear to be construct valid. There was, however, a problem in the self-statements: a significant positive correlation between the number of positive and negative self-statements clients made. This suggested that the verbal propensities of the client may have influenced the clients' scores on this measure. In order to control for this problem we used the algebraic sum of positive and negative self-statements as the third dependent measure. These three dependent measures were analyzed separately.

The number of clients who entered this module was somewhat smaller than the numbers entered in the modules previously described. There were three reasons for this. First, the module was implemented somewhat later than the others. Second, only clients who had "graduated" from Personal Information Training were eligible for participation in Self-esteem Training. The basis of this exclusion criterion was the belief that clients who were not oriented as to self, time, and place would not benefit from Self-esteem Training. Finally, during the period when this evaluation was conducted the experimental study of self-esteem (described earlier) was also carried out. Self-esteem Training was to be offered to members of the control group after the study was completed: however, some of these clients left the program before their training could begin.

Self-esteem Scale. Of the 79 clients initially assessed on this scale, 46 (58.2%) also had valid first progress and discharge assessments. Part of this attrition was due to the fact that usage of this scale was discontinued after about 15 months. The analysis of variance failed to disclose any differences between the clients in different groups or programs. There were no significant changes in scores across assessments.

Life Satisfaction Scale. Fifty-five of the 79 clients initially assessed on this scale (69.6%) also had valid first progress and discharge assessments. There were no differences between the (time-based) groups or day and residential clients. There was a significant main effect for assessments. The planned comparison of the assessment scores revealed that the clients' level of life satisfaction improved significantly from first progress to discharge assessment.

Self-statements. The difference score for residential clients was significantly higher than the score for day clients. This indicated that even when there was control for verbosity, the residential clients evidenced better self-esteem (as measured by this technique) than did day clients. There was no significant change in scores across assessments.

The evaluation of this module must take into account the results of the experimental study, presented earlier. The findings from this examination of the ongoing module and the experimental study both indicate that training in the module increases the clients' level of life satisfaction. Since this improvement was found in an experimental as well as in a quasi-experimental study, we may substantially exclude maturation as an alternative explanation of the changes that were found. In contrast to this positive finding, the data from the quasi-experimental evaluation indicate that the module did not impact self-esteem as measured by Rosenberg's scale or positive/negative self-statements. Thus, the module *as actually used in the program* was only partially successful. Obviously, further work is needed to determine the reason for the disparity in the results of the two investigations.

Summary

Overall, the results of the evaluations of the modules as they were used in the program were quite encouraging. In all instances there was significant improvement among the clients who received modular training. Although there were differences between the time-based groups and day and residential clients in the absolute level of their assessment scores and/or the magnitude of change which occurred, in all instances the changes which were found for one group were also found for the other. Thus, the effects of modular training did not seem to be peculiar to a particular time or group of clients. The fact that changes occurred within the various groups also enables us to exclude selection as an alternative explanation of the results. The major ambiguity in these evaluations is the extent to which general programmatic variables, history, or simple maturation may have produced the changes. In those modules where true experiments were conducted, these extraneous variables were excluded as alternative explanations of the results. However, in several of the modules maturation could not be excluded as an alternative explanation of the significant improvement among the clients. Until this can be done, caution must be exercised in the claims made for the efficacy of any particular module taken by itself. With this qualification in mind, it can be stated that, in the main, the modular training was effective in teaching the clients the targeted social and survival skills.

10

The Evaluation of the Program

Louis A. Penner, David A. Eberly, and Roger L. Patterson

The previous chapter addressed the effectiveness of specific components of the Gerontology Program. This chapter addresses the
effectiveness of the overall program. It asks a very simple question:
Did the program work? In order to begin answering this question, it
is necessary to have some specification of the goal or goals of the
program. At the risk of oversimplification, the primary goals of the
program were to prevent the institutionalization of "at-risk" elderly
clients and to return previously institutionalized elderly clients to the
community. It must be made clear that the program's goal was not
merely deinstitutionalization. Deinstitutionalization can be achieved
by simply releasing clients into the community irrespective of whether
these clients are ready to live in the community. As Erickson (1975)
has pointed out, programs which are simply directed at discharging
people into the community may produce two rather negative outcomes. The first is obvious. Clients are discharged into the community before they are ready and thus become recidivists within a short
period of time. This "revolving door" syndrome is not beneficial to
the client or to the society which supports mental health institutions.
A second possible negative outcome is the placement of clients in
community settings which are merely substitutes for the hospital from
which the client was discharged, a community-based residential program which is as restrictive as the institution the client has just left.
For example, the movement of an elderly client from a state mental
hospital to a nursing home would hardly be described as a successful
deinstitutionalization. The program goal was prolonged community
living after discharge in a less restrictive environment. Furthermore,

the client should function as an active member of the community, not someone in need of supervision or custodial care.

In order to determine the extent to which this goal was attained, a program must be able to compare the postdischarge status with the status of some control or comparison group. Ideally, one would want to create the following paradigm: A large group of elderly clients in need of treatment is identified. By means of random assignment, half are assigned to a treatment program and the other half are placed in a custodial care control group. Both groups are placed in facilities which, while separate, are physically quite similar. Clients remain in the facilities for comparable periods of time and are released into the community simultaneously. The status of both groups after discharge is followed to determine the long-term outcome. As discussed in Chapter 7 such an experimental program evaluation was not conducted for practical, methodological, and ethical reasons. The majority of this chapter is concerned with an alternative approach to the experimental method for relating the total program to the clients' status after discharge. There is, however, one other question which must be investigated before we can turn to the long-term effects of the program: Were the systematic changes in the clients' general behavior during the course of treatment? It would be hard to argue that the program affected long-term changes in the clients' general behavior (i.e., behavior after discharge) if we were unable to show any changes in their general behavior while they were in treatment. Therefore, we will begin our evaluation of the overall program by examining the behavior changes among the clients while they were in the program.

Behavioral Changes during Treatment

As the reader will recall, when clients entered the program they were rated on the NOSIE-30 and Community Adjustment Potential scale (CAP).[1] Ratings of each client on these scales were repeated every 4 weeks, with a final rating at discharge if more than 2 weeks had elapsed since the last progress rating.

The purpose of the analyses to be presented was to address three questions. First, did the clients' on-ward behavior change over the course of treatment? Second, were the changes found for both day and residential treatment clients? And third, were the same patterns

---

[1]The clients also were rated on the Social Adjustment Behavior Rating Scale (SABRS). The findings for this scale were practically identical to those obtained on the CAP. Therefore, they will not be presented here.

of change obtained for clients who entered the program at different points in time? As with the modular evaluations, the quasi-experimental, institutional cycle design was used. That is, the clients were broken into two groups based on when they entered the program. Group 1 entered the program between August 17, 1977 and March 23, 1978; clients in Group 2 entered the program between March 24, 1978 and December 1, 1978. Initial, progress, and discharge assessments were combined across clients within each group. Then mixed-model analyses of variance were used to answer the questions posed above. There were a sufficient number of assessments for statistical analyses to examine the client's scores at intake, after 4 and 8 weeks of treatment, and at discharge. In none of the analyses presented below were there any significant main effects or interactions involving the time when clients entered the program, that is, no differences between Group 1 and Group 2.

CHANGES ON THE NOSIE-30

The NOSIE-30 (Honigfeld *et al.*, 1966) was developed as a sensitive measure of the clients' on-ward behavior and the changes in that behavior over time. Data on the reliability of the NOSIE-30 are presented in Chapter 9. Of the 168 clients initially assessed on the NOSIE-30, 112 had valid initial, first progress, second progress, and discharge assessments.

The analyses of variance failed to disclose any significant changes on the Social Competence, Neatness, and Psychosis subscales. On the Neatness subscale, the day treatment clients were rated significantly higher than were the residential treatment clients. There were significant changes on the remaining three subscales.

Social Interest

This subscale provides a measure of a clients social behavior; for example, does the client talk to others? display appropriate affect with others? show interest in other people? Figure 22 presents the changes for day and residential treatment of clients on this subscale. As may be seen from the figure, the day treatment clients were rated significantly higher than residential treatment clients at all four assessment periods. For both groups, there was a significant increase in their ratings from the initial to first progress assessments. The last three assessments (i.e., first progress, second progress, and discharge) did not differ significantly from one another. Thus, the results of this analysis suggest that clients showed a significant improvement in

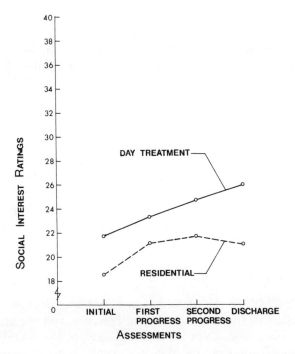

FIGURE 22. Changes on Social Interest ratings for day treatment and residential treatment clients.

their interactions with others during the first 4 weeks of their stay in the program.

Retardation

The retardation subscale measures the physical activity of the client. A high score on this subscale would indicate a client who sits alone or sleeps unless directed into an activity and who is slow-moving and sluggish. Figure 23 presents the changes on this scale for day and residential clients. As may be seen from this figure, the residential treatment clients tended to receive higher retardation ratings than did day treatment clients. Overall, there was a significant decline in retardation ratings from initial to first progress assessment, but it would appear that this decline was much greater for day treatment than residential clients. While the retardation scores of the day treatment clients continued to decline, the residential clients' scores showed a nonsignificant increase at the second progress assessment. These results suggest that clients (especially in day treat-

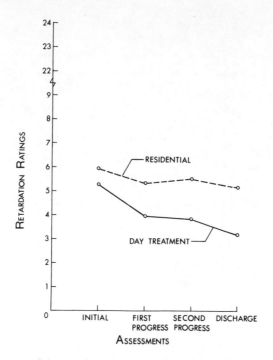

FIGURE 23. Changes on Retardation ratings for day treatment and residential treatment clients.

ment) did become more active and less withdrawn during the first 4 weeks of treatment and that this change was maintained over time.

Irritability

The Irritability subscale consists of five items concerning how angry and upset a client becomes, whether the client is irritable and impatient, and whether the client loses his temper. Figure 24 presents an unexpected finding. At the time of the first progress assessment, both day and residential treatment clients were rated as significantly more irritable than they had been during their first week in the program. There were no significant differences between the remaining assessments.

Obviously, it was not the intent of the program to make the clients more irritable and upset; therefore, this finding demands more explanation. The data from the modular assessments of communication and conversation skills and from the Social Interest and Retardation NOSIE-30 subscales suggest that when the clients (especially

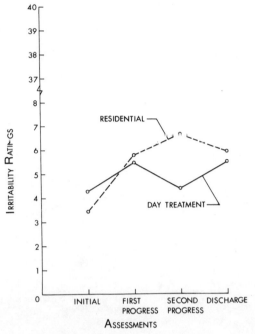

FIGURE 24. Changes on Irritability ratings for day treatment and residential treatment clients.

residential treatment clients) enter the program, they are withdrawn and inactive, lack conversational and communication skills, and are unwilling or unable to interact with others. Thus, when the initial irritability ratings of the clients are made, they are unlikely to display *any* sort of affect. After 4 weeks in the program, the clients are appreciably more outgoing and interact more with others. Thus, the increase in irritability ratings may simply reflect an increase in the clients' ability and/or willingness to display affect rather than a true increase in their level of irritability. There is some indirect evidence to support this conclusion. Those clients who had the greatest increase in irritability ratings during the first 4 weeks in the program were also the clients with the lowest initial ratings on the Social Interest subscale and the highest ratings on the Retardation subscale. That is, the clients who were the most withdrawn and inactive at admission were those who were most likely to show an increase in their irritability ratings. Thus, the increase in irritability may be an artifact of the clients' increased willingness and/or ability to display affect (both positive and negative) in their interactions with others.

Changes on the Community Adjustment Potential Scale (CAP)

The CAP contains 16 items which measure the clients' conversational and social skills and their ability to live independently in the community. A fuller description of the CAP and data on its reliability can be found in Chapter 9. Of the 168 clients with initial CAP assessments, 113 also had valid first progress, second progress, and discharge assessments. Figure 25 presents the changes in CAP scores across the four assessment periods for day and residential clients. As the figure indicates, the scores of the day treatment clients are significantly higher than those of the residential treatment clients at admission, although by discharge the scores of the two groups are quite close. Scores on the CAP increased significantly from the initial to first progress assessment and from the second progress to discharge assessment. These data suggest that both day and residential clients showed significant improvement in their conversational and social skills over the course of treatment and also were rated as much more likely to be able to live independently in the community after treatment.

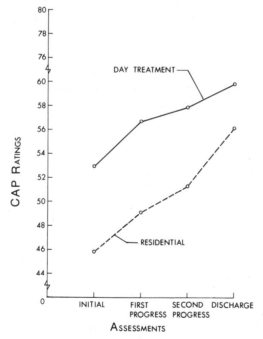

FIGURE 25. Changes on Community Adjustment Potential ratings for day treatment and residential treatment clients.

The Clients after Discharge

Several attempts were made to examine the long-term effects of the program. The first investigation focused on the clients enrolled in the program during Phase I of its operation (from the opening of the program in December 1975 through mid-August 1977). *Phase I* is used here to designate the developmental phase of the program. These clients were interviewed by telephone 1 and 3 months after discharge. In August 1977 the data collection system described in Chapters 7, 8, and 9 was implemented. This system permitted more extensive in-house and follow-up assessments of clients. During the period of time that the data from Phase II of the program were being collected (Phase II clients were those who were enrolled in the program from late August 1977 through July 1979, after the modular behavioral program was developed and in full operation), we conducted a retro-spective comparison of the length of stay, discharge, and recidivism statistics for a group of residential clients (from both Phase I and Phase II) with the same statistics for a group of clients at a state mental hospital which serves as one of the sources of clients for the Gerontology Program at FMHI. At the completion of Phase II, analy-ses were begun on the effects of the program on clients during the 12 months after their discharge.

Phase I Evaluation

During Phase I of the program's operation, the primary effort was directed at the development and implementation of the training modules. This factor, in combination with a shortage of staff, made it difficult to obtain detailed information on clients after they had left the program. In lieu of extensive face-to-face interviews, clients were contacted by telephone and a short 20-item questionnaire was admin-istered. The questionnaire addressed four areas: (1) how much the clients like their living situation, (2) how much they liked the social activities they engaged in, (3) how satisfied they were with the treat-ment they had received in the program, and (4) how much they like their jobs (since few of the clients worked, data on job satisfaction will not be presented). The clients were also asked to provide the name of someone who knew them well before and after treatment. In those cases in which the client could identify someone, this person was called and asked to answer a series of questions taken from the PARS V Community Adjustment Scale (Ellsworth, 1974). These ques-tions addressed such topics as the clients' personal hygiene habits and whether they had shown improvement after treatment. Since this was the crucial question asked of the significant others, only this one question will be presented in the evaluation of the long-term effects of the program during Phase I.

A total of 165 clients stayed in the program for more than 4 weeks and were discharged into the community. Eighty-nine of these were from the residential program and 76 were from the day treatment program. Because of unplanned discharges and refusals to participate in the follow-up, about 70% of the residential treatment and 60% of the day treatment clients were available for follow-up interviews. Only the data from the residential clients will be presented because there were two major problems with the day treatment clients' data which made them unusable. First, out of the 76 possible clients, interviews were conducted with only 37. This extremely high attrition rate raised the real possibility that those day treatment clients who were available for follow-up were not representative of the total group of day treatment clients. More important, all the day treatment clients had been living in the community before they entered treatment; and in the absence of pretreatment data it would be impossible to determine whether their level of functioning in the community after discharge represented any real change from that existing before treatment.

Of the 69 clients who were in the community and eligible or willing to participate in the follow-up, 58 (84%) responded to these questions during the first 3 months after discharge. Because of limitations in the follow-up procedure during Phase I of the program (being restricted to telephone interviews and mail responses and the moving of subjects out of the area), it was not possible to obtain sufficient data from the clients beyond three months after discharge.

Living Situation

Five questions concerned how much the clients like their living situation, that is, the place where they lived, the people they interacted with, and so forth. The items were presented on a Likert format with five alternatives for each item. The alternatives ranged from "I like it a great deal" to "I like it somewhat" as the midpoint. In order to obtain an overall score, client responses across the five items were summed and an average item response was computed. A number 1 indicated the most positive response and a 5 indicated extreme displeasure. Their average response to the living situation items was 1.47, which indicates rather strong positive attitudes toward their living situation.

Social Activities

Of the 69 clients available for follow-up interviews, 59 (85.5%) responded to the five social activities questions within three months of their discharge. As in the previous set of questions, the response alternatives ranged from "Like it a great deal" to "Don't like it at all." The average score was 2.62, which indicated a moderate amount of positive affect for social activities.

Satisfaction with the Program

Sixty one of the 69 clients (88%) responded to the item "My training at the Florida Mental Health Institute prepared me to move into the community." A five-point Likert format was used with the responses ranging from strongly agree (1) to strongly disagree (5); the midpoint was undecided (3). The mean score was 2.07, which indicated the clients agreed with the statement.

The Perceptions of Significant Others

Of the 69 clients, 32 (46.4%) were rated by a significant other. A large percentage of the clients were not rated because many of the clients did not return to where they had lived before treatment (indeed, many of these clients lived in institutions prior to entering the program). Thus, for these clients it was impossible to find someone who knew them equally well before and after participation in the program. The 32 significant others were asked to indicate whether the clients' level of adjustment was better, the same, or worse than before they entered the program. A five-alternative Likert format was used. The alternatives ranged from "Worse now than she/he was before treatment" (1) to "Very much better now than she/he was before treatment" (5); "Somewhat better now than she/he was before treatment" was the midpoint (3). The average response was 4.0, which corresponded to the alternative "Much better now than she/he was before treatment."

In summary, responses to the telephone interview indicate that the clients were quite satisfied with their living situations, only moderately satisfied with their social activities, and felt that the program had prepared them for community living. In the view of the significant others, the clients were much better than before they entered the program.

It is obvious that these findings must be interpreted with caution. There is a strong possibility that the significant others' ratings of the client and the clients' evaluation of the program were biased in a positive direction because the questions were asked by representatives of the Gerontology Program, with possible implicit pressure to make positive responses. There is no way to determine the extent to which this occurred, especially since there are no pretreatment or normative data on the questions asked of the clients or the significant others. However, these data can be viewed as positive responses by those who knew them prior to and after treatment. In this context, the data suggest that after treatment previously institutionalized clients reported that they liked where they were living, were satisfied with their social activities, and liked the program they had been in. The most direct evidence for the efficacy of the program came from the responses of the significant others. Their data suggest that the clients were functioning much better after treatment than before.

The data from the Phase I follow-up are admittedly sketchy and open to a number of alternative explanations. The Phase II follow-up was considerably more detailed and provided answers to many of the questions left unanswered by the Phase I evaluation (this was due primarily to the application of more staff time to the Phase I follow-up and the implementation of a computerized data reduction system for client assessments). But before the Phase II analysis is discussed, another investigation, which compared a group of clients to a group of elderly clients at a state mental hospital, will be presented.

A Comparative Study of the Long-Term Effects of the Program

The purpose of this study was to determine whether participation in the residential component of the Gerontology Program would affect (1) how long a person is institutionalized, (2) discharge destination, and (3) recidivism, as compared to geriatric wards of state hospitals. Unlike the other evaluation studies reported in this book, it was necessary to identify a group of elderly individuals who would provide the comparison with our clients. We were able to do this by using clients from one of the state mental hospitals which was also a referral source for clients to this program.

At periodic intervals, the Gerontology Program received from the state mental hospital a list of clients who were thought to meet the criteria for admission into the program. Staff members of the program conducted a screening visit to determine whether a client on the list met the admission criteria. After identifying those clients who were suitable for transfer, a screening team member described the program at the Florida Mental Health Institute and asked the clients to transfer into it. Since all admissions to the program were voluntary, a client had the right to refuse transfer to the program. About 50% of the clients who were screened as acceptable refused to transfer. Since both the clients who accepted transfer and those who refused had been selected and screened according to the same criteria and procedures, those who refused could be utilized as a comparison group for those who entered the program. There is obviously a possible selection bias in using the refusal group for the purposes of comparison, and this bias will be discussed later; but in the absence of any other obtainable group of elderly psychiatric patients, this comparison was a worthwhile investigation of a major program goal. Therefore, the refusal and the transfer groups were compared on three variables: length of stay in an institution after the date of refusal/transfer, percentage discharged into the community within one year of that date, and recidivism rate within one year after discharge.

The clients selected for study were those who were screened between December 30, 1975 and November 29, 1977. During this period of time 112 clients were screened. Of those 112 clients, 54 refused and 58 agreed to transfer to the program.

In order to conduct a valid and meaningful comparison, it was necessary to exclude certain clients from the data analysis. The first criterion for exclusion was that the client had died within the period of time when the screening visits were conducted or within one year of their date of discharge. This was done because of the rather obvious way in which death confounds an analysis of discharge rates, length of stay, and recidivism rates. One client from the refusal group was excluded on the basis of this criterion.

The second exclusion criterion was length of prior hospitalization that exceeded 14 years. This exclusion was based on the premise that the length of prior hospitalization is a strong predictor of the outcome measures in this study. We selected 14 years as our exclusion criterion because an analysis of data from state mental hospitals showed that less than 2% of their discharges are people who have been there for more than 14 years. Four clients from the refusal group and one from the transfer group were eliminated on the basis of this criterion.

Finally, we excluded clients who remained institutionalized for 30 days or less after the date of the screening visit. This exclusion criterion was based on the assumption that people who were discharged from the hospital or the program within 30 days of the decision date had not experienced sufficient treatment for any differential effect to be manifested. Since we wanted to compare the effectiveness of our program with the state mental hospitals, it was necessary to use clients who received treatment *after* the decision date. This final criterion resulted in the exclusion of eight refusal and

TABLE 13. Biographical and Demographic Characteristics of
Gerontology Program and State Hospital Clients

	Gerontology Program clients ($n=53$)	State hospital clients ($n=41$)
Sex		
Male	22 (42%)	18 (44%)
Female	31 (58%)	23 (56%)
Age		
Mean	63.1	68.7
Standard deviation	5.4	7.6
Marital status		
Married (with living spouse)	9 (17%)	12 (29%)
Not married (or spouse deceased)	44 (83%)	29 (71%)
Place of residence		
Counties near Gerontology Program	35 (66%)	19 (46%)
Counties near state mental hospital	18 (34%)	22 (54%)
Length of prior hospitalization		
Mean	364.28 (days)	500.21 (days)
Admitting diagnosis		
Psychotic, organic brain syndrome	9 (17%)	4 (10%)
Psychotic, no organic brain syndrome	29 (55%)	18 (44%)
Nonpsychotic, organic brain syndrome	10 (19%)	13 (31%)
Nonpsychotic, no organic brain syndrome	5 (9%)	6 (15%)

four transfer clients. In summary, 13 clients from the refusal group
and 5 clients from the transfer group were excluded from the data
analysis, leaving 41 in the former group and 53 in the latter.

The next step in this study was to determine whether the two
groups differed in their demographic characteristics and/or psychiatric
status. Although the two groups were comparable on the admission
criteria, it was possible that they differed significantly on demographic and psychiatric characteristics which are related to outcome
measures but were not admission criteria. On the basis of the data
available in hospital records, the following characteristics were used
for comparison: age, sex, marital status, county of residence, length of
prior hospitalization, and admitting diagnosis.[2] Table 13 presents the
comparisons. As Table 13 shows, the refusal group was 5.6 years

[2]This was the diagnosis when all clients entered the mental hospital. It was made by
staff of the hospital for all clients in both the refusal and the transfer groups.

older (68.7 versus 63.1), a statistically significant difference, but, although this difference is *statistically* significant, we are not sure that the age difference is meaningful. Both groups were relatively homogeneous in their age, which accounts for the fact that the five-year age difference was statistically significant. Other analyses that have been performed suggest that among this population a five-year age difference is of little practical import in a person's length of stay or probability of discharge. Because the state mental hospital was located some distance from the Florida Mental Health Institute, we suspected that the clients' place of residence might influence their decision to transfer or remain at the hospital. This hypothesis was confirmed. Whereas 68% of the clients who transferred lived in counties near the institute, only 46% of the clients who refused transfer lived in these counties. These percentages were significantly different, $\chi^2 (1) = 4.20$, $p < .05$. The difference may explain in part the reason for refusal but should not effect treatment outcomes. The two groups did not differ on any of the other characteristics we examined.

Table 14 presents the comparisons of the two groups on the outcome measures. First, discharges for one year following the date of

TABLE 14. Status of Gerontology Program and State
Mental Hospital Clients One Year Later

	Gerontology Program clients $(n=53)$	State hospital clients $(n=41)$
Discharge rates		
Still in psychiatric facility	8 (15%)	26 (63%)
Discharged to community	45 (85%)	15 (37%)
Discharge destination[a]		
Independent living	15 (33%)	2 (13%)
Boarding home	6 (13%)	1 (7%)
Foster home	8 (18%)	1 (7%)
Spouse, family	16 (36%)	11 (73%)
Recidivism rates (after one year)[a]		
Recidivists	3 (7%)	7 (47%)
Length of stay (discharged clients)[a]		
Mean	135.7 (days)	136.9 (days)
Standard deviation	52.9	85.5
Length of stay (all clients)		
Mean	170.3 (days)	281.5 (days)
Standard deviation	88.4	121.4

[a]These analyses were conducted only on those clients who were discharged from the Gerontology Program/State Hospital.

decision were examined. (The date of decision was used because in some cases clients were not transferred for three or four weeks after the screening visits. If the date of admission into the program had been used, some of the transferred clients would have had up to one month of institutionalization which would not have been reflected in this or other analyses. This could have biased the data in favor of the program.) Of the 53 clients who transferred into the program, 45 (85%) were discharged into the community within one year. By contrast, 15 of the 41 refusals (37%) were discharged into the community within the same period of time. This difference was statistically significant χ^2 (1) = 23.37, p < .001.

The data on length of stay were considered next. When we examined the average length of stay for the discharged clients only, we found no difference between the two groups. However, in light of the fact that only 37% of the refusal group were discharged, we felt that it was more appropriate to compare the average length of stay for all the clients in the two groups. When this comparison was made using the decision date for the refusal group and the date of transfer to the program, we found that the average length of stay for the transferred clients was about 170 days, whereas it was 281 days for the group which remained at the mental hospital. The difference of 111 days was statistically significant, t (92) = 4.94, p < .01.

Finally, we examined recidivism within one year of the time of discharge. Of the 15 discharged from the mental hospital, 7 (47%) were reinstitutionalized within one year. Only 3 out of the 45 discharges from the program (7%) were reinstitutionalized. This difference was statistically significant, χ^2 (1) = 8.05, p < .01.

Although the study only covered a one-year period after discharge, the clients were tracked for two years after discharge. Within two years of discharge, 60% of the refusal group and 9% percent of the transfer group had been reinstitutionalized.

In summary, the discharge rate from the program within one year was almost 2½ times as great as it was from the state hospital. The average length of treatment was about four months less, and the recidivism was less than 1/6 of the rate for the mental hospital. Overall, at the end of the time period examined, 79% of the clients who entered the program were living in the community; only 20% of the clients who elected to remain in the hospital were living in the community. Further study indicated that at the end of two years the difference in the rate of return to the institution in favor of those treated by the program actually *increased*.

As in any retrospective field study, there are a number of alternative interpretations of the results. As Cook and Campbell (1979) have pointed out, causal inference in such studies rests on the ability to exclude alternative explanations of the differences between the two groups. In the present study, the most plausible rival explanation of the differences is that the refusal group differed from the transfer group on characteristics which were related to discharge rates, length of stay, and recidivism. For example, the refusal group may have been much more "institutionalized" than the transfer group and as a result would have done worse than the transfer group did *even if the latter had not been admitted to the program.* Initial comparison of the two groups failed to disclose any differences on the demographic and/or psychiatric variables which could be directly tied to the outcome measures, but it is possible that the groups differed on characteristics which, although unmeasured, were responsible for the obtained differences. Attempts to obtain additional information on the reasons for refusal by developing a system for recording and coding the responses of the refusal group at the time of the screening indicate that responses were not reliable. That is, in analyzing the reasons for refusal given by clients who were interviewed more than once, it became apparent that their reasons changed from one interview to the next. Thus, it was not possible to go beyond the data initially collected in attempting to identify alternative explanations of the differences.

To support this study's results, it should be emphasized that the two groups did not differ on the two most obvious correlates of the outcome measures (i.e., length of prior hospitalization and admission diagnosis). Further, the one variable on which the two groups differed rather dramatically was their place of permanent residence. People who remained at the state hospital were likely to reside in the area near the hospital; people who came to the Florida Mental Health Institute were likely to reside in the area near the institute. This difference was probably attributable to the clients' desire to be in familiar areas which were near their friends and family and permitted visits (FMHI is 100 miles distant from the hospital). It does not appear to be a logical cause of the difference between the two groups on the outcome measures. Thus, while the possibility of a self-selection bias cannot be excluded as influencing the study's results, it was not possible to identify the source of such a bias.

A second alternative explanation of the results is that the differences were not due to the greater efficacy of treatment but rather that the program's discharge and placement procedures might have been superior to those of the state mental hospital. That is, our clients were discharged sooner and at a greater rate and were less likely to recidivate because more effort was devoted to discharge planning and the selection of appropriate placements for the state hospital clients. The staffing patterns at the two facilities suggest that this is probably true. As described in Chapter 6, the program treatment team included a social worker whose major responsibility was to work with the client, the team, family, friends, placement agencies, placement sites, and others exclusively for the 25–30 residential clients in the program at any one time. Individuals in the state hospital with placement responsibilities were at a considerable disadvantage for many reasons. They typically did not function as full-time members of treatment teams. The state hospitals did not use extensive behavioral assessments which provided valuable placement information. Many more placement sites were located close to the program, whereas the state hospital was in an isolated rural area. And finally, placement workers in the state hospital had about twice the client caseload. These important differences do not invalidate the results of this study. The Gerontology Program views the behavior modification and placement components as interdependent parts of the total treatment package. That is, the skills and new behaviors taught our clients would be of little value if a client were incorrectly placed, and placement in the community without the appropriate training would also lead to failure. Thus, what the study evaluated was the total program. The data presented in this section strongly suggest that this total program is quite effective in returning the institutionalized elderly into the community and enabling them to stay there, as compared to the total hospital program.

Phase II Evaluation

The first two evaluations of the long-term effects of the Gerontology Program produced encouraging outcomes. Therefore, a more detailed, in-depth evaluation was conducted to determine whether the program had had a positive long-term impact on its clients.

The clients studied were those individuals who entered the program between August 1977 and August 1979 and who had received at least four weeks of treatment. Two direct care staff members were assigned the responsibility of obtaining information on discharged clients at 1, 3, 6, and 12 months after discharge. For clients who signed at discharge an informed consent form agreeing to participate in follow-up, an attempt was made to conduct a face-to-face interview with them at 1, 3, 6, and 12 months if they resided within 50 miles of the institute.

In the face-to-face interview, the clients were given the Activities of Daily Living assessments (i.e., ADL I, ADL II, and ADL III) and the Personal Information Training assessment, filled out the Life Satisfaction Questionnaire, and answered several questions about their present living situation. In addition, the clients were asked to identify a "significant other"—someone who knew them quite well. This person was contacted and with the client's permission filled out the NOSIE-30 (cf. Chapter 9) on the client.

There were 275 clients enrolled in the program during the Phase II period. Forty-eight of them (17.5%) were not included in the follow-up sample because they either were in the program less than 4 weeks or were readmitted to the program after discharge (the vast majority of these exclusions fell into the former category). Obviously, it was not possible to track all of the 227 remaining clients for 12 months after discharge. The percentage of clients we could locate 1, 3, 6, and 12 months after discharge were 79%, 68%, 63%, and 54% respectively. Although this attrition rate is small by comparison with other follow-up studies, it did raise the possibility that the clients available for follow-up differed from those who were not. Therefore, before beginning to examine the data from these clients, analyses were conducted to determine whether the located clients differed from the "lost" clients.

To be more specific, the clients were divided into three groups: those who were located and agreed to be interviewed, those who were located but refused (or were unable to give) an interview, and those who were "lost" (i.e., they could not be located at the time of the interview). Then for each interview period (i.e., 1, 3, 6, and 12 months), the three groups were compared on five sets of variables: (1) their biographic/demographic characteristics such as age, education, income, length of hospitalization prior to admittance to the Gerontology Program, and psychiatric status at time of admission to the program; (2) their initial modular assessments; (3) their discharge assessments; (4) the NOSIE-30 and CAP ratings at intake; and (5) the NOSIE-30 and CAP ratings at discharge.[3]

The only consistent difference found among the three groups was in their age. The clients who agreed to an interview and those who refused did not differ on the variable (or any of the other variables), but the lost clients were reliably younger than the other two groups. To be more specific, comparisons of the agreers and the lost clients revealed that the clients who agreed to the 6- and 12-month interviews were significantly older than the clients who could not be

[3]The SPSS discriminant function analysis program was used to compare the three groups. Discriminant function analysis tells if groups differ on a set of variables considered individually and in the aggregate. The former is determined by looking at the univariate F ratio for each of the variables. The latter is determined by looking at the multivariate F ratio for comparison of the variables taken together.

located for these interviews. Comparisons of the refusers and lost clients revealed that the latter group was significantly younger than the former group at all four interview periods (i.e., 1, 3, 6, and 12 months).

It seems reasonable to propose that because the lost clients were younger than the other two groups they were more mobile and therefore more likely to move out of the area in which the Gerontology Program was located. This resulted in the follow-up team's being unable to locate these clients or their being outside the 50-mile radius that limited interviews.

The increasing attrition rate across interview periods and the age difference described above limited the representativeness of the sample of follow-up clients we could locate. However, we do not feel that there was a serious selection problem. First, the group differed on only one of the 25 variables we examined. There were no differences on some of the more obvious predictors of postdischarge status (e.g., prior hospitalization, income). Second, in prior analyses we have conducted, age has not been found to be a significant correlate of our clients' level of functioning (partially because of the restricted age range of our clients). Finally, if in fact age did impact postdischarge, the impact would have biased the results against the program. That is, it seems reasonable to propose that younger clients (i.e., the lost group) should suffer from fewer physical and mental deficiencies than older clients and thus should function at a higher level in the community. We decided, therefore, that although the located clients might not constitute a perfectly representative sample of our discharged clients, it was appropriate to use these data to assess the long-term effects of the program.

Where Were the Clients Living?

The first question asked of the follow-up data was a simple one. Where were discharged clients living after discharge? This is admittedly a rather gross measure of the program's long-term effectiveness, but it is an important indicant of the program's impact on the clients. Recall that the ultimate goal for the day treatment clients was to prevent institutionalization for other than medical reasons. Among the residential treatment clients, the ultimate goal was to enable a previously institutionalized population to live in a noninstitutional setting.

Three categories of living situations were used as residences in the community in the analyses: (1) private residences: a house or an apartment which was owned or rented by either the client, a relative of the client, or some individual (e.g., a friend of the client's) who was not receiving funds for housing the client; (2) foster homes: a house which was owned or rented by a person who received some form of compensation for housing the client and providing some degree of family interaction; and (3) boarding houses: congregate living facilities which typically housed from 5 to 20 individuals on a monthly fee for profit basis and provided minimal custodial services for the residents (e.g., meals, linen service). In none of the three community settings were medical or psychiatric services provided. Three categories were used for institutional settings: (1) medical hospitals: institutions where residents received skilled nursing and medical care for physical rather than mental illnesses; (2) nursing homes: licensed institutions where individuals who were unable to care for themselves received full custodial services plus skilled nursing or intermediate nursing care (all clients who entered nursing homes did so because of physical disorders); and (3) psychiatric hospitals: institutions which provided full custodial and medical care for residents who, because of psychiatric disorders, were unable to live in the community.

Day Treatment Clients

There were 101 day treatment clients who received at least 4 weeks of treatment and were discharged from the program. Table 15 presents living situation data on those clients who could be located and were alive 1, 3, 6, and 12 months after discharge. One client died in the month following discharge. Of the surviving 100 clients, we were able to locate 75. As the table shows, the vast majority of these

TABLE 15. Living Situation of Discharged Day Treatment Clients

	Months after discharge			
	1	3	6	12
Number located		64	61	53
Community				
Boarding home	12%	15.6%	16.4%	11.3%
Foster home	5 3%	4.7%	4.9%	5.7%
Private residence	64%	62.5%	62.3%	56.5%
Medical institutions				
Medical hospital	2.6%	3.1%	0%	3.8%
Nursing home	9.3%	7.8%	9.8%	13.2%
Psychiatric institutionalization	6.7%	6.3%	6.5%	9.4%

clients (81.3%) were living in the community. Nine clients were institutionalized for medical reasons (12%) and five (6.7%) were in a psychiatric facility. Two more clients died between one and three months after discharge. We located 64 of the surviving 98 clients. Over 82% of them were still living in the community. Seven clients (10.9%) were institutionalized for medical reasons and four (6.3%) were in a psychiatric facility.

Six months after discharge there were 97 surviving clients, 61 of whom could be located. Approximately 84% were still in the community; 9.8% were in medical facilities and 6.5% were in psychiatric facilities. There were no additional deaths between the 6- and 12-month interviews. We located 53 clients a year after discharge. Thirty-nine of them (73.5%) were living in the community; nine (17%) were in medical facilities and five (9.4%) were in psychiatric facilities.

All day treatment clients were, by someone's estimate, in danger of institutionalization. In contrast, the great majority of the residential clients were already in institutions at the time of admission to the program (a few were referred to FMHI directly from residential treatment rather than being transferred from another institution).

Residential Treatment Clients

There were 126 clients enrolled in the residential treatment program who had received at least 4 weeks of treatment. Table 16 presents living situation data on those clients who could be located and were alive 1, 3, 6, and 12 months after discharge. Two clients died within one month of their discharge. We located 101 of the 124 surviv-

TABLE 16. Living Situation of Discharged Residential Treatment Clients

| | Months after discharge | | | |
	1	3	6	12
Number located	101	84	78	60
Community				
Boarding home	25.7%	26.2%	26.9%	26.7%
Foster home	3.0%	1.2%	1.3%	1.7%
Private residence	52.5%	47.6%	44.9%	38.3%
Retirement hotel	2.0%	2.4%	1.3%	—
Medical institutionalization				
Medical hospital	0.9%	1.2%	2.6%	—
Nursing home	4.9%	7.1%	5.1%	6.7%
Psychiatric institutionalization	8.9%	14.3%	16.7%	26.7%

ing clients. Eighty-five percent of them were living in the community; 6 clients (5.9%) were institutionalized for medical reasons; and 9 (8.9%) were in psychiatric facilities. By three months after discharge, 3 clients had died. Eighty-four of the 123 surviving clients were located; 73.3% of them were residing in the community. Seven clients (8.3%) were in medical facilities and 12 (14.3%) were in psychiatric facilities.

There was an additional death between the 3 and 6-month interviews, leaving 122 clients. We located 78 of them. Of these 78, 59 (75.6%) were not institutionalized, 6 (7.7%) were institutionalized for medical reasons, and 13 were institutionalized for psychiatric reasons. One year after discharge there were 121 surviving clients; 60 of them were located. Forty (66.7%) were in the community, 4 (6.7%) were in medical facilities, and 16 (26.7%) were in psychiatric facilities.

The Clients after Discharge: Summary

As noted in the introduction to this chapter, the primary goals for the Gerontology Program were (a) to prevent the institutionalization of at-risk elderly clients and (b) to return previously institutionalized elderly clients to the community. What do the data from the Phase II clients and the comparison study tell us about the extent to which these goals were achieved?

Obviously, it is extremely difficult to answer the question about prevention. There was no untreated control group for the day treatment clients. Therefore, we do not know if the fact that less than 10% of our day treatment clients were in psychiatric institutions a year after discharge represents a significant improvement over what would occur without treatment.

A review of the gerontological literature also fails to provide us with a comparison figure. Atchley (1977) reported that at any given time less than 4% of people over 65 are living in long-term care institutions. But this percentage is based on the total elderly population, not the at-risk group treated in the day treatment program. Palmore (1976) succinctly described the state of our knowledge on the probability that an elderly person will be institutionalized: "We have no estimate (of the chances) of an older person being institutionalized" (p. 504).

We are, therefore, forced to evaluate the 10% figure in an absolute rather than a comparative fashion. That is, at this point we can merely acknowledge the obvious. This percentage is quite low, and despite the prediction that these individuals would soon need institutional care, less than 1 in 10 of the people located in follow-up were in fact institutionalized.

The follow-up data from the residential clients are somewhat easier to interpret. Although we were unable to find published studies that investigate recidivism rates among elderly deinstitutionalized clients, there are comparative data from other sources. Recall that in the comparison study, the one-year recidivism rate for clients who refused transfer to the Gerontology Program was 46.7%. A report on the recidivism rate for all clients discharged from state mental hospitals during the three-year period of fiscal year 1978 through fiscal year 1980 found that 50.9% of these clients were recidivist. Fairweather, Sanders, and Tournatzky (1974) reported that 18 months after discharge 72% of chronic psychotic clients and 55% of neurotic patients (irrespective of the type of treatment program employed) had been reinstitutionalized. By contrast, slightly more than 26% of our clients were recidivist. In other words, our clients' recidivism rate was about one-half the rate typically found among discharges from public mental hospitals. Further, it is likely that few if any of the clients lost in the follow-up were hospitalized, since such hospitalization would have been relatively easy to discover during the follow-up period. Therefore, we can reasonably estimate that the recidivism rate for the *entire* group of residential clients was probably closer to 15% than to 26%, a figure which is consistent with that obtained in the comparison study.

Whether one wishes to accept the 15% or 26% figure, the data lead to the same conclusion. The Gerontology Program does appear to have achieved one of its primary goals—the long-term deinstitutionalization of elderly psychiatric clients.

THE RELATIONSHIP BETWEEN CHANGES DURING TREATMENT AND POSTDISCHARGE STATUS

In Chapter 9 the training modules were shown in the main to be effective in teaching the clients certain social and survival skills. In the two studies just presented, there was evidence that the majority of clients who have experienced the modular training are able to live in the community after discharge. Thus, it would *appear* that the program was successful in reaching the proximal goals (i.e., teaching the clients certain social and survival skills) and that the obtaining of these skills enabled the clients to live in the community after discharge. We say *appear* because thus far evidence to establish a direct relationship between modular training and postdischarge status has not been presented. It is possible that factors other than the modular training were responsible for the finding that the majority of our previously institutionalized clients were able to live in the community for the year following their discharge. For example, their success in the community may be due to the single case behavioral treatments, medical services, or our placement activities rather than to the modular training. Or, alternatively, variables such as the clients' support systems in the community, rather than the modular training *per se*, may have been the primary cause of their low recidivism rate. The next study presented investigates this problem, that is, the relationship between the clients' performance in the program and their postdischarge status.

The specific question addressed in the study was: What is the relationship between the modular treatment of clients received while in the program and their ability to remain in the community after discharge? To answer this question the intake, first progress, and discharge assessments of the clients who were and were not institutionalized one year after their discharge were compared.[4]

If modular training was related to postdischarge status, institutionalized and noninstitutionalized clients should have had comparable skill levels at the time they entered the program (i.e., intake assessments), but the noninstitutionalized should have shown a higher level of skill acquisition than did the institutionalized clients. Only the data from residential clients were analyzed because few day treatment clients changed their place of residence after treatment and none was institutionalized when treatment began. Thus, it was not reasonable to conduct these analyses with the day treatment clients.

The clients used in this study were 56 individuals who could be located one year after discharge and were either living in the community (40) or in a psychiatric institution (16). These two groups of clients were first compared on their demographic/biographical characteristics. Then their initial, first progress, and discharge assessments in all of the basic modules and the behavior rating scales were compared.

The purpose of the biographical/demographic comparisons was to determine whether these nonprogrammatic variables were related to the clients' living situation one year after discharge. The two groups' members were compared on sex, age, marital status, education, in-

---

[4]The reader will recall that many clients received only the first progress assessment. Therefore, in order to maximize the number of clients for whom we had training data, we decided to use only the first progress assessment.

come, length of hospitalizations, number of prior hospitalizations, and diagnosis at the time of admission. The two groups did not differ on any of these variables.

The absence of any identifiable differences between the two groups on the nonprogrammatic variables having been established, the investigation of differences between them was conducted using a 2 × 3 mixed-model analysis of variance. The classification variables were postdischarge status (institutionalized one year after discharge versus not institutionalized one year after discharge) and assessments (initial, first progress, discharge). A separate analysis of variance was conducted for each of the following modular assessments: Activities of Daily Living I, Personal Information Training, Communication Training (both pleasure and displeasure), Conversation Training, and the Life Satisfaction scale from the Self-esteem Training. Separate analyses were also conducted for the six NOSIE-30 subscales and the Community Adjustment Potential scale. Each analysis was accompanied by planned comparisons of differences between the initial, first progress, and discharge assessments of the two groups. For all tests of main effects, interactions, and between-cell differences the significance level was set at .10. This significance level was used because of the small number of cases available for some of the analyses and the exploratory nature of this investigation. In the interest of clarity, the analyses for each of the modules and behavior rating scales will be reported separately.

Changes in Modular Skills, ADL I. Of the 56 clients, 22 had the three in-house assessments in the ADL I. Fifteen of these clients were not institutionalized 12 months after discharge and 7 were institutionalized. (The reader will recall that many clients did not require ADL I training. Thus, the number of clients available for this analysis was rather small.)

The analysis of variance failed to produce any significant differences between the two groups. However, the planned comparisons did reveal some differences between the rate of improvement on ADL I for the institutionalized and noninstitutionalized clients. The two groups' initial assessments were not significantly different, but by the time of the first progress assessment, the noninstitutionalized clients were significantly higher in ADL I. The reason for this difference was that although the noninstitutionalized clients showed significant improvement from their initial to first progress assessment, the institutionalized clients showed a nonsignificant *decline* in their assessment scores. The two groups did not differ in their discharge assessments.

Personal Information Training (PIT). There were 21 noninstitutional and 8 institutionalized clients with the three in-house assessments.

The analysis of variance failed to disclose any significant differences between the groups in their initial scores or rate of acquisition of the PIT skills. Both groups did show significant improvement in PIT.

Conversation Training. Thirty-eight noninstitutionalized and 15 institutionalized clients were used in this analysis. There was no significant difference between the groups, and the groups by assessments interaction was not significant. The planned comparisons did reveal a disparity of the rate of improvement between the two groups. Whereas the Institutionalized clients did not show a significant improvement across assessments, the noninstitutionalized clients did. Their first progress and discharge assessments were significantly higher than their intake assessments (the average change among the noninstitutionalized clients from the intake to discharge was 5.06 points; among the institutionalized clients it was 4.60).

Communication Training. There were 35 noninstitutionalized and 14 institutionalized clients with Communication Training assessments. Let us first consider the communication of pleasure. The *F* ratio for

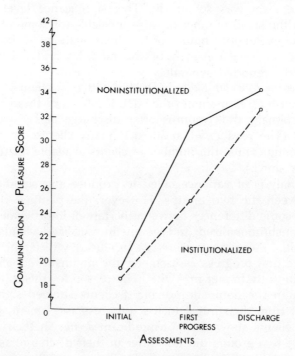

FIGURE 26. Within-treatment changes in Communication (of Pleasure) for clients living in the community or institutionalized one year after discharge.

differences between the groups was not significant, but the groups by assessments interaction was significant, F (2, 94) = 2.96, < .06. This interaction is presented in Figure 26.

As Figure 26 shows, the two groups did not differ at intake but did differ on the first progress assessment. Although both groups showed significant improvement from intake to the first progress assessment, the improvement of the noninstitutionalized clients was 1.90 times as great as that of the institutionalized clients. Between the first progress and discharge assessments, this pattern was reversed. Both groups showed significant improvement, but the rate of improvement of the institutionalized clients was 3.18 times as great as the rate among the noninstitutionalized clients. The pattern of results for the communication of displeasure was similar.

The assessment scores of the noninstitutionalized clients on displeasure were not significantly higher than those of the institutionalized clients. There was a significant groups by assessments interaction, F (2, 94) = 4.74, p < .01. The planned comparisons revealed the source of these significant F ratios. The two groups did not differ at intake but did differ significantly at the first progress assessment. The improvement of the noninstitutionalized clients was 1.93 times as great as that of the institutionalized clients. Again, the pattern reversed between the first progress and discharge assessments. The institutionalized clients' improvement was about 3.9 times as great as that of the noninstitutionalized clients.

Self-esteem Training. The analysis of Self-esteem Training was conducted using the Life Satisfaction scores of 15 noninstitutionalized and 7 institutionalized clients.

Although the F ratio for group differences was not significant, the group by assessments interaction was, F (2, 40) = 6.89, p < .01. This interaction is presented in Figure 27. As the figure shows, at intake the average Life Satisfaction score of the noninstitutionalized group was significantly *lower* than that of the institutionalized group. This pattern was also maintained at the time of the first progress assessment. But by the time of discharge the Life Satisfaction score of the independent living group was significantly *higher* than that of the institutionalized group.

To summarize the results of the analyses of changes in the skills taught in the modules, there was only one significant difference in the initial scores of the two groups. On the Life Satisfaction measure, the noninstitutionalized clients were significantly lower than were the institutionalized cilents. There were significant groups by assessments interactions in Communication of Pleasure, Communication of Displeasure, and Life Satisfaction. The first two interactions were at-

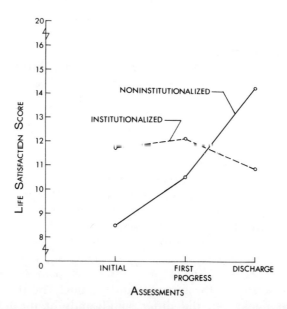

FIGURE 27. Within-treatment changes in Life Satisfaction for clients living in the community or institutionalized one year after discharge.

tributable to much greater initial improvement among the noninstitutionalized than among the institutionalized clients. The significant interaction on Life Satisfaction was due to the fact that the noninstitutionalized clients started at a significantly lower range but at discharge were significantly higher than the institutionalized clients. Finally, in ADL I and Conversation Training the noninstitutionalized clients showed significant improvement whereas the institutionalized clients did not.

Although in all comparisons the discharge assessment score of the noninstitutionalized clients was higher than the score of the institutionalized clients, this difference reached statistical significance only in the comparison of Life Satisfaction scores.

Thus, the following conclusions and differences between institutionalized and noninstitutionalized module-related skill acquisition would appear justified. The two groups did not differ statistically or meaningfully in the areas measured by the assessments when they entered the program. There was a consistent but statistically nonsignificant trend for the noninstitutionalized clients to have higher scores on the discharge assessments than the institutionalized clients. The major difference between the two groups was in the improvement in level of performance in the modules. Clients who remained in the community for a year after discharge typically showed significantly greater improvement from intake to the first progress assessment than did those clients who were institutionalized. Although the latter group of clients did show significant improvement, the magnitude of their improvement during the first 4 weeks of treatment was invariably less than the rate for the noninstitutionalized clients.

BEHAVIOR CHANGES DURING TREATMENT

The next series of analyses concerned the two groups of clients' general behavior while they were in treatment, as contrasted with performance in specific modules. We wanted to know if: (a) the institutionalized and noninstitutionalized clients differed in their general behavior ratings when they entered the program; (b) the two groups showed different rates of change in the behavior ratings while they were in treatment; and (c) the two groups differed in their general behavior ratings when they were discharged from the program.

The intake, first progress, and discharge ratings of the clients institutionalized and noninstitutionalized after discharge on the six NOSIE-30 subscales and the Community Adjustment Potential scale were examined in a series of 2×3 mixed-model analyses of variance. In the interest of clarity, these seven analyses will be presented separately.

Social Competence. There were 55 clients (16 were institutionalized after discharge; 39 were not institutionalized after discharge) with intake, first progress, and discharge assessments on this and the five other subscales of the NOSIE-30.

The analysis of variance disclosed that overall the scores of the noninstitutionalized group were significantly higher than those of the institutionalized group, F (1, 53) = 2.79, $p < .10$ (on this and the following two subscales higher scores indicate more positive behaviors). The planned comparisons revealed that at intake the noninstitutionalized clients were rated significantly higher than were the institutionalized clients. Neither group's ratings changed significantly across assessments.

Social Interest. The analysis of variance failed to disclose a significant difference in the ratings the two groups received on this subscale. Although the groups by assessments interaction was not significant, there was a difference in the rates of change between the two groups. Whereas the ratings of the noninstitutionalized group improved significantly from the initial to discharge assessments, the

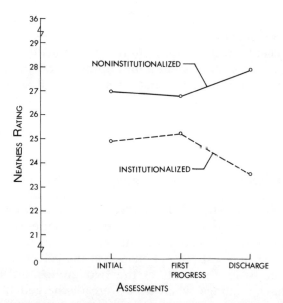

FIGURE 28. Within-treatment changes in neatness ratings for clients living in the community or institutionalized one year after discharge.

ratings of the institutionalized clients did not show a significant change.

Neatness. Overall, the noninstitutionalized clients were rated higher on this subscale than were the institutionalized clients, F (1, 53) = 2.78, $p < .10$. The planned comparisons revealed that although the two groups did not differ in their initial and first progress ratings, the discharge rating of the noninstitutionalized group was significantly higher than the discharge rating of the institutionalized group. Figure 28 shows the reasons for these differences. Whereas the ratings of the institutionalized clients decreased from the first progress to discharge assessments (nonsignificantly), the ratings of the noninstitutionalized clients increased (nonsignificantly).

Irritability. On this and the following two NOSIE-30 subscales *higher* scores indicate *less positive* behavior. Overall, there was no difference between the two groups on this subscale. The independent living group showed a significant increase in irritability from initial to first progress assessment, followed by a nonsignificant *decrease* in their ratings from first progress to discharge assessments. The institutionalized group showed a nonsignificant increase in irritability ratings from initial to first progress and first progress to discharge. At no point were the two groups rated differently.

Psychosis. There were no differences between the ratings of the two groups on this subscale, overall or on any of the three assessments. The planned comparisons did disclose that whereas the ratings of the noninstitutionalized clients did not change from the first progress to discharge assessment, the ratings of psychotic behavior of the institutionalized clients increased significantly over this same interval.

Retardation. Overall, the retardation ratings of the two groups did not differ. Nor were any differences found in the planned comparisons of the clients in each of the three assessments. Neither group's retardation ratings changed during treatments.

Community Adjustment Potential Scale. There were three in-house assessments of 39 noninstitutionalized and 16 institutionalized clients. Overall the noninstitutionalized clients were not rated more positively on the scale than the institutionalized clients. The planned comparisons revealed that although the two groups did not differ on the intake and first progress assessments, the noninstitutionalized group was rated significantly higher on the discharge assessment. These ratings are presented in Figure 29, which shows that while both

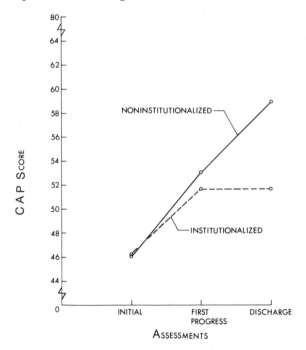

FIGURE 29. Within-treatment changes in Community Adjustment Potential ratings for clients living in the community or institutionalized one year after discharge.

groups' ratings increased, only the noninstitutionalized clients increased significantly from the initital to first progress and from the first progress to discharge assessment.

To summarize the findings from the analyses of the behavior rating scales, on two of the three NOSIE-30 subscales which concerned positive behaviors (Social Competence and Neatness), the noninstitutionalized clients received significantly higher overall ratings than did the institutionalized clients. No such differences were found on the other rating scales. There were differences in the rate of change between the groups on five of the seven scales. On the Social Interest subscale, the noninstitutionalized clients showed significant improvement from intake to discharge, whereas no change was found among the institutionalized clients. The same pattern was found on the CAP. On the Neatness subscale, the ratings of the noninstitutionalized clients showed an improvement, while the scores of the institutionalized clients declined. Turning to the scales which measured negative behaviors, the Irritability ratings of the noninstitutionalized clients increased significantly from the intake to first progress assessment, and the ratings of the institutionalized clients did not change significantly. The Psychosis ratings of the institutionalized clients increased significantly between the first progress and discharge assessments and the ratings of the noninstitutionalized clients did not change. At discharge, the ratings of the noninstitutionalized clients were significantly higher than those of the institutionalized clients on all three of the NOSIE-30 subscales which rated positive behavior and the CAP rating. However, these differences also existed at intake on the Competence and Social Interest subscales.

SUMMARY

The primary purpose of the analyses presented was to determine whether the clients' ability to live in the community after discharge was related to the treatment the clients received. What do the data tell us? We will attempt to draw some conclusions about the effect of the treatment on postdischarge status by posing a series of questions.

Can the clients' ability to live in the community be explained by the biographical/demographic or diagnostic variables? That is, were nonprogrammatic variables responsible for some clients' being in the community one year after discharge and others' being institutionalized? We would answer no to this question. Recall that none of the biographical/demographic or diagnostic variables we examined was found to be related to the clients' living situation after discharge. Certainly the variables we considered do not represent an exhaustive list of the characteristics which may impact on an elderly person's ability to live in a noninstitutional setting, but they do represent a good sampling of those variables which could be reasonably thought to be related to postdischarge status. More important, if there were unmeasured variables which were the sole or primary determinants of postdischarge status, we should not have found any relationship between within-treatment changes and living situations. For example, if a variable such as number of living children (which we did not measure) was a major determinant of whether a client was or was not institutionalized after discharge, then we should not have found that the rate at which clients acquired the modular skills was related to postdischarge status. To be sure, certain biographical/demographic characteristics, in combination with the treatment, could influence the clients' postdischarge status. Our data indicate that such variables or interactions are not more important than treatment-related effects.

Did the institutionalized and noninstitutionalized clients differ on the skills taught in the modules when the two groups entered treatment? More specifically, were the noninstitutionalized clients' skills higher than the institutionalized clients' before the modular training began? The answer to this question is no. There was only one significant difference between the two groups. The initial score of the noninstitutionalized clients on the Life Satisfaction scale was significantly *lower* than the score of the institutionalized clients. If we consider nonsignificant trends, we find that the noninstitutionalized clients were higher in four of the remaining five initial modular assessments. However, in only one instance did this difference exceed one point, and this was on a scale with more than a 30-point range (Communication Training assessment).

Could differences in the clients' general level of functioning at the time they entered treatment explain the difference in their postdischarge status? The answer to this question is given by the analyses of the NOSIE-30 subscales and CAP. These analyses suggest that the noninstitutionalized clients were functioning at a somewhat higher level when they entered the program than were the institutionalized clients. In six of the seven comparisons of the two groups' intake ratings, the noninstitutionalized group was rated more positively than the institutionalized groups. This difference was significant for the Competence and Social Interest subscales of the NOSIE-30. Does this mean that initial differences between the two groups rather than the training were responsible for the difference in the clients' postdischarge status? We do not believe so. Rather, we would suggest that these differences may partially explain why some clients improved in their modular training during treatment and others did not.

The rate of improvement, in turn, impacted the clients' postdischarge status. In other words, we believe that the clients' general level of functioning when they entered the program may have influenced how much the clients were able to acquire from the training.

Did the institutionalized and noninstitutionalized clients differ at the time of discharge from the program? The answer to this question is a rather tentative yes. On all six modular assessments and all seven behavior rating scales, the noninstitutionalized clients received more positive discharge scores than did the insitutionalized clients. Although this difference was significant on only one of the modular discharge assessments, the magnitude of the differences between the groups at the time of discharge was much greater than the difference at intake. On four of the seven behavior rating scales, the noninstitutionalized groups received significantly higher ratings at the time of discharge than did the institutionalized group.

Did clients who were institutionalized and clients who were not institutionalized one year after discharge differ in their rate of improvement during treatment? First, let us consider changes on the modular assessments. In five of the six modular assessments analyzed, there were differences in the rate of improvement between the institutionalized and noninstitutionalized clients. In three of the analyses there were significant group by assessments interaction terms, indicating that the two groups differed significantly in their rate of improvement in the modules. In two assessments, the interaction term was not significant. However, the planned comparisons of these assessments disclosed that, whereas the noninstitutionalized clients showed significant improvement, the institutionalized clients did not. Therefore, with regard to the modular training, the answer is yes. The clients who remained in the community acquired the skills more rapidly and/or at a greater rate than did the clients who were institutionalized. This would suggest that the modular training was related to postdischarge status.

The changes measured by the rating scales are hard to interpret. There were no differences between the two groups in the rate of change on the Competence and Retardation subscales of the NOSIE-30. On the Social Interest and Neatness subscales and the CAP, the noninstitutionalized clients showed improvement and the institutionalized clients' ratings either stayed the same or declined. The Psychosis ratings of the noninstitutionalized clients did not change, but the institutionalized clients were rated as significantly more psychotic at discharge than at the first progress assessment. All of these findings tend to support the conclusion that the noninstitutionalized clients improved more during treatment than did the institutionalized clients. The fact that Irritability ratings of the noninstitutionalized clients increased significantly might be viewed as an exception to this general pattern. However, as we have noted earlier, an increase in Irritability ratings may simply reflect an increase in the clients' ability and/or willingness to display affect. Thus, the findings from the analyses of the rating scales indicate that, in the main, the noninstitutionalized clients were more likely to improve during treatment than were the institutionalized clients. This conclusion must be tempered, however, by findings that there were initial group differences on two of the rating scales and no differences in rate of change on two of the scales. This makes it somewhat harder to argue that there was a clear-cut difference between the groups in how their behavior changed during treatment.

An admittedly speculative explanation of these findings is that some of the areas measured by the rating scales, most notably Competence, are not impacted by treatment (recall that in none of the analyses conducted were significant changes found on this subscale). Rather, a clients' level of general competence at intake may influence the degree to which he is able to acquire similar skills taught in the program. There are data to support this conjecture. The PIT assessments and Competence subscale of the NOSIE-30 seem to be measuring the same thing.[5] An analysis of the relationship between intake PIT scores and skill acquisition in the other modules was conducted which relates to this issue. This analysis showed that the higher a client's initial PIT score, the more likely the client was to acquire the skills taught in the other modules. Thus, the clients' level of intellectual competence when they entered the program may explain why some could acquire the skills better than others. The acquisition of the skills, in turn, influenced the clients' ability to live in the community.

The areas addressed by the other rating scales do seem to be affected by treatment. In those areas which are influenced by treatment, noninstitutionalized clients typically show more improvement than do institutionalized clients. (It must be noted that these conclusions only apply to our residential clients. Since we were unable to obtain an uncontaminated measure of postdischarge status for the day treatment clients, we are unable to argue that treatment is related to postdischarge status among these clients.)

Weiss (1972) has proposed that one evaluates a program by looking at three things: (1) the degree to which a program achieves its proximal goal(s), (2) the degree to which it achieves its distal goal(s), and (3) the extent to which this proximal goal facilitates the achieve-

---

[5]Cf. section on reliability and validity of measures in Chapter 9.

ment of the distal goal. With regard to the residential program, we can address these issues. The data presented in Chapter 9 indicate that the program was successful in reaching its proximal goals: the clients were able to learn the skills taught in the modules. The comparative and within-program analyses of the recidivism rates among our residential clients suggested that the program was successful in reaching its distal goal: the returning of previously institutionalized clients to the community. And, finally, the data from the analyses just presented suggest that the acquisition of the skills taught in the modules did play an important role in enabling the clients to live in the community.

PROGRAM IMPACT

In addition to answering questions concerning the program's effectiveness in meeting proximal and distal goals and the relationships between the two, there is the broader, overall evaluation question as to whether the program materially affected the delivery of mental health services to the elderly. More specifically, the evaluation of the program's impact attempts to answer the following questions: (1) Did the program produce changes in the system for delivering mental health services to the elderly in the state of Florida and, if so, what were these changes? and (2) did the program affect public policy of the state and, if so, what was the nature and content of the change?

Answers to these questions cannot be derived by the application of the techniques described in the previous two chapters. The answers must come from historical fact, and therefore causality cannot be inferred. That is, on a probabilistic basis, the same historical facts might have occurred in spite of the program. However, the information to be presented below leads us to discount pure historical coincidence as the cause of the changes which have occurred in the attitudes toward and treatment of elderly mental health clients in the state of Florida.

DELIVERY SYSTEM CHANGE

The overall mission of the Gerontology Program was to develop, demonstrate, evaluate, and disseminate treatment programs that would deinstitutionalize elderly mental health clients of the state and prevent institutionalization of elderly, at-risk clients residing in the community. The previous sections of this chapter have dealt with the effectiveness of the treatment program as related to *the clients of the Gerontology Program*. The question remains as to whether this program was disseminated to others and whether it was *effective with the clients of other service providers*. The first part of this question can be answered easily. The staff of the Gerontology Program carried on an extensive dissemination effort covering most of the traditional methods, that is, publication in journals, presentations at society meetings, reading papers at conferences, guest lecturing at various university and community college courses, and participating in workshops conducted by provider agencies. In addition, four specific program dissemination activities were undertaken to educate and train those interested in providing mental health services to the elderly. These activities were: (1) a series of one-day workshops conducted every 3 months which covered the skill training modules; (2) on-site training and consultation visits by program staff to those agencies which wished to adopt the program or some of its components; (3) a once-a-month residency "training week" for intensive instruction, hands-on practice, and supervised clinical experience for those who wanted to provide direct service; and (4) producing training manuals for each of the skill training modules. The manuals were used in conjunction with the workshops and the residency training weeks. Although the workshops were well attended with several hundred participants during the period when they were offered, they were concluded in mid-1978 to concentrate dissemination efforts on training weeks and consultation visits with agencies that wished to adopt the program. This effort was directed to the second part of the question—whether or not the program was effective with clients of other service providers in other settings.

Two types of agencies were chosen as dissemination targets. The first was large state mental health hospitals and the second, community agencies, most frequently comprehensive community mental health centers. Although almost all providers in the state sent participants to workshops and many had staff attend residency training weeks, with only six community agencies was there continuing consultation and on-site training. Although all of these six agencies are continuing to utilize some of the program components, only one community agency, the Santa Rosa Mental Health and Rehabilitation Facility, Inc., has incorporated the total program. Their Geriatric Residential Center is providing treatment to approximately 150 elderly clients a year, of whom approximately 40% are transferred from state mental health hospitals and others are admitted directly from psychiatric facilities in the community. Approximately 10% of the discharges from this center are to psychiatric inpatient facilities; another 10% are discharged to nursing homes. The remaining 80% are discharged to less restrictive settings in the community. Although these highly successful achievements of the Santa Rosa Center cannot be attributed to the Gerontology Treatment Program from which it was adopted, it should be noted that their outcome results are comparable percentages to those reported in Chapter 8 for the discharge destination of Gerontology clients. It also should be noted that the Santa Rosa Center is approximately 350 miles distant from the FMHI Gerontology Program, operating in a different geographical, economic, and cultural area from that of the Institute. It would appear, therefore, that the program can be effective with clients of other service providers in quite different settings. Other community agencies are continuing to utilize various gerontology program treatment components such as the ADL module series, communication and conversation training, assessment instruments and techniques, and the application of client criteria for screening and admission to treatment programs.

Replication of the program in the large state hospitals absorbed the majority of the dissemination effort from 1978 to 1981. On-site consultation and training and residency training of hospital staff at FMHI were initiated in early 1978 and have continued with all four state hospitals. The first replication effort was at Florida State Hospital, the oldest and largest of the four, with over 1,200 patients age 55 and older representing approximately 57% of the patient census. Gerontology Program staff assisted the hospital administration and clinical staff in planning, developing, and initiating Project New Directions, a direct replication of the gerontology residential treatment program with the objective of deinstitutionalizing and returning to the community elderly long-term patients. The only programmatic departure from the Gerontology Program was the clients transferred to Project New Directions would be 65 years of age and older, instead of 55 years as in the Gerontology Program at FMHI. From February 1978 through November 1980, Project New Directions admitted 143 patients by transfer from other units of the hospital. Of these 143 patients, 42 were still in treatment, while 91 had been discharged from the project. Sixty-five of the discharges were to less restrictive community settings; 23 were returned to their hospital units (rehospitalized); one died; one eloped; and one was transferred to another state hospital. The success rate of Project New Directions can be viewed as 73% (65 of 89), with 27% not being discharged or deinstitutionalized. This is a remarkable achievement when one realizes that the average age of the clients of Project New Directions was 74 years and their average length of continuous stay at Florida State Hospital was 17.9 years. Only 7 of the 65 community discharges had been rehospitalized as of

November 1980 but as of that date some of the discharged clients had been in the community only one month. Still, for this population, an 11% short-term recidivism rate is extremely low. It would appear that the Gerontology Program can be replicated in a different institutional setting and be effective with appropriate clients of state hospitals.

In summary, changes have occurred in the system for delivering mental health services to elderly clients since the Gerontology Program has been conducting its dissemination efforts. These changes are recognition at both the community and state levels that it is possible to deinstitutionalize certain categories of elderly long-term clients, that it is possible to select such clients from the total elderly hospitalized population, and that it is possible to provide a psychosocial rehabilitation treatment program that will enable these clients to reside in less restrictive community settings. The rehabilitation treatment developed by the Gerontology Program has demonstrated how this can be done and has been incorporated in its entirety by one community agency and one state hospital with positive results. Other community agencies and other state hospitals are using various parts of the program, and their increased use indicated relative satisfaction with their efficacy. Through impact on public policy and on the state of gerontological practice, as discussed in the following two sections, it is expected that the treatment methodology and the program technology will be utilized to an ever increasing extent in changing the delivery of mental health services to the elderly.

Public Policy Change

Public policy affecting mental health services in the state of Florida is promulgated in two basic ways: by an act of the legislature and by administrative rules and direction of the state government, the latter in the offices of the Secretary of the Department of Health and Rehabilitative Services (DHRS) and the Staff Director of the Mental Health Program Office. Until 1977, Florida public policy toward the elderly hospitalized mental health patient was to provide the highest possible level of custodial care under the assumption that hospitalization would be required for the rest of the client's life. Rehabilitation and return to community living were not considered a viable option for geriatric clients. During the 1977 legislative sessions, the Florida Legislature mandated a broad deinstitutionalization program for DHRS institutions. From this program a deinstitutionalization plan was developed by PDMH for the state mental health facilities, and the Gerontology Program Director was asked to participate in representing the needs of older persons in the planning process. The concept that elderly clients could be trained in several areas of skill which enable them to obtain adequate environmental support to reside in the community was injected into public policy planning.

In January 1980, on the basis of an interim status report and the accomplishments of Project New Directions at Florida State Hospital, the DHRS directed the transfer of the Gerontology Program to other institutions and stated that "the treatment program . . . can be significant in resolving the basic problem of adequately preparing mental health patients to return to their communities" (Pingree, 1980). In the spring of 1980 the legislature appropriated funds to initiate two pilot programs for the deinstitutionalization of elderly patients through community-based geriatric residential and treatment systems. Gerontology staff have been consulting with these two systems and training their staff in the program components and modules. The preliminary evaluation of these legislated programs acknowledges the role of the Gerontology Program in shaping treatment and assessment methods (DCI Research Associates, 1981).

Confirmation of the impact of the Gerontology Program on public policy is contained in the *Comprehensive Plan for Deinstitutionalization of Geriatric State Hospital Patients* prepared in March 1981 by PDMH. This plan was in direct response to the Florida Senate, which directed DHRS to submit to the legislature "a comprehensive plan for the deinstitutionalization of those state hospital patients over age 55 who do not meet the criteria for involuntary hospitalization" (*Official Florida Statutes* § 394.4674). The 6-year plan credits the Gerontology Program as being the "model for the subsequent development of additional . . . programs" (Florida Department of Health and Rehabilitative Services, 1981).

THE PROGRAM AND THE PRACTICE

During the time that the Gerontology Program has been in existence there have been changes in the practice of mental health for the elderly in the state of Florida. These changes are significant and, as we have pointed out in the above sections, they involve the system for the delivery of service as well as the type of treatment. In addition, there have been basic changes in the attitudes toward the elderly mental health patient as reflected in changes in public policy including statutory amendments. The major elements of these changes are:

- Recognition that many of the hospitalized elderly or those at risk of institutionalization need not be placed in such restrictive or custodial care environments

- Acceptance of the fact that the elderly who suffer from cognitive and psychosocial deficits can be rehabilitated through behavioral treatment and acquire the skills necessary to reside in less restrictive community settings
- Initiation of a spectrum of community-based treatment and rehabilitation programs emphasizing behavioral approaches to develop and maintain environmental support systems
- A 30% decline in geriatric (55 years and older) admissions to state hospitals despite an increase of approximately 120% for this age group in the population as a whole; and a drop of almost one-third in the number of elderly in state hospitals (2800 to 1900)

Although it is not possible to attribute these changes directly to the Gerontology Program at FMHI, we like to believe that we had some effect and that the program of treatment and rehabilitation described in this book was instrumental in improving the living situation of many of Florida's older residents.

References

Albee, G. W. *Mental health manpower trends* (Monograph No. 3 of the Joint Commission on Mental Illness and Health). New York: Basic Books, 1959.

American Psychiatric Association, Contract Survey Board. *A survey of the mental health needs and resources in Florida.* Washington, D.C.: Author, 1963.

American Psychiatric Association. *Remotivation technique: A manual for use in nursing homes.* Washington, D.C.: Author, 1968.

Atchley, R. C. *The social forces in later life: An introduction to social gerontology.* Belmont, Calif.: Wadsworth, 1977.

Atthowe, J. M., & Krasner, L. Preliminary report on the application of contingent reinforcement procedures (token economy) on a "chronic" psychiatric ward. *Journal of Abnormal Psychology,* 1968, *73,* 37–43.

Aumack, L. A social adjustment behavior rating scale. *Journal of Clinical Psychology,* 1962, *13,* 436–441.

Ayllon, T., & Azrin, M. *The token economy: A motivational system for therapy and rehabilitation.* New York: Appleton-Century-Crofts, 1968.

Azrin, N. H. A strategy for applied research: Learning based but outcome oriented. *American Psychologist,* 1977, *32,* 140–149.

Baffa, G. A., & Zarit, S. H. Age differences in the perception of assertive behavior. *The Gerontologist,* 1977, *15*(5), 36.

Baltes, M. M., & Baltes, P. B. The ecopsychological relativity and plasticity of psychological aging: Convergent perspectives of cohort effects and operant psychology. *Zeitschrift für Experimentelle und Angewandte Psychologie,* 1977, *24,* 179–194.

Baltes, M. M., & Barton, E. M. New approaches toward aging: A case for the operant model. *Educational Gerontology,* 1977, *2,* 383–405.

Baltes, M. M., & Zerbe, M. B. Reestablishing self-feeding in a nursing home resident. *Nursing Research,* 1976, *25,* 24–26. (a)

Baltes, M. M., & Zerbe, M. B. Independence training in nursing home residents. *The Gerontologist,* 1976, *16,* 428–432. (b)

Baltes, P. B., & Willis, S. L. Toward psychological theories of aging and development. In J. E. Birren & K. W. Schaie (Eds.), *Handbook of the psychology of aging.* New York: Van Nostrand Reinhold, 1977.

Bandura, A. *Principles of behavior modification.* New York: Holt, Rinehart & Winston, 1969.

Bandura, A., Ross, D., & Ross, S. A. A comparative test of the status envy, social power, and the secondary-reinforcement theories of identificatory learning. *Journal of Abnormal Social Psychology,* 1963, *67,* 527–534.

Barrett, J. H. *Gerontological psychology.* Springfield, Ill.: Charles C Thomas, 1972.

279

Bates, H. D. *Gerontology proposal*. Tampa, Fla.: Florida Mental Health Institute, 1975.

Becker, A., & Schulberg, H. D. Phasing out state hospitals—a psychiatric dilemma. *The New England Journal of Medicine*, 1976, *294*, 255–261.

Bellack, A. S., & Hersen, M. (Eds.). *Research and practice in social skills training*. New York: Plenum Press, 1979.

Birren, J. E., Butler, R. N., Greenhouse, S. W., Sokoloff, L., & Yarrow, M. R. (Eds.). *Human aging*. Washington, D.C.: U.S. Government Printing Office, 1963.

Blackman, K. D., Howe, M., & Pinkston, E. M. Increasing participation in social interaction of the institutionalized elderly. *The Gerontologist*, 1976, *16*(1), 69–76.

Bourostom, N. C., Wolff, R. J., & Davis, H. R. Prognostic factors in elderly mental patients. *Journal of American Geriatric Society*, 1961, *9*, 150–155.

Bower, W. H. Recent developments in mental health manpower. *Hospital and Community Psychiatry*, 1970, *21*, 11–17.

Bureau of Economic and Business Research. *Florida statistical abstract*. Gainesville, Fla.: University Presses of Florida, 1980.

Butler, R. N. Age-ism: Another form of bigotry. *Gerontologist*, 1969, *9*, 243–246.

Butler, R. N. *Why survive? Being old in America*. New York: Harper & Row, 1975.

Butler, R. N. Ageism: A foreword. *Journal of Social Issues*, 1980, *36*, 8–11.

Butler, R. N., & Lewis, M. I. *Aging and mental health*. St. Louis, Mo.: C. V. Mosby, 1973.

Butler, R. N., & Lewis, M. I. *Aging and mental health* (2nd ed.). St. Louis, Mo.: C. V. Mosby, 1977.

Campbell, D. T., & Fiske, D. W. Convergent and discriminant validation by the multitrait-multimethod matrix. *Psychological Bulletin*, 1959, *56*, 81–105.

Campbell, D. T., & Stanley, J. C. *Experimental and quasi-experimental designs for research*. Chicago: Rand-McNally, 1963.

Cautela, J. R., & Mansfield, L. A behavioral approach to geriatrics. In W. D. Gentry (Ed.), *Geropsychology: A model of training and clinical service*. Cambridge, Mass.: Ballinger, 1977.

Clark, M., & Anderson, B. *Culture and aging*. Springfield, Ill.: Charles C Thomas, 1972.

Cohen, H. L., & Filipczak, J. *A new learning environment*. London: Jossey–Bass, 1971.

Comprehensive plan for the deinstitutionalization of geriatric state hospital patients. Tallahassee, Fla.: Mental Health Program Office, Department of Health and Rehabilitative Services, 1981.

Cook, T. D., & Campbell, D. T. *Quasi-experimentation: Designs and analysis issues for field settings*. Chicago: Rand-McNally, 1979.

Corby, N. Assertion training with aged populations. *The Counseling Psychologist*, 1975, *5*(4), 69–74.

Cowen, E. L. Some problems in community program evaluation research. *Journal of Consulting and Clinical Psychology*, 1978, *46*, 792–805.

DCI Research Associates. *Interim report of the evaluation component of the Mental Health Geriatric Residential and Treatment System for Institutionalized Elderly (GRTS) in Sarasota and Manatee Counties*. Bradenton, Florida, April 1981.

Dee, C. K. *Memory development*. Poster session presented at the second annual Nova Behavioral Conference on Aging, Fort Lauderdale, Florida, January 1980.

DiScipio, W. J., & Feldman, M. C. Combined behavior therapy and physical therapy in the treatment of a fear of walking. *Journal of Behavior Therapy and Experimental Psychiatry*, 1971, *2*, 151–152.

Ellis, A., & Grieger, R. *Handbook of rational emotive therapy*. New York: Springer, 1977.

Ellsworth, R. B. *Personal adjustment and role skills (PARS) scales*. Roanoke, Va.: Institute for Program Evaluation, 1974.

Erickson, R. C. Outcome studies in mental hospitals: A review. *Psychological Bulletin*, 1975, *82*, 519–540.

Fairweather, G. W., Sanders, D. H., & Tournatzky, L. *Creating change in mental health organizations*. New York: Pergamon, 1974.

Fairweather, G. W., Sanders, D. H., Maynard, H., & Cressler, D. L. *Community life for the mentally ill: An alternative to institutional care*. Chicago: Aldine, 1979.

Favell, J. *The power of positive reinforcement: A handbook of behavior modification*. Springfield, Ill.: Charles C Thomas, 1977.

Florida Department of Health and Rehabilitative Services, Alcohol, Drug Abuse, and Mental Health Program Staff. *Client assessment survey*. Tallahassee, Fla.: Author, September 1981.

Foxx, R. M., & Azrin, N. H. Restitution: A method of eliminating aggressive-disruptive behavior of retarded and brain-damaged patients. *Behavior Research and Therapy*, 1972, *10*, 15–27.

Foxx, R. M., & Azrin, N. H. The elimination of autistic self-stimulatory behavior by overcorrection. *Journal of Applied Behavior Analysis*, 1973, *6*, 1–14.

Fry, L. J., & Miller, J. P. The impact of interdisciplinary teams on organizational relationships. *The Sociological Quarterly*, 1974, *15*, 417–431.

Gaitz, C. M. Barriers to the delivery of psychiatric services to the elderly. *Gerontologist*, 1974, *14*, 210–214.

Geiger, O. G,. & Johnson, L. A. Positive education for elderly persons: Correct eating through reinforcement. *The Gerontologist*, 1974, *14*, 432–436.

Gergen, K. J. *Experimentation in social psychology: A reappraisal*. Invited address to Division 8 of the American Psychological Association, Chicago, August–September 1975.

Glass, G. V., & Ellet, F. S. Evaluation research. *Annual Review of Psychology*, 1980, *31*, 211–228.

Goldfried, M. R., & Davison, G. C. *Clinical behavior therapy*. New York: Holt, Rinehart & Winston, 1976.

Goldstein, A. P. *Structured learning therapy*. New York: Academic Press, 1973.

Goldstein, A. P., Sprafkin, R. P., & Gershaw, N. J. *Skill training for community living: Applying structured learning therapy*. New York: Pergamon, 1976.

Gurin, G., Veroff, J., & Field, S. *Americans view their mental health: A nationwide interview study*. New York: Basic Books, 1960.

Gutride, M. E., Goldstein, A. P., & Hunter, G. F. The use of modeling and role playing to increase social interaction among schizophrenic patients. *Journal of Consulting and Clinical Psychology*, 1973, *40*, 408–415.

Gutride, M. E., Goldstein, A. P., & Hunter, G. F. Structured learning therapy with transfer training for chronic inpatients. *Journal of Clinical Psychology*, July 1974, 277–280.

Hersen, M. Complex problems require complex solutions. *Behavior Therapy*, 1981, *12*, 15–29.

Hersen, M., & Barlow, D. H. *Single case experimental designs*. New York: Pergamon, 1976.

Hersen, M., Eisler, R. M., & Miller, P. M. *Progress in behavior modification* (Vol. 9). New York: Academic Press, 1980.

Hogarty, G. E., & Ulrich, R. The discharge readiness inventory. *Archives of General Psychiatry*, 1972, *26*, 419–426.

Homans, G. C. *The human group*. New York: Harcourt, Brace, 1950.

Honigfeld, G., Gillis, R. D., & Klett, C. J. The nurses' observation scale for inpatient evaluation. *Journal of Consulting Psychology*, 1966, *21*, 69–77.

Horowitz, J. J. *Team practice and the specialist.* Springfield, Ill.: Charles C Thomas, 1970.

Hoyer, W. J. Application of operant techniques to the modification of elderly behavior. *Gerontologist*, 1973, *13*, 18–22.

Hoyer, W. J. Aging as intraindividual change. *Developmental Psychology*, 1974, *10*, 821–826.

Hoyer, W. J., Kafer, R. A., Simpson, S. C., & Hoyer, F. W. Reinstatement of verbal behavior in elderly mental patients using operant procedures. *The Gerontologist*, 1974, *14*(2), 149–152.

Hoyer, W. J., Mishara, D. L., & Reidel, R. G. Problem behaviors as operants: Applications with elderly individuals. *Gerontologist*, 1975, *15*, 452–456.

Ingersoll, B., & Silverman, A. Comparative group psychotherapy for the aged. *Gerontologist*, 1978, *18*, 201–206.

Jackson, G. M., & Schonfeld, L. I. *The behavioral treatment of orafacial tardive dyskinesia.* Paper presented at the 2nd Annual Nova Behavioral Conference on Aging, Fort Lauderdale, January 1980.

Jackson, G. M., & Schonfeld, L. I. Multielement baseline/multiple schedule comparisons of visual feedback, instructional prompts, and discrete prompting in the treatment of orafacial tardive dyskinesia. *The International Journal of Behavioral Geriatrics*, in press.

Jenkins, W. O. *An innovative approach to the analysis and alteration of human behavior: Behavior evaluation, treatment and analysis (BETA).* Montgomery, Ala.: Beta Systems, 1977.

Johnson, R., Frallicciardi, V., & Patterson, R. L. *A multiple baseline evaluation of a reality orientation procedure for disoriented geriatric clients.* Paper presented at the 23rd Annual Meeting of the Southeastern Psychological Association, Hollywood, Florida, May 1977.

Kahn, R. L., & Zarit, S. H. Evaluation of mental health programs for the elderly. In P. O. Davidson, F. W. Clark, & L. A. Hamerlynek (Eds.), *Evaluation of behavioral programs in community residential and social settings.* Champaign, Ill.: Research Press, 1974.

Kalish, R. A. *The later years.* Belmont, Calif.: Wadsworth, 1977.

Kastenbaum, R. Perspectives on the development and modification of behavior in the aged: A developmental-field perspective. *Gerontologist*, 1968, *8*, 280–283.

Kastenbaum, R. Personality theory, therapeutic approaches, and the elderly client. In M. Storandt, I. C. Siegler, & M. F. Elias (Eds.), *The clinical psychology of aging.* New York: Plenum Press, 1978.

Katz, D., & Kahn, R. L. *The social psychology of organizations* (2nd ed.). New York: Wiley, 1978.

Kazdin, A. E. Statistical analyses for single-case experimental designs. In M. Hersen & D. H. Barlow (Eds.), *Single case experimental designs.* New York: Pergamon Press, 1976.

Kogan, N., & Wallach, M. Age changes in values and attitudes. *Journal of Gerontology*, 1961, *16*, 272–280.

Kramer, M., Taube, C. A., & Redick, R. W. Patterns of use of psychiatric facilities by the aged: Past, present, and future. In C. Eisdorfer & M. P. Lawton (Eds.), *The psychology of adult development and aging.* Washington, D.C.: American Psychological Association, 1973.

Kulka, R. A., & Tamir, L. *Patterns of help-seeking and formal support.* Paper presented at the meeting of the Gerontological Society, Dallas, Texas, November 1978.

Langer, E., Rodin, J., Beck, P., Weinman, C., & Spitzer, L. Environmental determinants of memory improvement in late adulthood. *Journal of Personality and Social Psychology*, 1979, *37*, 2003–2013.

Lankford, D. A., & Herman, S. H. *Behavioral geriatrics: A critical review*. Paper presented at the 1st Nova Behavioral Conference on Aging, Port St. Lucie, Florida, May 21–25, 1978.

Lawton, M. P. Clinical geropsychology: Problems and prospects. *JSAS Catalog of Selected Documents in Psychology*, 1979, *9*, 32 (MS. No. 1847).

Levine, M. Adapting the jury trial for program evaluation. *Evaluation Program Planning*, 1978, *1*, 177–186.

Liberman, R. P., King, L. W., DeRisi, W. J., & McCann, M. *Personal effectiveness*. Champaign, Ill.: Research Press, 1975.

Libow, L. S. Senile dementia and "pseudo-senility": Clinical diagnosis. In C. Eisdorfer & R. O. Friedel (Eds.), *Cognitive and emotional disturbance in the elderly*. Chicago: Year Book Medical Publishers, 1977.

Lindsley, O. R. Geriatric behavior prosthetics. In R. Kastenbaum (Ed.), *New thoughts on old age*. New York: Springer, 1964.

McClannahan, L. E., & Risley, T. R. A store for nursing home residents. *Nursing Homes*, June 1973, 26–31.

McClannahan, L. E., & Risley, T. R. Design of living environments for nursing home residents. *The Gerontologist*, 1974, *14*, 236–240.

McGuire, W. J. The Yin and Yang of progress in social psychology: Seven Koan. *Journal of Personality and Social Psychology*, 1973, *26*, 446–456.

Miller, L. K. *Principles of everyday behavior analysis*. Monterey, Calif.: Brooks/Cole, 1975.

Miller, L. M. *Behavior treatment of alcoholism*. New York: Pergamon, 1976.

Miller, L. M. Toward a classification of aging behaviors. *The Gerontologist*, 1979, *19*, 283–290.

Mueller, D. J., & Atlas, L. Resocialization of regressed elderly residents: A behavioral management approach. *Journal of Gerontology*, 1972, *27*(3), 390–392.

Murphy, R., Doughty, N., & Nunes, D. Multielement designs. *Mental Retardation*, 1979, *17*, 23–27.

Nathan, P. E., & Lansky, D. Common methodological problems in research on the addictions. *Journal of Consulting and Clinical Psychology*, 1978, *46*, 713–726.

National Center for Health Statistics. Profile of chronic illness in nursing homes. In *Vital and health statistics* (Series 13, No. 29). Hyattsville, Md.: U.S. Department of Health, Education and Welfare, 1977.

Neugarten, B., Havighurst, R., & Tobin, S. The measurement of life satisfaction. *Journal of Gerontology*, 1961, *16*, 134–143.

Official Florida Statutes (17th ed.). Tallahassee, Fla.: Author, 1979.

O'Sullivan, M. J., Eberly, D. A., Patterson, R. L., & Penner, L. A. *An experimental study of improving life satisfaction by older people by increasing self-esteem through behavioral training*. Paper presented at the 26th Annual Meeting of the Southeastern Psychological Association, New Orleans, March 1979.

Palmore, E. B. Social factors in mental illness of the aged. In E. W. Busse & E. Pfeiffer (Eds.), *Mental illness in later life*. Washington, D.C.: American Psychiatric Association, 1973.

Palmore, E. B. Total chance of institutionalization among the aged. *Gerontologist*, 1976, *16*, 504–507.

Pascal, G. R., & Jenkins, W. O. *Systematic observation of gross human behavior*. New York: Grune & Stratton, 1961.

Patterson, R. L. Individualized treatment using token economy methods. In R. L. Patterson (Ed.), *Maintaining effective token economies*. Springfield, Ill.: Charles C Thomas, 1976.

Patterson, R. L., & Jackson, G. M. Behavior modification with the elderly. In M. Hersen, R. M. Eisler, & P. Miller (Eds.), *Progress in behavior modification* (Vol. 9). New York: Academic Press, 1980. (a)

Patterson, R. L., & Jackson, G. M. Behavioral approaches to gerontology. In L. Michelson, M. Hersen, & S. Turner (Eds.), *Future perspectives in behavior therapy*. New York: Plenum Press, 1980. (b)

Patterson, R. L., Smith, A. G., Goodale, P., & Miller, C. *Improving communication abilities in psychogeriatric clients*. Paper presented at the 29th Annual Meeting of the Southeastern Psychological Association, Atlanta, March 1978. (a)

Patterson, R. L., Smith, A. G., Goodale, P., & Miller, C. *Three studies on improving communication abilities in psychogeriatric clients*. Poster session presented at the Nova Behavioral Conference on Aging, Port St. Lucie, Florida, May 1978 (b)

Patterson, R. L., O'Sullivan, M. J., & Spielberger, C. D. Measurement of state and trait anxiety in elderly mental health clients. *Journal of Behavioral Assessment*, 1980, 2, 89–97.

Patterson, R. L., Penner, L. A., Eberly, D. A., & Harrell, T. L. Behavioral assessments of intellectual competence, communication skills, and personal hygiene skills of elderly persons. *Behavioral Assessment*, in press.

Paul, G. L. The chronic mental patient: Current status—future directions. *Psychological Bulletin*, 1969, 71, 81–94.

Paul, G. L., & Lentz, R. J. *Psychosocial treatment of chronic mental patients: Milieu versus social learning programs*. Cambridge, Mass.: Harvard University Press, 1977.

Peterson, R. G., Knapp, T. J., Rosen, J. O., & Pither, B. F. The effects of furniture arrangement on the behavior of geriatric patients. *Behavior Therapy*, 1977, 8, 464–467.

Pfeiffer, E. A short portable mental status questionnaire for the assessment of organic brain deficits in elderly patients. *Journal of the American Geriatric Society*, 1975, 23, 433–436.

Pfeiffer, E. Psychopathology and social psychology. In J. E. Birren & K. W. Schaie (Eds.), *Handbook of the psychology of aging*. New York: Van Nostrand Reinhold, 1977.

Pingree, D. S. (Secretary, Florida Department of Health and Human Services). Personal communication, Tallahassee, Florida, January 21, 1980.

Popham, W. J., & Carlson, D. Deep dark deficits of the adversary evaluation model. *Education Research*, 1977, 6, 3–6.

Ray, T. S. *Operation Hope: Evaluation of impact on the well-being of placement of elderly mental hospitalized patients in alternate care facilities*. A report to the Southern Conference on Mental Health Statistics. Atlanta, November 16, 1971.

Reagles, K. W. *Program evaluation in rehabilitation settings*. Presentation at the University of South Florida, Tampa, Florida, December 5, 1980.

Rebok, G. W., & Hoyer, W. J. The functional context of elderly behavior. *Gerontologist*, 1977, 17, 27–34.

Redick, R. W., Kramer, M., & Taube, C. A. Epidemiology of mental illness and utilization of psychiatric facilities among older persons. In E. W. Busse & E. Pfeiffer (Eds.), *Mental illness in later life*. Washington, D.C.: American Psychiatric Association, 1973.

Rehabilitation Research Foundation (RRF) Publications. *Measurements and evaluations, 1977*. Box BV, University, Alabama, 1977.

Reichenfeld, H. F., Csapo, K. G., Carriere, L., & Gardner, R. C. Evaluating the effect of activity programs on a geriatric ward. *The Gerontologist*, 1973, 13, 305–310.

Repp, A. C., Dietz, E. D., Boles, S. M., Dietz, S. M., & Repp, C. F. Differences among common methods for calculating interobserver agreement. *Journal of Applied Behavior Analysis*, 1976, 9, 104–113.

Richards, W. S., & Thorpe, G. L. Behavioral approaches to the problems of later life. In M. Storandt, I. Siegler, & M. Elias (Eds.), *The clinical psychology of aging*. New York: Plenum Press, 1978.

Riley, M., & Foner, A. *Aging and society: Volume I. An inventory of research findings.* New York: Russell Sage Foundation, 1968.

Risley, T. R., & Edwards, K. A. *Behavioral technology for nursing home care: Toward a system of nursing home organization and management.* Paper presented at the Nova Behavioral Conference on Aging, Port St. Lucie, Florida, May 1978.

Risley, T. R., Gottula, P., & Edwards, K. A. *Social interaction during family and institutional style meal service in a nursing home dining room.* Paper presented at the Nova Behavioral Conference on Aging, Port St. Lucie, Florida, May 1978.

Rodin, J., & Langer, E. Aging labels: The decline of control and the fall of self-esteem. *Journal of Social Issues,* 1980, *36,* 12–29.

Rosenberg, M. *Society and the adolescent self-image.* New York: Basic Books, 1965.

Rusin, M. J. *Role-play training of self-care skills with geriatric psychiatric patients.* Master of Science thesis, Florida State University, 1978.

Schwartz, A. N. An observation on self-esteem as the linchpin of quality life for the aged: An essay. *Gerontologist,* 1975, *15*(5), 470–472.

Sidman, M. *Tactics of scientific research: Evaluating experimental data in psychology.* New York: Basic Books, 1960.

Siegal, S. *Nonparametric statistics for the behavioral sciences.* New York: McGraw-Hill, 1956.

Skinner, B. F. *The technology of teaching.* New York: Appleton-Century-Crofts, 1968.

Sommer, R., & Ross, H. Social interaction on a geriatric ward. *International Journal of Social Psychiatry,* 1958, *4,* 128–133.

Stake, R. E. A theoretical statement of responsive evaluation. *Studies in Educational Evaluation,* 1976, *2,* 19–22.

Stake, R. E., & Easley, J. A., Jr. *Case studies in science education* (Vols. 1 & 2). Urbana, Ill.: Circe, 1978.

Sulzer-Azaroff, B., & Mayer, G. *Applying behavior analysis procedures with children and youth.* New York: Holt, Rinehart & Winston, 1977.

Taulbee, E. S., & Wright, H. W. A psychosocial behavioral model for therapeutic intervention: IV. The geriatric reality orientation program. *Topics in Clinical and Community Psychology,* 1971, *3,* 71–75.

Todd, J. Covarant control of self-evaluative responses in the treatment of depression: A new use for an old principle. *Behavior Therapy,* 1972, *3,* 91–94.

U.S. Bureau of the Census. *Statistical abstract of the United States; 1978* (99th ed.). Washington, D.C.: U.S. Government Printing Office, 1978.

U.S. Bureau of the Census. *Illustrative projections of world populations to the 21st century* (Current population reports: Special studies service, p. 23, No. 79). Washington, D.C.: U.S. Government Printing Office, 1979.

U.S. President's Commission on Mental Health. *Task panel reports* (Vol. III, Appendix). Washington, D.C.: U.S. Government Printing Office, 1978.

Van Viervliet, A. Program evaluation research: Its importance for applied behavior analysis and its basic components. *Behavior Therapist,* 1979, *2,* 3–7.

Waters, E., Fink, S., & White, B. Peer group counseling for older people. *Educational Gerontology,* 1976, *1,* 157–169.

Watson, L. S. Shaping and maintaining behavior modification skills in staff using contingent reinforcement techniques. In R. L. Patterson (Ed.), *Maintaining effective token economies.* Springfield, Ill.: Charles C Thomas, 1976.

Webster, D. R., & Azrin, N. H. Required relaxation: A method of inhibiting agitative-disruptive behavior of retardates. *Behavior Research and Therapy,* 1973, *11,* 67–78.

Webster's new collegiate dictionary. Springfield, Mass.: Merriman, 1979.

Weed, L. W. *Medical records, medical education, and patient care.* Chicago: Year Book Medical Publishers, 1970.

Weiss, C. H. *Evaluating action programs*. Boston, Mass.: Allyn & Bacon, 1972.

Wiener, N. *The human use of human beings*. Boston, Mass.: Houghton Mifflin, 1950.

Wilson, G. T. On the much discussed nature of the term "behavior therapy." *Behavior Therapy*, 1978, *9*, 89–98.

Wolf, M. M. Social validity: The case for subjective measurement, or how applied behavior analysis is finding its heart. *Journal of Applied Behavior Analysis*, 1978, *11*, 203–214.

Wolman, B. B. (Ed.). *Dictionary of behavioral science*. New York: Van Nostrand Reinhold, 1973.

Index